The Presence of Montaigne
In the *Lettres Persanes*

The Presence of Montaigne
In the *Lettres Persanes*

by

John M. Bomer

SUMMA PUBLICATIONS, INC.
Birmingham, Alabama
1988

Copyright 1988
Summa Publications, Inc.

ISBN 0-917786-68-8
Library of Congress Catalog Number 88-62882

Printed in the United States of America

CONTENTS

CONTENTS (cont'd)

Note to the Reader

My work is an extension of past source studies on the *Lettres persanes*. Vernière in his Garnier edition catalogues the large number of hidden sources in the *Information* section of his introduction (pp. xvii-xxviii). But for particular examples of borrowings see, in this edition, note 1, p. 120; note 1, p. 113; note 2, pp. 90-91; note 4, p. 174. These documented sources show how Montesquieu was closely inspired by his readings.

✻　✻　✻

I would like to thank François Rigolot for helping me revise the bibliography and find a publisher.

Alfred Glauser inspired this work and accepted it as a dissertation, guiding it to successful completion.

Without the love and support of my wife, Hilde Stalzer, *The Presence of Montaigne in the "Lettres persanes"* would not have been written.

—*J. M. B.*

INTRODUCTION

For MANY YEARS LITERARY CRITICS have been aware of the close relationship between Montaigne and Montesquieu. The parallels in their lives and thoughts are too striking to ignore, for they are both nobles from the province of Gascony, representatives of the landed gentry, magistrates and, above all, writers, humanists, and advocates of enlightenment.

Connoisseurs of these two philosophers have noted the liveliness of their style. Sainte-Beuve was the first who compared one with the other, adding a subjective value judgment as well. Montesquieu, he writes, possessed a "tour d'imagination prompte qui revêtait aisément la pensée et la maxime d'une forme poétique, comme faisait son compatriote, Montaigne; mail il était moins aisé que Montaigne, et n'avait pas la fleur comme lui."[1] Sainte-Beuve alludes to the famous *saillies* of Montesquieu's style, a facet of his personality which links him with Montaigne. Albert Sorel associates this trait with Gascon nature in general, implying the author's kinship with the essayist on the question of conversational wit and verve.[2] More important, Sorel was probably the first critic to hint that Montesquieu in addition to Montaigne followed in the humanist tradition of compiling and commenting on the writing of others:

> Montesquieu aime Montaigne: il le range parmi les grands poètes; il s'en délecte, il s'en nourrit et, par moments, il le ressuscite. . . . Possédé de la passion des lectures, il voyage à travers sa bibliothèque, il s'y promène, il y chasse, il y butine; il barbouille ses livres de notes. Cette battue en forêt anime constamment et féconde sa pensée.[3]

But, added Sorel, Montesquieu attacks his sources with a greater sense of order and construction: "Montaigne a dispersé sa pensée; Montesquieu a besoin de rassembler la sienne."[4] More often he needs to explain the causes behind the multicolored nature of man. Sorel did not clarify which writings of Montesquieu reflect his quoting instinct and his predilection for historical anecdotes (so similar to Montaigne's), but he probably meant the *Lettres persanes* as well as *L'Esprit des lois*, even though Montesquieu annotated his many sources only in the latter work. As Sainte-Beuve generalized, "Les ouvrages de Montesquieu ne sont guère que le résumé philosophique et la reprise idéale de ses lectures."[5] Sorel could have discreetly been referring to both masterpieces of the author's literary career without mentioning either.

A little known work on our two writers is perhaps the greatest precedent to the present undertaking. In an obscure journal of Orléans in 1882 a certain Eugène Bimbenet published two articles which dealt only with the relationship between Montaigne and Montesquieu. This study contains many valid thoughts, some of which foreshadow our own comparisons. Bimbenet endeavored to draw parallels between these two Gascons' lives and ideas—their similar social status, profession, voyages through Europe, chauvinistic attitudes toward women, deistic beliefs (counterbalanced by a Catholic exterior), objections to laws against suicide, divorce, etc. The two articles, however, have too large a scope. Bimbenet tried to say all in less than a hundred pages; il simply cannot be done. And despite some very relevant comparisons, many (notably those between the *Essais* and *L'Esprit des lois* in the "Seconde Partie" of his study) do not seem valid to us. Particularly his treatment can be criticized, for, overcome by textual resemblances, the poor scholar felt above all inclined to quote, preferring long excerpts to speak for themselves rather than limit them and add much of his own commentary. Not once did he note stylistic similarities. Finally, and most to his disadvantage, Bimbenet sought comparison for comparison's sake, arriving rarely at any synthesis. As a result Montesquieu emerges hardly as an individual distinct from the essayist. We are not surprised that a colleague of Bimbenet's who answered both articles with a critique was lead to say, "Je suis sûr que l'on pourrait, en y mettant de la malice, amener le savant auteur du mémoire à convenir que Montesquieu se ressemble moins à lui-même, qu'il ne l'a fait ressembler à Montaigne."[6] Nevertheless, we render hommage to our predecessor who was intuitively right in so many of his observations and who sought to make only a sketch, not a definitive study of the two writers. We are surprised that twentieth-century editors of Montesquieu's *Lettres persanes* have not paid the slightest attention to his *mémoire*.

Fortunat Strowski considered Montaigne and Montesquieu in a new, comprehensive light. He felt Montesquieu's complex physiognomy was divided into two conflicting halves—one side "l'homme de la raison divine," the other "l'homme ondoyant et divers." Malebranche, writes Strowski, was most influential in forming the absolute character of Montesquieu's thought, whereas Montaigne "a appris à Montesquieu que tout est ondoyant et divers, la nature aussi bien que l'homme."[7] Montesquieu himself admitted the double influence of these thinkers in one of his oft quoted *pensées:* "Ces quatre grands poètes: Platon, Malebranche, Shaftesbury, Montaigne."

Pierre Barrière has been the critic probably most interested in the deep relationship between Montaigne and Montesquieu. His long book on Montesquieu (wrongly underrated by Cabeen) is scattered with brief comparisons and contrasts concerning the two writers. He points out Montesquieu's moderation and impartiality in the Bull *Unigenitus* affair.[8] Our noble *homme de robe* urged acceptance of the Bull but appealed forcibly to the king to show a spirit of magnanimous toleration. He was not so much a partisan of either Parliament or Court as a lover of peace. Such tradition was illustrated during the religious wars of two hundred years before by that other Gascon, Montaigne, and that other magistrate, L'Hospital.[9] Barrière emphasizes Montesquieu's freedom of judgment in confronting the many problems of his life, and he places this characteristic in the light of Montaigne's example.[10] Typical representatives of their class and environment, both men shared similar views toward love, marriage and infidelity.[11] They had a great facility for adapting to the atmosphere of a new country.[12] Montesquieu's travel journal is the first important French document of its kind since Montaigne's. Barrière believed that Montaigne's voyage served as a stimulus to Montesquieu's own. "L'exemple de Montaigne est là, comme une obsession," he writes.[13] Montesquieu's ideas on conversation are reminiscent of the essay, "De l'art de conferer." For both men conversation demanded a veritable method of execution.[14]

In a sort of conclusion on their common traits Barrière compares Montesquieu with Montaigne and Cicero. He felt that both the Roman and the Gascon *gentilhomme* were our author's true models, both in life and writing. They share the same predilection for sanity and peace of mind, the same sense of moderation in all aspects, the same adaption and conformity to the necessities of life, the same belief in their aptitude for affairs of state, the same conception of their roles as mediators and guides in an unstable society.[15]

This broad analysis, however, was not Barrière's last word on their relationship. Most interesting is his suggestion that Montaigne's playful dialectic influenced Montesquieu. Somewhat affected by Strowski's interpretation of the essayist, Barrière speaks of Montesquieu's "dilettantism." But he adds a new sense to the word:

> Dans sa double attitude de l'homme sérieux et badiné se révèle un certain dilettantisme, une certain tendance à jouer avec les idées. Montesquieu, comme Montaigne, est sincère, mais d'une sincérité un peu momentanée, dans les idées comme dans l'amour; ainsi que les gens trop sensibles, il passe trop vite d'un point de vue à un autre et déroute les esprits moins mobiles qui cherchent chez un écrivain et un penseur une attitude fixe. . . . Lui aussi essaie les idées; ondoyant et divers, il est tantôt d'un côté, tantôt de l'autre de son argumentation, et il pourra s'étonner . . . qu'on prenne certaines expressions plus à la lettre qu'il ne les a prises lui-même.[16]

Barrière suggests more than anyone before him the complex protean character of thought we find exemplified in the *Lettres persanes*, the author's double nature, his duplicity. The continual dialectic of Montesquieu's thought is one of his closest ties with Montaigne. These two men of law were sensitive to the pro and contra of every concept. They could not see one side of an issue without altering it by a comment, either contradicting or varying it, placing it in another light, another context. Here is the very premise of conversation. In the *Essais* Montaigne converses with his sources and his readers. In the *Lettres persanes* Montesquieu adds another dimension, for he speaks through his Persians as well as his sources. His wit and gentle malice are the sparks of friction when one idea rubs against another, and neither survives in its original, fixed form. Barrière was sensitive to Montesquieu's love of contradictions which compare so well with paradoxes in the *Essais*. But he claims that the author of the *Lettres persanes* displays them with a smile Montaigne was incapable of expressing.[17] And yet, we ask, does the essayist not also smile behind his accumulation of paradoxes? Montesquieu's humor and irony are simply more obvious.

A significant contribution which Barrière has made to our knowledge of Montesquieu is his discovery of autobiographical elements in the *Lettres persanes*. The critic goes a bit too far with his theory, particularly when comparing the hypothetical nature of Montesquieu's marriage and love life with the intrigues of Usbek's harem. But much of what he says is valid. And the conclusion he tentatively draws from all this is what pertains here. The *Essais*, he feels, were responsible for drawing out the author's *moi* —a *moi* which was by nature very timid and reluctant to show itself. As Montaigne had dared to choose himself as the subject of the *Essais*, Montesquieu turns the reflection of the *Lettres persanes* back against his own life. The author himself, in a certain measure, is the topic under discussion. Barrière suggests that his work is the result of an "expérience sur soi-même" and an "effort permanent de sincérité inquiète." As a sort of conclusion near the end of his article he writes: "Son œuvre, si nettement influencée par celle de Montaigne, apparaît comme un véritable examen de conscience intellectuel et moral."[18]

However, Barrière believed that searching for Montesquieu's written sources was an illusory task—especially when one simply compares ideas instead of the form and style in which they are expressed. As though in answer to Sorel before him, Barrière remarks: "Par prudence Montaigne tenait à se couvrir du paravent des anciens; Montesquieu revendique la personnalité et la responsabilité de ses idées." And he quotes *Mes Pensées* to prove his argument against a possibly valid source study of Montesquieu's work.[19]

It is surely true that coincidences do not necessarily indicate plagiarism. Montesquieu could have thought himself what others thought before him. If he speaks of love and marriage, of law and customs in a manner similar to another writer, this may indicate nothing more than analogous tradition which precedes them both. But we must not forget the other side of the coin in determining its authenticity. Montesquieu was quite proud of his large libraries in Paris and La Brède. He collected books and several editions of important works. More than a mere bibliophile, his capacity for reading would surely impress anyone today. In his reading Montesquieu saw how the same idea could be found many times over the ages. A concept he had sensed to be unique in his own time could suddenly reappear in the writings of an ancient Greek. For example, he was astounded and amused to discover that all the theologian's principles on usury could be found already word for word in Aristotle's *Politics*.[20] Montesquieu was lucid concerning plagiarism. He was intelligent and well-read enough to know when an idea was stolen or even unconsciously borrowed. Proud to weed out plagiarism in dissertations submitted to the Academy of Bordeaux, (see *pensée* 856; 794), Montesquieu was probably chosen by his colleagues because of his immense learning and excellent memory. Originality was naturally one of the principal goals which members of the Academy sought in their scientific research. But literature was another matter. Plagiarism or imitation was a traditional device of composition since antiquity. No writer sought out originality for its own sake. He used another name or names before him as his model:

> Comme le Tasse a imité Virgile, Virgile, Homère, Homère a pu avoir imité quelque autre. Il est vrai que l'Antiquité se taît à cet égard. Quelques-uns ont pourtant dit qu'il n'avoit fait que ramasser les fables de son temps. (*Pensée* 424; 864)

Montesquieu's attachment to tradition was an essential part of his nature. He was immensely proud of his noble heritage. Vain enough to make up a genealogy, he was also curious to know the sources of a writer's ideas and artistic method, in brief, his literary ancestors. Probably he was insulted to discover himself a literary relative of Voltaire (since among other debts the latter was directly inspired by Persian letter 125 for "Le Bûcher" and by letter 46 for "Le Souper" episodes in *Zadig*): "Voltaire a une imagination plagiaire," writes Montesquieu; "elle ne voit jamais une chose si on ne lui en a montré un côté" (*pensée* 2235; 935). The roots of a tree are hidden, but they are no less important to its life than its leaves and branches: "Sans l'*Iliade* et l'*Odyssée*, il y a apparence que nous n'aurions pas l'*Enéide*" (*pensée* 2179; 865).

Montesquieu read the ancients with a delight and assiduity reminiscent of Montaigne's. Through Usbek he reproaches those short-sighted, ill-read journalists of his day who, like most of mankind, were only familiar with their own era and environment:

> Le grand tort qu'ont les journalistes, c'est qu'ils ne parlent que des livres nouveaux; comme si la vérité était jamais nouvelle. Il me semble que, jusqu'à ce qu'un homme ait lu tous les livres anciens, il n'a aucune raison de leur préférer les nouveaux.[21]

With an air of superiority he writes once in *Mes Pensées* that ancient literature is for authors, contemporary literature for readers (see *pensée* 703; 850). As a creator and not simply a passive reader Montesquieu considered himself an exception to the rule. Connoisseurs of the ancients did not abound in the society around him.

Thus, although Montesquieu defended the originality of a great author like Descartes and knew that the critics who accused this philosopher of plagiarism were oversimplifying unfairly (see *pensée* 50; 793), he was also a keen observer of true plagiarism—its use and abuse. Although he knew it was absurd to claim that there is a source for everything, whether in Horace, Theocrites, or some other ancient, the tradition of imitation in literature was too strong to be ignored. Montesquieu was aware that the great writers of antiquity had imitated their illustrious predecessors. Given the essential spark of ability, it was possible to increase the value of one's work through the choice of a great model. Corneille, Racine, La Fontaine, Boileau, Ronsard, Rabelais, Montaigne and many others had done so.

Montesquieu's contemporaries accused Montaigne of being a mere commentator of the ancients, so that Voltaire felt obliged to come to his defense. We know that Montaigne's genius saves him from being a mere plagiarizer. A large part of the *Essais'* frame is built of what others have said. But the author has made this superficial structure into a work of art through commentary of great quality and through personal reflections. We might say the same of the *Lettres persanes*. With characteristic ambiguity Montesquieu indirectly criticizes glossators and commentators in one context (*Lettres persanes*, p. 209) and praises them in another (ibid., p. 285). Being a compiler in itself is no great sin or virtue. How one does it determines whether a writer is poor or excellent. This double-edged lesson is agreeably illustrated by a conversation in the convent library which Rica visits:

> Voici, me dit-il, les grammairiens, les glossateurs et les commentateurs. —Mon Père, lui dis-je, tous ces gens-là ne peuvent-ils pas se dispenser d'avoir du bon sens? —Oui, dit-il; ils le peuvent, et même il n'y paraît pas: leurs ouvrages n'en sont pas plus mauvais; ce qui est très commode pour eux. —Cela est vrai, lui dis-je, et je connais bien des philosophes qui feraient bien de s'appliquer à ces sortes de sciences. (p. 285)

Rica's last words are nothing less than Montesquieu's reflection on his own creative process. The author realized that his work was to a large extent a compilation of and commentary on his readings. Yet he believed and hoped the method had its purpose if applied in the right way.

The history of research on the *Lettres persanes* has developed over the last half a century in the light of Rica's conversation above. Scholars have increasingly discovered that the author's reading was all the more influential in that it was of encyclopedic proportions. Montesquieu's contacts with past and contemporary literature seem to have multiplied over the decades. Elie Carcassonne was the first to present the public a critical edition of this work where the more immediate models were discussed—Addison, Dufresny, and above all, Marana.[22] Bringing to light Montesquieu's debt to seventeenth-century voyagers, the editor also provided notes suggesting specific passages which could have been of direct inspiration to the author. Antoine Adam continued the same approach, enriching the sources to include ancient and contemporary historians, philosophers, geographers, writers of memoirs and Persian *contes*.[23] Only six years later in 1960 appeared the first edition where this and other material collected by scholars over the years was reevaluated and classified.[24] Paul Vernière has carefully catalogued sixty possible, probable, or sure sources into their correct period or genre. This important edition clarifies to what extent Montesquieu read and commented on his reading in composing the *Lettres persanes*.

Vernière's method of judging the validity of a source is not simply to seek out similar ideas and place them at the foot of the page. He searches for specific words which Montesquieu could have lifted from his reading, for apparently the author took notes on any work he felt might be useful to his own writings. A paragraph, a sentence, small phrases, even a few key words in common suggest Montesquieu's task of compiler and his sketchy, note-taking method of preparation which preceded the formal act of writing.[25] Robert Shackleton was also aware of Montesquieu's ability to quote from or allude to classic sources. He says that Usbek's description of the bishop in letter 101 as " 'un gros homme avec un teint vermeil' is a probable echo of the servant's description of Tartuffe in Molière's play: 'gros et gras, le teint frais, et la bouche vermeille.' "[26]

Sources for a single paragraph or episode often overlap. In one notable instance Montesquieu has as many as three predecessors. Treating a traditional theme, *les embarrass de Paris*, he is surely aware of Boileau's classic satire. But also Marana's *L'Espion turc* has its place in contributing certain expressions which Montesquieu uses and transforms at the same time. Not even Dufresny should be excluded as a participant. Boileau would seem to be Montesquieu's model. The introduction to Rica's description takes on the nature of a title: ". . . quand tout le monde est descendu dans la rue, il s'y fait un *bel embarras*" (p. 54). The title of Boileau's *Satire VI* probably had its influence on the important position of this word, accented as it is at the end of a sentence, and serving as a transition to the essential treatment of the theme. Vernière's choice of two verses from Boileau's poem (see p. 55, fn. 2) is pertinent to Montesquieu's text, even though they share no specific vocabulary. Unlike Dufresny's Siamese visitor, Boileau and Rica are caught in the midst of the tumult, pushed, shoved and splashed by the rushing Parisians: "Guénaud sur son cheval en passant *m'éclabousse*, writes Boileau (line 68). ". . . car encore passe qu'on *m'éclabousse* depuis les pieds jusqu'à la tête," writes Rica (p. 55). Vernière might also have made the above comparison to further suggest Montesquieu's awareness and recent reading of Boileau's satire.

Montesquieu may also have been inspired by La Bruyère's Giton in drawing his portrait of the vain and haughty "grand seigneur" of Paris (see letter 74). The latter, Usbek surmises, "fait sentir à tous les instants la supériorité qu'il a sur tous ceux qui l'approchent." Is this not the same air that Giton exudes? Both portraits represent archetypes of their class (the court nobility), and they seem to share certain gestures peculiar to this breed of homo sapiens:

> (Giton) déploie un ample mouchoir, et *se mouche* avec grand bruit; il *crache* fort loin . . .

Usbek writes:

> Il prit une prise de tabac avec tant de hauteur, il *se moucha* si impitoyablement, il *cracha* avec tant de flegme . . . (p. 158)

The semantical relationship between these two excerpts cannot be denied.

In conclusion it must be said that specific words and expressions are the surest key to the question of sources. They are no proof in themselves, for judgment must decide in each individual case. Nevertheless, if Montesquieu is treating a traditional theme, either consciously or unconsciously he may repeat the vocabulary of his predecessors. It is the indication of his assiduous, monumental amount of reading, the notes taken on it, and his unfailing desire to create new literature from the old. He was aware that many themes were enriched by their age. Through imitation he might likewise acquire merit, a rational, justified merit. His models would clarify openly to what extent he was original. The public, or rather the learned public who knows his sources, could judge for themselves.

"L'imitation n'est pas esclavage," writes La Fontaine. Montesquieu is no slave of tradition.

Montaigne was also a compiler and commentator. He relied as heavily upon Seneca and Plutarch as did Montesquieu upon Marana and Chardin. As the former would borrow a choice anecdote from Laertius, the latter lifts a particularly amusing tale from Froger. This aspect of Montaigne's creative method is understandably less interesting to us today than the author's personality behind his sources. Yet during the first of this century scholars were astounded by the bulk of Montaigne's plagiarism in certain essays. And the essayist was well aware of the problems of excessive compilation. Notably in "Des livres" he attacks those abominable writers of comedies who pile five or six tales of Boccacio into a single work. In letter 66 Rica also pronounces a scathing tirade against plagiarists, although his position parallels Montaigne's only on a superficial plane. Montaigne with his more staid wisdom censures only those compilers who indulge excessively, whereas Rica condemns them all. Therefore, either Rica is a biting critic of Montesquieu, or he is ironic. The less playful Montaigne would not consider snubbing all plagiarists. In fact, on another occasion he openly admits borrowing passages from Seneca or Plutarch without telling the reader of his deed. In our opinion it was this frank confession which provoked Rica's mock attack on compilers. Let us compare that excerpt from "Des livres" with Rica's harangue in letter 66:

> Ez raisons et inventions que je transplante en mon solage et confons aux miennes, j'ay à escient ommis parfois d'en marquer l'autheur, pour tenir en bride la temerité de ces sentences hastives qui se jettent sur toute sorte d'escrits, notamment jeunes escrits d'hommes encore vivants, et en vulgaire, qui reçoit tout le monde à en parler et qui semble convaincre la conception et le dessein, vulgaire de mesmes. Je veux qu'ils donnent une nazarde à Plutarque sur mon nez, et qu'ils s'éschaudent à injurier Seneque en moy. Il faut musser ma foiblesse souz ces grands credits.[27]

> De tous les auteurs, il n'y en a point que je méprise plus que les compilateurs, qui vont, de tous côtés, chercher des lambeaux des ouvrages des autres, qu'ils plaquent dans les leurs, comme des pièces de gazon dans un parterre. Ils ne sont point au-dessus de ces ouvriers d'imprimerie qui rangent des caractères qui, combinés ensemble, font un livre où ils n'ont fourni que la main. Je voudrais qu'on respectât

les livres originaux, et il me semble que c'est une espèce de profanation
de tirer les pièces qui les composent du sanctuaire où elles sont,
pour les exposer à un mepris qu'elles ne méritent point. (*Lettres
persanes*, p. 136)

Two important factors link these excerpts. First of all, Rica has turned
Montaigne's idea upside down, grandiloquently, ironically abhorring the
fact that the true author whose work has been pillaged is unfairly exposed to
scorn by the plagiarist. Is it by pure coincidence that he reverses the essayist's very method? Montaigne makes fun of his critics who are ignorant of
his sources, who think that everything he says is his own invention or even
his own opinion, who can be offended by concepts as old as Mother Earth.
The essayist's point of view is similar to Usbek's, when he speaks of journalists in letter 108. Their error, writes the Persian, is in thinking that every
new book by nature possesses original ideas. They are unaware of tradition
and totally blind to ancient literature, speaking only of the new. "Ils n'ont
garde de critiquer les livres dont ils font les extraits, quelque raison qu'ils en
aient" (p. 226). Thus, like Montaigne, Montesquieu imagined that he
would be the victim of the same sort of petty critic who attacked particular
passages without realizing that they belonged in reality to writers who lived
long before him. Naturally Montesquieu responded immediately to Montaigne's method of escape. He would quote authors without indicating a
source and let his self-appointed judges make fools of themselves.

Secondly, thinking such a general objection to Montaigne's thievery
insufficient to place the reader on the right track, Rica has chosen to re-
phrase his victim's sturdy Renaissance image: "Ez raisons et inventions que
je transplante en mon solage"; his version is: ". . . qu'ils plaquent dans les
leurs, comme des pièces de gazon dans un parterre." Actually he deforms
Montaigne's image of transplanting, for the essayist later broadens the
metaphor, calling the passages uprooted from others' works "flowers":
"mon terrior n'est aucunement capable d'aucunes fleurs trop riches que j'y
trouve semées . . ." (*Essais*, II, ch. 10, pp. 84-85). Rica, on the other
hand, has dug up pieces of sod to plant them in a flower garden. He
reverses not only Montaigne's idea, but his image as well. He whistles the
essayist's tune, but backwards. Moreover, he whistles it jauntily, for the
familiarity of Montaigne's style rubs off on Rica's own. The word
"plaquent" is a bit brusk, so much so that the editor of the second 1721
edition changed it to "placent" —a calmer, more reasoned and deliberate

verb (see Vernière's variants for p. 136). Such an alteration, of course, belied Montesquieu's wishes.

Rica's concrete metaphor is an exception to the rarely figurative style of the *Lettres persanes*, but Montaigne, the vigorous manipulator of images, uses such comparisons often. The idea of pieces serves to connote the form of the *Essais*, of man, and even the social structure.[28] Like the famous *marqueterie mal jointe* the image of transplanting fragments into another whole suggests his patchwork method of writing. With similar comparisons he may modestly underestimate his own originality or attack other authors' lack of originality. The presence of such an image and especially the pompous rebuttal of the very procedure Montaigne adopts regarding Seneca and Plutarch—these two factors provide the most convincing evidence of direct contact between our two writers.

Probably the most prevalent type of imagery we find in Montesquieu's work is drawn from the vegetable world. Reading the epic poets of antiquity instilled in him a taste for the rich, noble similes between man and nature. Moreover, in the country he was sensitive to the many plants and flowers which surrounded him, especially those at La Brède where he did most of his reading and writing. One suspects the same was true of Montaigne. The life-giving source for both these rural nobles was the earth. Montesquieu had all his wealth tied up in land; he often speaks with pride and affection of "mes terres" on which he roamed either alone or with guests. Land provided both Montaigne and Montesquieu their insularity against the outside world. It is a symbol of their independence from the crown, of their rank among fellow nobles, of their dominion over the peasants they employed and over the crops, mostly vineyards, which nourished them all. "Pour lui (Montesquieu) comme pour Montaigne la seule existence, quand on n'est pas d'épée, est de vivre sur ses terres. . . ."[29] Montesquieu cherished his land and endeavored to render it beautiful. He had an English garden designed at La Brède with its freely winding paths and charming, contrived disorder. Rica's image, "pièces de gazon dans un parterre," was doubly derogatory to Montesquieu. Transplanting sod into a flower garden seems foolish and futile enough to us. But the Baron of La Brède felt a certain disdain for *parterres* in themselves—petty, geometrical structures. With such creations man inhibited the free and thriving nature about him. On another occasion the author compares modern literature to parterres, clearly showing what category they deserved to be placed in alongside the "belles et vastes campagnes" of the ancients (see *pensée* 117;

451). Rica's image of "pièces de gazon (plaquées) dans un parterre" is thus more than a reversal of Montaigne's *fleurs*. It belongs to Montesquieu's psychology. It reflects a part of his nature he shares with Montaigne, not simply a detail he stole from him. And we believe it expresses the author's irony at his own expense, not at Montaigne's. He is examining his own creative method with lucid, skeptical eyes, asking himself and the reader, "Is such a procedure valid in view of my illustrious predecessor?"

Montesquieu also applies the concept of transplanting to his Persian's "tout à coup transplantée en Europe, c'est-à-dire dans un autre univers" ("Quelques réflexions sur les *Lettres persanes*," 1753).[30] The significance of this detail lies in the real fact that Montesquieu in a sense transplanted himself into another universe to write the *Lettres*. He drew upon many great names of literature (the outer spectrum) but transposed his personality into the characters of Rica and Usbek (the inner spectrum). This dual method of composition suggests protection and guarantees detachment. Clearly the author, who published his work anonymously, is involved in the objectivity and distance of his "transplanting" metaphor.

Our suggestion that Rica in letter 66 is playfully contradicting Montaigne, only to adopt his method of composition, is in no way conclusively proved. However, if we find that Montesquieu compiles and comments upon the ideas not only of Chardin and Tavernier, Pascal and La Bruyère (as is well known), but on those of Montaigne, then there is stronger reason for believing our interpretation of Rica's important paragraph. One of the principal aims of the present work is to show that Montesquieu does indeed refer to the *Essais* and is inspired by them. We shall see that he transplanted sections, sentences, and metaphors from them into the *Lettres persanes*. Some of the passages reflect the *Essais* greatly in spirit but are not truly plagiarisms. Others seem to be designed as inspired borrowings and go well beyond Montaigne. One must, thus, show what Montesquieu does with his source, how he alters it or places it in a context where it may lose its original shade and tone. One must remember that anything which is transplanted continues to grow. We are dealing here with more than a mere mechanical game of word hunting. Montaigne's ideas are alive and become continually transformed and rejuvenated when planted on Montesquieu's soil. More than once Montesquieu appears to contradict his predecessor, as he does in letter 66. On other occasions he seems to answer him, as if to outdo the essayist. Youth has its ambition, and Montesquieu's is a very challenging and contradicting train of mind. When we believe there is a special rapport either through similar ideas, contradiction, or response, we shall quote one text underneath another and italicize key words.

But beyond this textual study we shall compare the general tenure of thought common to both philosophers, the similar nature of their private lives and lastly Montesquieu's self-portrait as concealed in the *Lettres persanes* and its relationship to Montaigne's. In order to reveal a less disguised Montesquieu and to explain some of his obscure thought we shall rely rather heavily on *Mes Pensées*—the three volumes of notes which the author compiled little by little throughout his lifetime. In sum, we hope to develop the same essential ideas both Sorel and Barrière had the intuition to grasp, and to further clarify Montaigne's relationship to Montesquieu in regard to the *Lettres persanes*.

I
THEMES FROM ANTIQUITY

The Senses

EARLY IN THE *LETTRES PERSANES* Usbek seeks freedom from the restraints of Oriental thought. His voyage to Europe is the most significant expression of his will to broaden his scope of knowledge. However, soon he is struck down by the relative state of insecurity which his travels lead him into, and in letter 17 he seeks vainly to find a path back to the consoling limits of conformity: "J'ai des doutes; il faut les fixer. Je sens que ma raison s'égare; ramène-la dans le droit chemin" (p. 41). The issue in this letter is a double one. Almost in spite of himself Usbek doubts certain taboos of strict Moslem dogma—the laws against eating pork and other so-called unclean meats, and those against touching a corpse. The target of his skepticism is religion, but the means of his attack are philosophical. That is, through analysis of the senses he touches upon man's preconceived ideas of purity and impurity. Through the physical he reaches the spiritual.

Moreover, Usbek steps onto a philosophical island quaking with relativity, an island which is part of Montaigne's territory. Certainly, it does not belong to him alone, but rather to many sects of antiquity from which he derived his last development in the *Apologie*—the discussion of man's senses and his abortive grasp at knowledge. In both texts we find that the instability of truth depends on three facts: 1) that judgment is acquired through the senses; 2) that every man judges according to his own individual tastes; 3) and that since each of us senses things differently from the other, there is no fixed and ordered basis on which to found *one* opinion. Thus, things possess in themselves no definable essence. Rather we give form to matter—a slippery and unsure shape which deceives through its diversity.[1] These essential ideas we find illustrated in the following comparison:

> Pour le jugement de l'action des sens, il faudroit donc que nous en fussions . . . d'accord . . . entre nous mesmes. Ce que nous ne sommes aucunement; et entrons en debat tous les corps de ce que l'un oit, void ou goute quelque chose autrement qu'un autre; et debatons, autant que d'autre chose, de la diversité des images que les sens nous raportent. . . . Nous recevons les choses autres et autres, selon que nous sommes et qu'il nous semble. (*Essais*, II, ch. 12, pp. 310-11)

> Les sens, divin, Mollak, doivent donc être les seuls juges de la pureté ou de l'impureté des choses. Mais, comme les objets n'affectent point les hommes de la même manière, que ce qui donne une sensation agréable aux uns en produit une dégoutante chez les autres, il suit que le témoignage des sens ne peut servir ici de règle à moins qu'on ne dise que chacun peut, à sa fantaisie, décider ce point et distinguer, pour ce qui le concerne, les choses pures d'avec celles qui ne le sont pas. (*Lettres persanes*, p. 42)

Certain words apparent in the *Apologie* reappear in Montesquieu's text—notably *juges* and *fantaisie* :

> Si les sens sont nos premiers *juges* . . . (*Essais*, II, ch. 12, p. 308)

> Les sens . . . doivent donc être les seuls *juges* . . . (*Lettres persanes*, p. 42)

> Nostre *fantasie* ne s'applique pas aux choses ains elle est conceue par l'entremise des sens; . . . la *fantasie* et apparence n'est pas du subject, ains seulement de la passion et souffrance du sens . . . (*Essais*, II, ch. 12, pp. 313-14)

> De cette extreme difficulté (due à l'incertitude de nos sens) sont nées toutes ces *fantasies*; que chaque subject a en soy tout ce que nous y trouvons; qu'il n'a rien de ce que nous y pensons trouver. (Ibid., p. 301)

> . . . chacun peut, à sa *fantaisie*, décider ce point et distinguer . . . (*Lettres persanes*, p. 42)

Usbek maintains that what is an agreeable sensation to one man is disagreeable to another: "ce qui donne une sensation agréable aux uns en produit une dégoutante chez les autres." Do we not see this principle illustrated in concrete and abstract terms in the *Apologie*?

> *Tantaque in his rebus distantia differitas que est,*
> *Ut quod alis cibus est, aliis fuat acre venunum. . . .*
> (*Essais*, II, ch. 12, p. 309)

> La variété et la différence sont si grandes en ces matières que l'aliment des uns est pour d'autres un âcre poison.
> (Lucretius, IV, p. 633) (Ibid., p. 309)

> . . . de ce que le miel estoit doux à l'un et amer à l'autre, il (Democritus) argumentoit qu'il n'estoit ni doux, ny amer. (Ibid., p. 297)

Most suggestive of Montaigne is an instance of doubt and suspension of judgment in the form of a paradox. Usbek states that mud is no more filthy than gold or diamonds, that we react to it negatively only because it affects our subjective sense of sight:

> La boue ne nous paraît sale que parce qu'elle blesse notre vue ou quelque autre de nos sens; mais, en elle-même, elle ne l'est pas plus que *l'or et les diamants.* (*Lettres persanes*, p. 41)

Was he inspired by a verse of Ovid's in the same section of the *Apologie*? The latter placed gold and gems in a similarly skeptical and negative light to the mind's eye.

> . . . la veue nous force d'en trouver le subject plus aimable et plus agreable, contre toute raison. Car en cela il n'y a rien du sien.

> *Auferimus cultu; gemmis auroque tequntur Crimina: pars minima est ipsa puella sui. . . .* (*Essais*, II, ch. 12, p. 305)

> Nous sommes séduits par la parure; *les gemmes et l'or* cachent les tares; la jeune fille est la moindre partie d'elle-même. (*Remèdes à l'amour*, I, p. 343) (Ibid., p. 305)

Both writers show that nothing is true, but that thinking makes it so. If we question our sense of sight, even gold and gems are no longer pure and beautiful in themselves. Whatever Montesquieu owes Montaigne in our letter is concealed and limited in its overall scheme. For Usbek's ultimate purpose is to question the essence of purity and impurity, not the power of the senses per se. His argument is primarily on a theological plane where the bias of dogma appears a bit foolish. The taboos of Islam reunite with another theme dominant in the *Lettres*—tolerance and common sense. Nevertheless, Usbek's query into his own faith remains a question in the form of invigorating doubt and, as such, reflects the skepticism of Montaigne's *Apologie*.

Stoicism

In a letter entitled "Insanité des pompes funèbres, des tristesses et des joies humaines" Usbek expresses his general skepticism concerning ceremony accompanying the dying and the dead. He deems vain *oraisons funèbres* and the lugubrious deathbed entourage of the moribund. Naturally Montesquieu is speaking of the rites accorded the French nobility, and it appears that he had Montaigne in mind for one of the above themes. In a rather unstoical moment in a very Stoic essay our author conjures up and declaims the last frightful moments experienced by the average member of his class. Montesquieu was sensitive to his description, as we see in the following comparison:

> A quoi servent les cérémonies, et tout l'attirail lugubre qu'on fait paraître à un mourant dans ses derniers moments, les larmes mêmes de sa famille et la douleur de ses amis, qu'à lui exagérer la perte qu'il va faire? (*Lettres persanes*, pp. 86-87)

> Je croy à la verité que ce sont ces mines et appareils effroyables, dequoy nous l'entournons, qui nous font plus peur qu'elle (la mort): une toute nouvelle forme de vivre, les cris des mères, des femmes et des enfans, la visitation de personnes estonnées et transies, l'assistance d'un nombre de valets pasles et éplorés, une chambre sans jour, des cierges allumez, nostre chevet assiegé de medecins et de prescheurs; somme, tout horreur et tout effroy autour de nous. Nous voylà desjà ensevelis et enterrez. (*Essais*, I, ch. 20, p. 99)

Usbek's philosophy on death raises him to dizzy heights. Both he, Montaigne and the ancients reason that death should not provoke our tears, that our birth has more tragic consequences:

> il faut pleurer les hommes à leur naissance, et non pas à leur mort.
> (*Lettres persanes*, p. 86)

> Non seulement plusieurs sectes, mais plusieurs peuples, maudissent leur naissance et benissent leur mort. (*Essais*, III, ch. 5, p. 104)

Did Montaigne's soaring relativity inspire Usbek, when the latter denies our free will, leaving man's ultimate happiness or misfortune to a power outside himself? Has Montesquieu condensed a passage of the *Apologie*? We find the philosophical Persian in a state of indifference and hopelessness concerning the human condition:

> Nous sommes si aveugles que nous ne savons quand nous devons nous affliger ou nous réjouir: nous n'avons presque jamais que de fausses tristesses ou de fausses joies. (*Lettres persanes*, p. 87)

Here is part of the long passage in the *Apologie* which may have influenced Montesquieu to write the above lament:

> Il me semble, entre autres tesmoignages de nostre imbecillité, que celui-cy ne merite pas d'estre oublié, que par desir mesmes l'homme ne scache trouver ce qu'il luy faut; que, non par jouyssance, mais par imagination et par souhait, nous ne puissions estre d'accord de ce de quoy nous avons besoin pour nous contenter. Laissons à nostre pensée tailler et coudre à son plaisir, elle ne pourra pas seulement desirer ce qui luy est propre, et se satisfaire:
> *quid enim ratione timemus*
> *Aut cupimus? quid tam dextro pede concipis, Ut te conatus non paeniteat votique Peracti?* (*Essais*, II, ch. 12, p. 283)

> Quand la raison règle-t-elle nos craintes ou nos désirs? Quel projet formé avec assez de bonheur pour qu'on n'ait pas à se repentir de l'avoir entrepris et mené à bonne fin? (Juvenal, X, 4) (*Ibid.*, p. 283)

> Dieu pourroit nous octroyer les richesses, les honneurs, la vie et la santé mesme, quelquefois à nostre dommage; car tout ce qui nous est

plaisant, ne nous est pas tousjours salutaire. Si, au lieu de la guerison,
il nous envoye la mort ou l'empirement de nos maux . . . il le fait par
les raisons de sa providence, qui regarde bien plus certainement ce qui
nous est deu que nous ne pouvons faire; et le devons prendre en bonne
part, comme d'une main très-sage et très-amie. . . . Car de les requerir
(les dieux) des honneurs, des charges, c'est les requerir quils vous jettent
à une bataille ou au jeu de dez, ou telle autre chose de laquelle l'issue
vous est incognue et le fruit doubteux. (Ibid., pp. 284-85)

Usbek's short paragraph quoted above is perhaps an abstraction of
what Montaigne demonstrates more concretely. Montesquieu would seem
to reduce the essayist's fine development of thought to the lowest common
denominator. "Fausses tristesses" in letter 40 suggest man's lamentation
over death or ever worsening ills of life which Montesquieu says God may
send us as an act of providence. "Fausses joies" in Usbek's text would be
the riches, honors, good health, and even life itself which, according to the
essayist, might all come to our ultimate detriment. Like Midas, we might
regret the fulfillment of our deepest wishes. The final comparison of man's
happiness or misery to a throw of the dice connotes the power of sheer
chances over and above providence. Was it not man's helplessness in the
midst of such a force which Montesquieu wished to express when calling us
"aveugles?" Very possibly the author created his succinct paradox from his
knowledge of the ancients and Montaigne.

The Rejection of Stoicism

What a contrast Usbek's stoical reflections in letter 40 make with a
brief paragraph on the benefit and pleasure derived from drinking! Here is a
better cure to man's unhappiness than stoic philosophy, declares Usbek:

Lorsqu'il arrive quelque malheur à un Européen, il n'a d'autre ressource
que la lecture d'un philosophe qu'on appelle Sénèque; mais les Asiatiques, plus sensés qu'eux, et meilleurs physiciens en cela, prennent des
breuvages capables de rendre l'homme gai et de charmer le souvenir de
ses peines. (p. 72)

Having alluded to Seneca, Usbek proceeds to reject the Roman's philosophy in the next paragraph:

> Il n'y a rien de si affligeant que les consolations tirées de la nécessité du mal, de l'inutilité des remèdes, de la fatalité du destin, de l'ordre de la Providence, et du malheur de la condition humaine. C'est se moquer de vouloir adoucir un mal par la considération que l'on est né misérable. Il vaut bien mieux enlever l'esprit hors de ses réflexions, et traiter l'homme comme sensible, au lieu de le traiter comme raisonnable. (Pp. 72-73)

Or is it only *Seneca's* philosophy that the author sweeps aside? Montaigne and Pascal also appear to be present in this undesirable cure to suffering. Usbek uses a phrase coined by the essayist[2] and later taken up with slight variation by the author of the *Pensées*—"la condition humaine." We find it used by Montaigne most often in his early so-called Stoic essays, where Seneca exercises his greatest influence. However, it is Pascal who, in depicting man's misery without God, foreshadows what Usbek terms "malheur de la condition humaine." Following we quote from Pascal's discussion of *divertissement* :

> Mais quand j'ai pensé de plus près, et qu'après avoir trouvé la cause de tous nos malheurs, j'ai voulu en découvrir la raison, j'ai trouvé qu'il y en a une bien effective, qui consiste dans *le malheur naturel de notre condition faible et mortelle, et si miserable, que rien ne peut nous consoler, lorsque nous y pensons de près.*[3]

The pleasures and bustle of life are considered vain and useless by Pascal, who challenges us to contemplate ourselves in "solitary confinement," as it were. Then we are faced with the harsh truth of our pitiful condition.

> La seule chose qui nous console de nos misères est le divertissement, et cependant c'est la plus grande de nos misères. Car c'est cela qui nous empêche principalement de songer à nous, et qui nous fait perdre insensiblement.[4]

When Usbek writes, "Il n'y a rien de si affligeant que les consolations tirées de la fatalité du destin, de l'ordre [i.e., le plan, l'équilibre] de la Providence," again he may be refuting Jansenist doctrine which placed man in very limited control of his destiny or salvation.

Suicide

Usbek's famous letter on suicide begins as an open attack upon European laws which punish these victims of despair. He vigorously assails society's religious and civil code which humiliated the dead by depriving their family of the deceased's property and, as a mark of infamy, by displaying the casket to all the citizenry. Usbek argues primarily in the form of rhetorical questions, one of Cicero's favorite devices. Montesquieu's purpose is analogous to that of the great Roman orator. Through forceful logic as a kind of prosecutor of the state, he aims to convince society that its laws are absurd, cruel, and useless.

The first five paragraphs, that is, approximately the first half of Usbek's letter appear to be a kind of commentary and development upon Montaigne's discussion of suicide in "Coustume de l'Isle de Cea," the only essay devoted entirely to that subject.[5] Each comparison we make below, where important words are underlined, is not conclusive in itself of any rapport between the two authors. But the accumulation of similar ideas cannot be the product of mere chance.

In his opening thesis Montaigne takes the point of view of the ancients, recounting many tales of suicide as the only cure to an intolerable life. He sees death as a "remède" to one's unbearable ills:

> Et ce n'est pas la *recepte* [le remède] à une seule maladie: la mort est la recepte à tous maux. (*Essais*, II, ch. 3, p. 20)

> Aux plus fortes maladies les plus forts *remedes*. (Ibid., p. 21)

> "C'est une recepte, dit-il, qui ne me peut jamais manquer, et de laquelle il ne se faut servir tant qu'il y a un doigt d'esperance de reste; . . ." (Ibid., p. 27)

> . . . le souverain *remede* de sa delivrance estoit qu'il se recommandast à tel sainct, avec tel et tel veu, et qu'il fut huit jours sans prendre aucun aliment, quelque defaillance et foiblesse qu'il sentit en soy. (Ibid., p. 27)

Usbek also considers suicide a remedy to suffering and moreover questions the laws that prohibit it:

> Il me paraît, Ibben, que ces lois sont bien injustes. Quand je suis accablé de douleur, de misère, de mépris, pourquoi veut-on m'empêcher de mettre fin à mes peines, et me priver cruellement d'un *remède* qui est en mes mains? (*Lettres persanes*, p. 160)

Usbek's terms—"douleur," "misère," and "mépris"—suggest especially the various states of mind which might drive a person justifiably to suicide. For it is through the mind that we suffer, whether the pain is mental or physical. Such description of pain could be an abstraction of many specific anecdotes Montaigne draws from antiquity, and it probably also reflects Montesquieu's own acquaintance with the classics.

There is semantic evidence suggesting that Montaigne's style inspired Montesquieu. Let us compare an anecdote of the essayist's with Usbek's portrayal of contemporary suicide victims' fate:

> . . . et nous lisons en outre, des vierges Milesienes, que, par une conspiration furieuse, elles se pendoient les unes apres les autres, jusqu'à ce que le magistrat y pourveust, ordonnant que celles qui se trouveroyent ainsi pendues, fussent *trainées du mesme licol, toutes nues, par la ville*. (*Essais*, II, ch. 3, pp. 24-25)

> Les lois sont furieuses en Europe contre ceux qui se tuent eux-mêmes: . . . ils sont *traînés indignement par les rues;* . . . (*Lettres persanes*, p. 160)

Is Usbek's phrase not an indignant and spontaneous reaction to this ancient custom of humiliating the dead, hardly more barbaric than what was taking place in eighteenth-century Europe? Montesquieu has associated a bizarre episode of the past immediately with the present. Society's punishment of the dead has scarcely become more civilized, he implies. His use of the word "traînés" is metaphorical, for in reality no one was actually dragged bodily along the streets; they were at least rolled by in carriages. However, Usbek's hyperbole, perhaps inspired by Montaigne, renders their fate more tragic and gripping.

Did Montesquieu perhaps also make an association between the ignominy cast upon criminals during the Roman emperor Tiberius's reign and the same rejection suffered by wayward Christians of his own time? Both were deprived of their property and an honorable burial:

> Les condamnez qui attendoyent l'execution, du temps de Tibere, per-
> doient leurs biens et estoient privez de sepulture. (*Essais*, II, ch. 3,
> p. 32)

> on les note d'infamie; on confisque leurs biens. (*Lettres persanes*,
> p. 160)

Beyond the above resemblances in vocabulary and ideas, the
strongest link between the two authors is one of contrast. With typical
objectivity or even duplicity Montaigne interrupts his humanistic apology of
suicide to reflect on the Catholic laws against it, and for several pages he
becomes absorbed in his new antithesis. Montesquieu, on the other hand,
directs his attack against the very principles which Montaigne, for the moment, upholds. Usbek's following questions seem to be addressed as much
to Montaigne as to the Catholic and civil code which outlawed suicide.

> Cecy ne s'en va pas sans contraste. Car plusieurs tiennent que nous ne
> pouvons abandonner cette garnison du monde sans le commandement
> exprès de celuy qui nous y a mis; et que c'est à Dieu, qui nous a icy
> envoyez, non pour nous seulement, ains pour sa gloire et service
> d'autruy, de nous donner congé quand il luy plaira, non à nous de le
> prendre; que nous ne sommes pas nez pour nous, ains aussi pour nostre
> pais; les loix nous redemandent conte de nous pour leur interest, et ont
> action d'homicide contre nous; autrement, comme deserteurs de nostre
> charge, nous sommes punis en l'autre monde.[6] (*Essais*, II, ch. 3,
> pp. 21-22)

> Pourquoi veut-on que je travaille pour une société, dont je consens de
> n'être plus? Que je tienne, malgré moi, une convention qui s'est faite
> sans moi? La société est fondée sur un avantage mutuel. Mais
> lorsqu'elle me devient onéreuse, qui m'empêche de renoncer? La vie
> m'a été donnée comme une faveur; je puis donc la rendre lorsqu'elle ne
> l'est plus: la cause cesse; l'effet doit donc cesser aussi.
>   Le prince veut-il que je sois son sujet quand je ne retire point
> les avantages de la sujétion? Mes concitoyens peuvent-ils demander ce
> partage inique de leur utilité et de mon désespoir? Dieu, différent de
> tous les bienfaiteurs, veut-il me condamner à recevoir des grâces qui
> m'accablent? (*Lettres persanes*, pp. 160-61)

In the above quotations it is apparent that both authors consider the individual's responsibility to society and to God. Montaigne affirms it (albeit in the name of "plusieurs," the Catholics); Montesquieu questions it in view of the fact that life may become an unwanted favor. Note that the expression, "service d'autruy," in the essay appears to have been transposed by Montesquieu into "avantage mutuel"; God's "gloire" becomes the pejorative "grâces qui m'accablent." However, in comparing life to a favor which one is at liberty to return, Usbek rationalizes somewhat like Montaigne, who writes elsewhere: "le sage vit tant qu'il doit, non pas tant qu'il peut" (II, ch. 3, p. 20); "La vie despend de la volonté d'autruy; la mort, de la nostre" (ibid.).

The Persian's final paradox concerning the individual versus society compares favorably with a paragraph in our essay. Arguing for suicide, Montaigne reasons playfully that one is not held responsible to laws against criminals, if one is the perpetrator and victim of one's own destruction. Usbek's logic is similarly elusive. He maintains that laws hold dominion over the living, not the dead:

> Comme je n'offense les loix qui sont faictes contre les larrons, quand j'emporte le mien, et que je me coupe ma bourse; ny des boutefeuz, quand je brusle mon bois: aussi ne suis je tenu aux lois faictes contre les meurtriers pour m'avoir osté ma vie. (*Essais*, II, ch. 3, p. 21)

> Je suis obligé de suivre les lois, quand je vis sous les lois. Mais, quand je n'y vis plus, peuvent-elles me lier encore? (*Lettres persanes*, p. 161)

In conclusion, then, Montesquieu has maintained a discernible distance from Montaigne, while at the same time remaining in touch with him. Both authors, influenced by the Stoic philosophers, consider suicide a "remedy" to any fate worse than death itself. When life is no longer bearable, then suicide is a logical, necessary escape. But whereas Montaigne is content with reiterating contemporary Christian and social laws totally in disagreement with the ancients, Montesquieu speaks out strongly in favor of the individual's freedom of choice. He is a more complete skeptic than Montaigne, and his irony is a biting commentary on the absurdity of the status quo:

> Les lois sont furieuses en Europe contre ceux qui se tuent eux-mêmes: on les fait mourir, pour ainsi dire, une seconde fois; . . . (*Lettres persanes*, p. 160)

Much later, of course, Montesquieu provided a sort of weak antithesis to his apology of suicide which had created a furor among the public. Ibben's letter 77, added in the 1754 edition, is a reply which halfway condones society's laws on this matter. Its last paragraph shows that late in life Montesquieu returned to a more conservative stance which is in accord with Montaigne's reservations:

> Si un être est composé de deux êtres, et que la nécessité de conserver l'union marque plus la soumission aux ordres du Créateur, on en a pu faire une loi religieuse. Si cette nécessité de conserver l'union est un meilleur garant des actions des hommes, on en a pu faire une loi civile. (*Lettres persanes*, p. 163)

Usbek's original paradoxical reasoning reflects the young author's bold criticism. As a humanist, skeptic, and reformer, he is more interesting and admirable. Pleading for the most extreme expression of man's free will—through suicide—Montesquieu ranks as a philosopher. Ibben's subsequent response holds less weight, as it was grudgingly written to accommodate the author's critics. Also one should note that Ibben merely states that society has made these laws; he does not say he agrees with them.

II
LOVE, MARRIAGE, AND INFIDELITY

Cuckoldry

IN SPEAKING OF FRANCE FROM A foreigner's point of view, Montesquieu chose to treat the subject of cuckoldry. The infidelity of French wives and the ultra-permissiveness of French husbands would shock a Persian. And Montesquieu probably considered the theme an antithesis to the Oriental system, where wives were imprisoned slaves often without a man to love them. The reader is well aware of the problems Usbek encounters with his harem. Rica, however, tells us in letter 55 that French wives are neither enslaved nor imprisoned and that they may have as many men to love them as they wish. Such was the glaring contrast between East and West, both customs equally extreme and equally amusing.

Cuckoldry is a traditional theme in French literature, visibly as old as the *fabliaux* of the middle ages and Rabelais's *Tiers Livre. L'Ecole des femmes, L'Ecole des maris, Le Cocu imaginaire* by Molière have immortalized jealous, maniacal French husbands, the laughing stock of society. But Rica's observations show that most husbands in France are far from jealous. His gaiety and detachment reflect Cotolendi's *Lettre écrite par un Sicilien à un de ses amis:*[1]

> C'est ici le pays du plaisir; les amants n'y soupirent guère, la jalousie ne tourmente personne . . . ; L'adultère y passe pour une galanterie dans l'esprit même des maris qui voyent tranquillement faire l'amour à leurs femmes. (Quoted by Vernière in *Lettres persanes*, p. 117, fn. 1)

Montesquieu, familiar with literary tradition and knowing what would surely please his audience, also undertook to renew an old cliché and infuse it with his own wit. To Rica, after all, there was nothing trite about cuckoldry. And the French reader, seeing himself through Persian eyes, might be surprised as well by his own customs. Montesquieu could very well have had Cotolendi's text in mind when composing letter 55, but it also appears that he received certain inspiration from Montaigne who takes up the problem of cuckoldry in the essay most entirely devoted to conflicts between love and marriage, "Sur des vers de Virgile" (III, ch. 5).

In the following résumé of sections from Montaigne's essay and letter 55 we shall recapitulate the content of the two works somewhat side by side so that the reader may associate Montaigne's theme and ideas with Montesquieu's. It will point out contrasts as well as parallels in the two texts. Also it will bring together the specific words that the two writers use in treating the same subject. We do not pretend that any one parallel of ideas or that any one word repetition is conclusive in itself, but the total accumulation of similar themes and vocabulary should suggest a definite rapport between all of letter 55 (except the first paragraph) and "Sur des vers." Consistent resemblance cannot be the product of mere chance.

Montaigne lets it be understood that cuckoldry is so common, so inevitable, that a faithful spouse is more exceptional than an unfaithful one. He plays counselor to an imaginary *cocu* who fears the shame and ridicule cast upon him by rumor of his fate. Wise old Montaigne, detached from the whole problem, well over the hill and out of Cupid's range, stands back and rationalizes, offering philosophical comfort to his patient.

"Mais jusques aux dames, elles s'en moqueront!"

"Et dequoy se moquent elles en ce temps plus volontiers que d'un mariage paisible et bien composé?" (*Essais*, III, ch. 5, p. 93)

Such was the license of the times; even women gossiped maliciously about their victims. Let them, implies Montaigne. We men know each other's worth. Accusing his male audience in general, Montaigne asks them to remember a simple fact: "chacun de vous a faict quelqu'un coqu" (ibid., p. 93). Then he adds logically that Nature is reciprocal; man should expect retaliation on a woman's part. "La frequence de cet accident en doibt meshuy avoir moderé l'aigreur; *le voilà tantost passé en coustume*," he exclaims (ibid.). Under such circumstances the final philosophical advice is clear and simple. The only antidote to this fateful disease of cuckoldry is a touch of indifference. "Serions nous pas moins coqus si nous craignions moins de l'estre? . . ." asks the essayist (ibid., p. 94). Resignation is the surest cure. Women are forced to accept your infidelity. Why not accept theirs?

Rica's letter is like a brighter, sharper reflection of the permissive society Montaigne reveals around him and the casual attitude which he recommends that husbands cultivate. According to the Persian's observations, marriage in eighteenth-century France is merely a law. But it is not the custom which appeals to the population's instincts.[2] A certain "convention tacite" determines their actual behavior. It allows them freedom outside the bounds of marriage; "elle fait le bonheur de l'un et de l'autre sexe." Both Montaigne and Rica believe, then, that infidelity is not simply an aberration from the status quo; it *is* the status quo. The bargain of love is made according to a "convention tacite" agreed upon between the sexes. Montaigne encourages his readers to cultivate a philosophical attitude of permissiveness towards their "amies." Rica says that those who do not do so vis-a-vis their wives are depriving their colleagues of a place in the sun.

If permissiveness eases that pain of cuckoldry, jealousy certainly aggravates it. For Montaigne, jealousy is a passion wherein man loses his self-control, his dignity, and his superiority over the weaker sex. Wise men bear up to being cuckolded like the brave Romans, Lucullus, Caesar, Pompeius, Antonius, Cato, and others. "Il n'y eust, en ce temps la, qu'un sot de Lepidus qui en mourut d'angoisse" (*Essais*, III, ch. 5, p. 85). Jealousy is the most vain and destructive illness which can afflict the human mind. Society ridicules the jealous husband who tries to prevent his wife's affair just as much as the man who is ignorant of it (ibid., p. 92). In fact, prying into the business can have vicious consequences. Wanting to know more can make things worse: "la honte s'augmente et se publie principalement par la jalousie" (ibid., p. 92). Rica goes a step farther on this point. The jealous husband receives worse treatment than any other, he claims. Such a man is "scorned," "hated," and never consoled (p. 116).

Both writers agree then that cuckoldry in itself is no great catastrophe; jealousy alone makes it so. Man's challenge is to conquer this rage by reason (as Montaigne sees it) or by nonchalance (as Rica sees it). Both authors feel that a true gentleman is not dishonored by being cuckolded. Rather he is admired for having suffered his fate without needless passion:

Je sçay çant honestes hommes coqus, honnestement et peu indecem-
ment. Un galant homme en est pleint, non *pas desestimé*. Faites que
vostre vertu estouffe vostre mal'heur, que les gens de bien en maudis-
sent l'occasion . . . (*Essais*, III, ch. 5, p. 92)

Il y a eu des maris qui ont *souffert cet accident*, non seulement sans
reproche et offence envers leurs femmes, mais avec singulier obligation
et recommandation de leur vertu. (Ibid., p. 90)

Un homme qui, en général, *souffre les infidelités* de sa femme n'est
point désapprouvé; au contraire, on le loue de sa prudence: il n'y a que
les cas particuliers qui déshonorent. (*Lettres persanes*, p. 117)

Rica declares with great exaggeration that there is no country in the
world where there are so few jealous husbands as in France. A husband's
peace of mind is not founded on confidence in his wife, but on the bad
opinion he has of her (p. 116). Expecting only the worst, he can never be
dispappointed. With similar tongue-in-cheek philosophy, Montaigne emphasizes the importance of not knowing one is cuckolded. You must be
clever and lucid to avoid such a painful and useless realization, he says.
The Romans had an effective method. Returning home from a trip, they
would send messengers ahead to announce their arrival, so as not to surprise their wives in bed with a stranger (III, ch. 5, p. 92).

The medecine of the Roman method is preventive and foolproof,
unlike that other sort—guarding and spying on one's wife to hold her in
check. Both writers believe that trying to force a woman to conform to
marriage can only backfire. This paradox of jealousy is older than the
fabliaux. Montaigne quotes Juvenal who relates how useless it is to lock up
one's wife and have her guarded; she will begin her revolt by seducing the
guards (ibid., p. 91). Rica states that the Asian custom of veils, prisons,
and vigilant eunuchs only encourages feminine ingenuity. They will escape
authority that much more quickly under such oppression (p. 116). Is this
not the lesson of Molière's two "Ecoles" as well as the point of Usbek's
failure with Roxane? On this same theme it seems that Montesquieu may
have borrowed the word "industrie" from Montaigne and applied it to the
opposite sex. In both texts it has the sense of "ingenuity" or "cleverness":

Et puis quel fruit de cette penible solicitude? Car, quelque justice qu'il y
ait en cette passion [la jalousie], encores faudroit il voir si elle nous

charrie utilement. Est-il quelqu'un qui les [les femmes] pense boucler par son *industrie*? (*Essais*, III, ch. 5, p. 91)

Toutes les sages précautions des Asiatiques . . . leur paraissent [aux Français] des moyens plus propres à exercer l'*industrie* de ce sexe qu'à la lasser. (*Lettres persanes*, p. 116)

If the husband endeavors to force or intimidate his wife into fidelity, Montaigne warns, he is defeating his own purpose by making the pursuers keener and the wives more eager to be pursued. "By increasing the value of the fortress, we increase the value and desire of conquest," he concludes. Rica shrugs off the danger and, using Montaigne's metaphor of "place" to a different effect, retorts playfully: "a king consoles himself over losing one fortress by taking another." Note that the exact meaning of "place" in both texts is *place-forte*, a stronghold:

Regardons aussi que cette grande et violente aspreté d'obligation que nous leur enjoignons en produise deux effets contraires à nostre fin: asçavoir qu'elle esguise les poursuyvants et face les femmes plus faciles à se rendre; car, quand au premier point, montant le pris de la *place*, nous montons le pris et le desir de la conqueste. (*Essais*, III, ch. 5, p. 94)

Ce titre de mari d'une jolie femme, qui se cache en Asie avec tant de soin, se porte ici sans inquiétude: on se sent en état de faire diversion partout. Un prince se console de la perte d'une *place* par la prise d'une autre. (*Lettres persanes*, p. 117)

Neither Rica nor Montaigne exclude the possibility of there existing virtuous, unyielding French ladies—providing they are ugly enough, that is:

. . . quand je les oy se vanter d'avoir leur volonté si vierge et si froide, je me moque d'elles; elles se reculent trop arriere. Si c'est une vieille esdenté et decrepite, ou une jeune seche et pulmonique, s'il n'est du tout croyable, au moins elles ont apparence de le dire. (*Essais*, III, ch. 5, p. 89)

Ce n'est pas qu'il n'y ait des dames vertueuses, et on peut dire qu'elles sont distinguées: mon conducteur me les faisait toujours remarquer.

Mais elles étaient toutes si laides qu'il faut etre un saint pour ne pas
haïr la vertu. (*Lettres persanes*, p. 117)

Such women as the above are rarities in a society where intercourse
between the sexes is so common and where sympathy for the cuckolded so
lacking that they have no one to confide in. To whom does one dare entrust
one's sorrow, asks Montaigne. If your listener doesn't react by laughing at
your story, he will use the information in order to cut a piece of the cake for
himself. Rica jumps a step beyond Montaigne's cynical opinion. Frenchmen almost never speak of their wives, he claims. They are afraid they
might be talking to people who know their partners better than they do; so if
Montaigne remarks that the man you confess to will try to make inroads into
the quarry, Montesquieu outdoes him with the answer: "What do you
mean? He may already have done so!" Better to remain silent in such an
environment. Any communication about the pleasures or pains of marriage
may make your confident curious to see for himself, that is if he hasn't
already penetrated the matter:

Miserable passion, qui a cecy encore, d'estre incommunicable . . .

car à quel amy osez vous fier vos doleances qui, s'il ne s'en rit, ne s'en
serve d'acheminement et d'instruction pour prendre luy-mesme sa part à
la curée?
   Les aigreurs, comme les douceurs du mariage, se tiennent secrettes
par les sages. Et, parmy les autres importunes conditions qui se
trouvent en iceluy, cette cy, à un homme languager comme je suis, est
des principales: que la coustume rende indecent et nuisible qu'on
communique à personne tout ce qu'on en sçait et qu'on en sent.
(*Essais*, III, ch. 5, p. 93)

Les Français ne parlent presque jamais de leurs femmes; c'est qu'ils ont
peur d'en parler devant des gens qui les connaissent mieux qu'eux.
(*Lettres persanes*, p. 116)

In conclusion, both philosophers agree that to set bounds for a game
without rules is nonsense. *Amor ordinem nescit.* Cupid subjugates all
other forces to his dominion. Frenchmen like the ladies the way Isocrates
said people liked Athens: everyone enjoyed wandering around and spend-
ing time there, but no one loved the city enough to settle there. If someone

were to lament the inconstancy of love in Montaigne's presence, the philo-sopher would reply: "Mon amy, tu resves; l'amour, de ton temps, a peu de commerce avec la foy et la preud'hommie" (*Essais*, III, ch. 5, p. 117). "C'est contre la nature de l'amour s'il n'est violant, et contre la nature de la violance s'il est constant" (ibid., p. 111).

One notes that Montaigne defends his own inconsistency by main-taining that he never swore or promised more attachment to a lady than he actually felt. Rica appears to take up the same idea at the close of his letter, perhaps borrowing the concept of "swearing" and "promising" from the *Essais*. However, Montaigne reveals himself in this regard. Rica uncovers a trait of the French male in general and embroiders on the pattern with facetious logic. "How can you accuse me of deceit or unfaithfulness, when I have made so few promises and have even kept most of them?" asks Montaigne. "How can Frenchmen be accused of infidelity, when their promises are relative to the charms of their spouses?" asks Rica in turn:

> je ne leur ay *tesmoigné* aux dames de mon affection que ce que j'en sentois, et leur en ay representé naïfvement la decadence, la vigueur et la naissance, les accez et les remises. On n'y va pas tousjours un train. J'ay esté si espargnant à *promettre* que je pense avoir plus tenu que promis ny deu. (*Essais*, III, ch. 5, p. 115)

> Après ce que je t'ai dit des mœurs de ce pays-ci tu t'imagines facilement que les Français ne s'y piquent guère de constance. Ils croient qu'il est aussi ridicule de *jurer* à une femme qu'on l'aimera toujours, que de soutenir qu'on se portera toujours bien ou qu'on sera toujours heureux. Quand ils *promettent* à une femme qu'ils l'aimeront toujours, ils supposent qu'elle, de son côté, leur promet d'être toujours aimable, et, si elle manque à sa parole, ils ne se croient plus engagés à la leur. (*Lettres persanes*, pp. 117-18)

More interesting than the above concept of not promising love, Montesquieu also focuses on Montaigne's metaphor of love and health. The old essayist, quite aware of his own physical ups and downs, speaks of affection as though it were a delicate organic problem in man: "je . . . leur en ay repre-senté naïfvement . . . les accez et les remises." Rica replies: "Ils croient qu'il est aussi ridicule de jurer à une femme qu'on l'aimera toujours, que de soutenir qu'on se portera toujours bien . . ."

Rica's specific repetition of words in Montaigne's text (or synonyms to these words), his recapitulation of two metaphors (comparing the object of one's love to a *place-forte* and the inconstancy of love to one's health), and perhaps, above all, the similar ideas in both works—all these elements together suggest direct contact between our two authors.

Montesquieu had several reasons for basing letter 55 on parts of "Sur des vers de Virgile." Surely the author was struck by the similarity of Montaigne's era and his own. He had perhaps thought the license of Parisian society unique, without great precedence. He had once taken the free social and sexual climate for granted. What surprise then to discover in his readings that almost a century and a half ago things were hardly different! As the essayist himself summed up the issue: "Bonne femme et bon mariage se dict non de qui l'est, mais duquel on se taist" (III, ch. 5, p. 92).

One of Montesquieu's purposes was to seize a certain ethnic characteristic of the Frenchman as a sexual being, to speak of him with the same ironic detachment he does of the Spanish, Italians, and Russians in other letters. Rica is of course one instrument of such objectivity. But Montaigne is another. For Montesquieu, Montaigne was symbolic of the French male—his prudence, detachment, and nonchalance in loving, his gaiety and mockery in speaking of love and marriage. These are the qualities of letter 55 one sees reflected in Montaigne.

Love and Marriage

Pierre Barrière has uncovered Montesquieu's personal reflexions on his own marriage in letter 116. The purpose of this letter would seem to be purely social propaganda. It is incorporated into a long, playful treatise deploring the depopulation of the contemporary world. For the most part Usbek speaks grandiloquently against the Catholic obligation to remain eternally tied to one woman. He preaches the virtue of divorce. The inability to escape one's wife limits man's ability to reproduce, he says. But Barrière realized that the letter revealed a disguised confession on the author's part.[3] Montesquieu's own physiognomy is present behind the veil of abstract philosophy, rather dull and dry in itself. Interpreted as autobiography, letter 116 comes alive. Evidently the author was bewildered by his own incompatible wife forced upon him by his family. (La Brède was obliged to give up a romance in order to marry Jeanne de Lartigue, hardly attractive but endowed with a good size fortune.) "A peine a-t-on trois ans de mariage qu'on en néglige l'essentiel; on passe ensemble trente ans de froideur," writes Usbek. At the date of this letter, 1718, Montesquieu had been married precisely three years and had only one child. A large family was important to him, and being one of several children himself, he hoped to carry on his noble lineage. Besides, children are often a consolation to an unhappy marriage. The thought of not producing additional offspring seems to haunt Montesquieu. The theme of death inserts itself into the language of Usbek's letter three times over: one is married until "death"; in union a wife's body is like a "corpse"; she "buries" her husband in refusing him sexual relations. Is there not personal, caustic criticism of his wife's frigidity, when Usbek (i.e., Montesquieu) threatens to visit a brothel? "Bientôt un homme dégoûtée d'une femme éternelle se livrera aux filles de joie: . . . (*Lettres persanes*, p. 244).

Letter 116 is autobiographical, but it is also a compilation. Montesquieu almost quotes Montaigne in two paragraphs. The specific personality of the essayist's paradoxes emerges suddenly from Montesquieu's style. Restless in the eternal state of Christian marriage, he remembered another nobleman of times past who shared his prejudices against the wedding band. Like Usbek, Montaigne felt that a husband's affection is actually diminished by the law designed to hold it in office:

> Nous avons pensé attacher plus ferme le *neud* de nos mariages pour avoir osté tout moyen de les dissoudre; mais d'autant s'est depris et *relaché* le neud de la volonté et de l'affection, que celuy de la contrainte s'est estroicy. (*Essais*, II, ch. 15, p. 330)

> [En défendant le divorce aux Chrétiens] on ôta non seulement toute la douceur du mariage, mais aussi l'on donna atteinte à sa fin: en voulant resserrer ses *nœuds*, on les *relâcha*; et, au lieu d'unir les cœurs, comme on le prétendait, on les sépara pour jamais.[4] (*Lettres persanes*, p. 243)

The parallel between our two texts continues:

> Et, au rebours, ce qui tint les mariages à Rome si long temps en honneur et en seurté fut la liberté de les rompre qui voudroit. Ils gardoient mieux leurs femmes d'autant qu'ils les pouvoient perdre; et, en pleine licence de divorces, il se passa cinq cens ans et plus avant que nul s'en servist. (*Essais*, II, ch. 15, p. 330)

> Rien ne contribuait plus à l'attachement mutuel que la faculté du
> divorce: un mari et une femme étaient portés à soutenir patiemment les
> peines domestiques, sachant qu'ils étaient maîtres de les faire finir, et ils
> gardaient souvent ce pouvoir en mains toute leur vie sans en user, par
> cette seule considération qu'ils étaient libres de le faire. (*Lettres
> persanes*, p. 244)

Montesquieu vaguely attributed such fidelity to antiquity. But he disagreed
with Montaigne's claim above that precisely in Rome marriages were so
honored that more than five hundred years passed before divorce occurred,[5]
and, a bit like Fénelon, he smiled down on Montaigne's idealization of the
ancients with the passing comment that in Roman times, unlike his day,
women passed in and out of husbands' hands:

> Le divorce est aboli; les mariages mal assortis ne se raccommodent
> plus; les femmes ne passent plus, comme chez les Romains, succes-
> sivement dans les mains de plusieurs maris, qui en tiraient, dans le
> chemin, le meilleur parti qu'il était possible.[6] (*Lettres persanes* p. 245)

The same essay—"Que nostre desir"—was perhaps Montesquieu's
source for another comment on antiquity. Usbek alludes to the Republic of
Lacedaemon where citizens were forever inhibited by strange and petty laws
governing love and marriage (p. 245). Very likely this general, historical
remark was inspired by Montesquieu's reading of Plutarch[7] or other ancient
historians and at the same time by a concrete detail related in "Que nostre
desir": To keep love alive, Licurgus ordained that couples of Lacedaemon
could have sexual relations only in secret, and that they should be as
ashamed when discovered in bed together as they would be when caught
sleeping with a lover. Montesquieu could have had this point in mind when
alluding to certain "lois singulières et subtiles":

> Pour tenir l'amour en haleine, Licurgue ordonna que les mariez de
> Lacedemone ne se pourroient prattiquer qu'à la desrobée, et que ce seroit
> pareille honte de les rencontrer couchés ensemble qu'aveques d'autres.
> (*Essais*, II, ch. 15, p. 326)

> J'ose le dire: si, dans une république comme Lacédémone, où les
> citoyens étaient sans cesse genés par des lois singulières et subtiles, et
> dans laquelle il n'y avoit qu'une famille, qui était la République, il

avoit été établi que les maris changeassent de femmes tous les ans, il en serait né un peuple innombrable. (*Lettres persanes*, p. 245)

However, the social, historical point of view must be seen in the light of the writers' private lives. Montaigne and Montesquieu idealize the past and also complain of the present in personal terms. The duration of marriage assured the duration of troubles and complications:

Quant aux mariages, outre ce que c'est un marché qui n'a que l'éntrée libre [sa *durée* estant contrainte et forcée, dependant d'ailleurs que de nostre vouloir], et marché qui ordinairement se fait à autres fins, il y survient mille fusées estrangieres à desmeler parmy, suffisantes à rompre le fil et toubler le cours d'une vive affection. (*Essais*, I, ch. 27, p. 201)

Il n'en est pas de même des Chrétiens, que leurs peines présentes déses-pèrent pour l'avenir: ils ne voient dans les désagréments du mariage que leur *durée* et, pour ainsi dire, leur éternité. (*Lettres persanes*, p. 244)

Let us remember Montesquieu's words that one does not marry for oneself, but for posterity, for one's family; that essentially love and marriage are two separate states, one refusing the company of the other. Here is precisely Usbek's point of view in his desire to have more children and in the following complaint: Ils [les Chrétiens] ne le font pas [le mariage] consister dans le plaisir des sens; au contraire, comme je te l'ai déjà dit, il semble qu'ils veulent l'en bannir autant qu'ils peuvent" (p. 245). Is Montesquieu not speaking for himself when writing: "Le mariage . . . est un contrat susceptible de toutes les conventions, et on n'en a dû bannir que celles qui auraient pu en affaiblir l'objet" (p. 245)? These "conventions" might be the same already mentioned above in connection with letter 55, those which allow a man sexual freedom to love outside Hymen's boun-dary. The "objet" Usbek refers to above is, of course, offspring and immortality of the family tree.[8] A roaming heart and other feminine objects of pursuit increase a man's potency at home, implies Montesquieu.

III
CHANGE AND INSTABILITY

ONE OF THE MOST ALL PERVASIVE THEMES in the *Lettres persanes* is that of change, mutation, or more precisely, inconstancy and instability. We have just seen it illustrated concerning love relationships. And one finds it implied in the very titles of several letters: "Inconstance des principes professés chez les Chrétiens par les particuliers et par les princes" (letter 75), "Inconstance de la fortune des modes et des mœurs en France" (letter 99), "Instabilité des fortunes en France" (letter 132), "Changements auxquels la Terre est sujette; . . ." (letter 113). It is with this viewpoint in mind that the author begins his long treatise on depopulation (letters 102 to 122). Man himself, not the earth alone, is caught up in a kind of Pascalian cosmos; he is subject to annihilation by a threatening environment:

> Les hommes, dans une demeure si sujette aux changements, sont dans un état aussi incertain: cent mille causes peuvent agir, capables de les détruire et, à plus forte raison, d'augmenter ou de diminuer leur nombre. (*Lettres persanes*, p. 236)

He is subordinate to the capricious laws of nature around him, but, more important, he is capricious himself, in religion, morality, politics, economy, law, custom and fashion. From a detached, objective point of view Montesquieu observes man's ever-changing nature. Sometimes his unpredictable moods and fancy create humorous consequences, sometimes tragic ones. Our author wishes to educate society and offer it an ideal at which to aim (best exemplified by the second society of Troglodytes), but he does not forget that man (and especially the Frenchman) is what he *is* and not what he ought to be. Both Montesquieu and Montaigne shake their heads at ever-changing French modes, which vary as unpredictably as a woman's fickle nature:

> Quant il [le peuple français] portoit le busc de son pourpoint entre les mamelles, il maintenoit par vives raisons qu'il estoit en son vray lieu; quelques années après, le voylà avalé jusques entre les cuisses: il se moque de son autre usage, le trouve inepte et insupportable. (*Essais*, I, ch. 49, p. 329)

> Quelquefois, les coiffures montent insensiblement, et une révolution les fait descendre tout à coup. Il a été un temps que leur hauteur immense mettait le visage d'une femme au milieu d'elle-même. Dans un autre, c'étaient les pieds qui occupaient cette place: les talons faisaient un pié-destal qui les tenait en l'air. Qui pourrait le croire? Les architectes ont été souvent obligés de hausser, de baisser et d'élargir leurs portes, selon que les parures des femmes exigeaient d'eux ce changement, et les règles de leur art ont été asservies à ces caprices. (*Lettres persanes*, p. 206)

Each writer attacks the subject with a tone of hyperbole to express the rapidity of change which erases one style after another:

> Par ce que nostre changement est si subit et prompt en cela, que l'invention de tous les tailleurs du monde ne sçaurait fournir assez de nouvelletez, il est force que bien souvent les formes mesprisées reviennent en credit, et celles là mesmes tombent en mepris tantost après; (*Essais*, I, ch. 49, p. 329)

> Que me servirait de te faire une description exacte de leur habille-ment et de leurs parures? Une mode nouvelle viendrait détruire tout mon ouvrage, comme celui de leurs ouvriers, avant que tu eusses reçu ma lettre, tout serait changé. (*Lettres persanes*, p. 205)

If Montaigne was Montesquieu's source of inspiration in describing capri-cious modes in France, then one must concede that he contributed to the theme's gaiety. In addition to the above excerpts one need only read more of letter 99 to note fully the author's genius at mocking the vanity of every changing fashion during the Regency.

To illustrate the inconstancy of French morality Montesquieu brings to light the contradictory attitudes of certain "Christian kings" concerning slavery. What they abolished during one era they allow in another. Thus, an ethical principle is less powerful than mere expediency and self-interest. After this example Montesquieu punctuates with a sort of exclamation point that stirs our memory: *"Vérité dans un temps, erreur dans un autre"* (p. 159). One should immediately recall Pascal in these words, and through Pascal, Montaigne:

> "Pourquoi me tuez-vous? —Eh quoi! ne demeurez-vous pas de l'autre côté de l'eau? Mon ami, si vous demeuriez de ce côté, je serais un assassin et cela serait injuste de vous tuer de la sorte; mais puisque vous demeurez de l'autre côté, je suis un brave, et cela est juste:
> *Vérité au deça des Pyrénées, erreur au delà*[1]

Following are Montaigne's comments which inspired Pascal:

> Que nous dira donc en cette necessité la philosophie? Que nous suyvons les loix de nostre pays? C'est à dire cette mer flotante des opinions d'un peuple ou d'un Prince, qui me peindront la justice d'autant de couleurs et la reformeront en autant de visages qu'il y aura en eux de changemens de passion? Je ne puis pas avoir le jugement si flexible. Quelle bonté est-ce que je voyois hyer en credit, et demain plus, et que le traict d'une riviere faict crime?
> *Quelle verité que ces montaignes bornent, qui est mensonge au monde qui se tient au delà?* (*Essais*, II, ch. 12, p. 287)

What Pascal demonstrates relative to place, Montesquieu shows in relation to time, while Montaigne (the most universal of the three) discusses fluctuating morality in respect to place and time. But the points of the three moralists are all similar: that man indeed lacks a stable, guiding principle and that even his laws fail to hold up immutable standards of justice and morality.

Human (not Divine) justice is relative to that group in power, for it is the strong who decide what is a crime; the weaker party must suffer its laws. During a revolution those judged guilty of treason are, of course, the losers. He who has gained the upper hand determines what is treason. Montaigne touches on this relative state of crime in considering France's wars of religion. Montesquieu offers us a similar paradox illustrated by English history; his example is more witty, concrete and playful, yet the same principle holds in both cases. Treason is a relative affair:

> Et chez nous icy, j'ai veu telle chose qui nous estoit capitale, devenir
> legitime; et nous, qui en tenons d'autres, sommes à mesmes, selon
> l'incertitude de la fortune guerriere, d'estre un jour criminels de lèze
> majesté humaine et divine, nostre justice tombant à la merci de l'injus-
> tice, et, en l'espace de peu d'années de possession, prenant une essence
> contraire. (*Essais,* II, ch. 12, p. 287)

> Le crime de lèse-majesté n'est autre chose, selon eux, que le crime que
> le plus faible commet contre le plus fort en lui désobéissant, de quelque
> manière qu'il lui désobéisse. Aussi le peuple d'Angleterre qui se trouva
> le plus fort contre un de leurs rois déclara-t-il que c'était un crime de
> lèse-majesté à un prince de faire la guerre à ses sujets. . . .
>
> Les Anglais disent qu'un de leurs rois, ayant vaincu et fait
> prisonnier un prince qui lui disputait la couronne, voulut lui reprocher
> son infidelité et sa perfidie: "Il n'y a qu'un moment, dit le prince
> infortuné, qu'il vient d'être décidé lequel de nous deux est le traître."
> (*Lettres persanes*, pp. 216-17)

Sir John Harrington (1561-1612) explained the paradox in a different way:
"Treason doth never prosper; what's the reason? Why, if it prosper, none
dare call it treason."

In letter 75, entitled "Inconstance de principes professés chez les
Chrétiens par les particuliers et par les Princes," Usbek is shocked by the
unpredictable nature of faith in Christian France. The upper classes, that
libertine society of the Regency, are defined basically as non-believers, a
group of natural rebels who shook off the yoke of religion almost before it
touched their shoulders. But, more surprising is that these *esprits forts* are
not stable atheists but change their attitudes towards philosophy as well as
religion, depending on their mood or whim. "Certes, c'est un subject
merveilleusement vain, divers et ondoyant, que l'homme. Il est malaisé d'y
fonder jugement constant et uniforme" (*Essais*, I, ch. 1, p. 5). As Montaigne introduces man to us in the *Essais*—an unpredictable and downright
capricious creature—so we find him here in letter 75. The wavering atheist
who confides in Usbek resembles Bion of antiquity. For both characters
good health means freedom from the vexing thought of God and a nebulous
afterlife, but once death threatens them they huddle safely into the lap of
religion:

Ils [les athées] establissent, . . . par la raison de leur jugement, que ce qui se recite des enfers et des peines futures est feint. Mais, l'occasion de l'experimenter s'offrant lors que la vieillesse ou les maladies les approchent de leur mort, la terreur d'icelle les remplit d'une nouvelle creance par l'horreur de leur condition à venir. . . . Ils recitent de Bion qu'infect des atheismes de Theodorus, il avoit esté longtemps se moquant des hommes religieux; mais, la mort le surprenant, qu'il se rendit aux plus extremes superstitions, comme si les dieux s'ostoyent et se remettoyent selon l'affaire de Bion. (*Essais*, II, ch. 12, p. 124)

Quand le médecin est auprès de mon lit, le confesseur me trouve à mon avantage. Je sais bien empêcher la religion de m'affliger quand je me porte bien; mais je lui permets de me consoler quand je suis malade: lorsque je n'ai plus rien à espérer d'un côté, la religion se présente et me gagne par ses promesses; je veux bien m'y livrer et mourir du côté de l'espérance. (*Lettres persanes*, p. 159)

Of course, in the above comparison Montesquieu's *esprit fort* is or was baptized Christian; Bion was a pagan. The atheist's irreverent creator has dared a step farther in his licentious portrait; he responds to the reality of his own era but also perhaps he is reacting to Montaigne who prudently refrains from defining a Christian in the same terms:

Et ce que dit Plato, qu'il est peu d'hommes si fermes en l'atheisme, qu'un dangier pressant ne ramène à la recognoissance de la divine puissance, ce rolle ne touche point un vray Chrestien. C'est à faire aux religions mortelles et humaines d'estre receues par une humaine conduite. (*Essais*, II, ch. 12, pp. 123-24)

Usbek demonstrates that there exists neither a "true Christian" nor a true atheist in his French environment. Christianity, implies Montesquieu, is also subject to the laws of relativity which govern man. Montaigne, on the other hand, disassociates Christianity from atheism and seeks to isolate it from the turmoil of contradictory opinions found in antiquity's innumerable sects.

The *esprit fort* is the most vacillating and inconstant of philosophers. He attaches himself to one doctrine after another, rejecting none, absorbing all according to his humor:

> Je crois l'immortalité de l'âme par semestre; mes opinions dépendent
> absolument de la constitution de mon corps: selon que j'ai plus ou
> moins d'esprits animaux, que mon estomac digère bien ou mal, que l'air
> que je respire est subtil ou grossier, que les viandes dont je me nourris
> sont légères ou solides, je suis spinosiste, socinien, catholique, impie
> ou dévot. (*Lettres persanes*, p. 159)

However more playful and capricious we find this fellow than any similar
creature in the *Essais* or their author himself, Montaigne's *Apologie*
apparently inspired Montesquieu to create such a humorous chameleon.
The essayist also considers the body's continual and ever-changing
influence upon the mind. Cleomenes of antiquity resembles Montesquieu's
philosopher in that his health changes his opinions, or rather, his
"fantasies." When reproached by his friends for being inconsistent, the
Greek replied:

> je croy bien . . . ; aussi ne suis-je pas celuy que je suis estant sain;
> estant autre, aussi sont autres mes opinions et fantasies. (*Essais*, II,
> ch. 12, p. 269)

Montaigne also illustrates this example in more abstract terms:

> Combien diversement jugeons nous des choses?
> Combien de fois changeons nous nos fantasies?
> (Ibid., p. 267)

> Toutefois que la fortune nous remue cinq cens fois de place, qu'elle ne
> face que vuyder et remplir sans cesse, comme dans un vaisseau, dans
> nostre croyance autres et autres opinions, tousjours la presente et la
> derniere c'est la certaine et l'infallible. (Ibid., p. 268)

The atheist of Usbek's letter maintains that his philosophy depends
on the "constitution" of his body—whether his stomach digests well,
whether his meat is light or heavy. Besides offering us the amusing anecdote above concerning Cleomenes, Montaigne speaks of fevers and drinks
which overturn his judgment (ibid., p. 269); if his stomach is empty, he
feels and thus thinks differently than when it is full (ibid., p. 271). The
body's influence on the mind is constant and inescapable:

> Il est certain que nostre apprehension, nostre jugement et les facultez de
> nostre ame en general souffrent selon les mouvemens et alterations du
> corps, lesquelles alterations sont continuelles. (Ibid., p. 269)

> à peine se peut il rencontrer une seule heure en la vie où nostre juge-
> ment se trouve en sa deue assiete, nostre corps estant subject à tant de
> continuelles mutations . . . (Ibid., p. 270)

One factor which determines the constitution of the atheist's body
and the inclination of his spirit is the very air he breathes: "selon . . . que
l'aire que je respire est subtil ou grossier . . . " Here it appears that
Montesquieu picked up the adjectives "subtil" and "grossier" from the Latin
"tenue" and "crassum" in a text of Cicero's:

> nostre estre despend de l'air . . .
> *Athenis tenue caelum, ex quo etiam acutiores putantur Attici; crassum*
> *Thebis itaque pinques Thebani et valente. . .*

> L'air d'Athènes est *subtil*, et c'est pourquoi les Athéniens sont réputés
> avoir l'esprit plus délicat; celui de Thébes est *épais* [i.e., grossier]; aussi
> les Thébains passent-ils pour gens grossiers et vigoureux. (*De fato*, IV)
> (Ibid., p. 282)

Usbek conveys the vacillating faith and incredulity of society's
esprits forts with an image of movement implying water:

> Aussi ne sont-ils pas plus fermes dans leur incrédulité que dans leur foi;
> ils vivent dans *un flux et reflux* qui les porte sans cesse de l'un à
> l'autre. (*Lettres persanes* p. 159)

Such is the most prominent type of metaphor in the same section of the
Apologie. Usbek's metaphor, "flux et reflux," (flood tide and ebb tide)
specifically denotes the ocean's regular rolling movement back and forth
from shore, a natural flowing in and out. Was this image inspired by
Virgil's poetry combined with Montaigne's commentary on his own
fluctuating opinion?

> Autant que je m'estois jetté en avant, je me relance d'autant en arriere:
> *Qualis ubi alterno procurrens qurqite pontus Nunc ruit ad terras,*
> *scopulisque superjacit undam, Spumeus, extremamque sinu*

perfundit arenam; Nunc rapidus retro atque aestu revoluta resorbens
Saxa fugit, litusque vado labente relinquit.

Telle la mer, dans un mouvement périodique, tantôt se rue vers la terre,
couvre d'onde les rochers et se répand au loin sur le rivage, tantôt,
retournant sur elle-même et entraînant dans son reflux les cailloux
qu'elle avait apportés, elle fuit et, abaissant ses eaux, laisse la plage à
découvert. (Virgile, *Enéide*, XI, p. 624) (*Essais*, II, ch. 12, p. 275)

Yet at the same time let us remember that this commonplace of metaphors
had been in the writer's vocabulary since an early *mémoire* on "Le Flux et le
reflux de la mer" which he composed prior to the *Lettres persanes*.

The *esprit fort*'s remark—"je crois l'immortalité de l'âme par
semestre"—could have been inspired by Montaigne's long discussion of the
soul in the *Apologie*. In imitation of Cicero the author brings together many
conflicting opinions and dogmas concerning the human soul, among others,
whether it is immortal or not (see II, ch. 12, pp. 153-54). Usbek's *esprit
fort* refuses to attach himself to one dogma alone, but will, like Montaigne,
accept any one at a given time in order to mock all of them in the same
breath. However, he condenses his disdain more ironically than Montaigne, ridiculing the debate on the soul's immortality by embracing sides
both for and against, according to the month of the year. Through his character's satirical pose Montesquieu is able to elaborate or even outdo the
philosophical detachment already demonstrated by Cicero and Montaigne.
His playfulness is more immediately obvious, his nonchalance more accen-
tuated by sarcasm.[2]

IV

LAW

Skepticism

USBEK'S LETTER 129 BEGINS AS an attack upon law and legislators in France. Its first part is composed of several short, succinct paragraphs the criticisms of which are directed at the prejudiced and narrow minds of French lawmakers, the petty details and childish formalities of justice and, finally, the absurdity of having written certain laws in Latin. One can find all these complaints already in Montaigne. They are not uttered in the same tone (for the essayist revealed greater bitterness and exasperation in his attacks), but one finds that identical flaws existed in the *ancien régime's* judicial system at the end of the sixteenth century as at the beginning of the eighteenth. The process of justice, like the entire hierarchy of that society, was so complicated, confused and distorted by inequality that any magistrate not upset by his professional environment must have had a heart of lead. Neither Montaigne nor Montesquieu was such a creature.

Montesquieu, under the guise of Usbek, speaks more cooly and with greater detachment than his predecessor, abstracting (we believe) certain concrete episodes found in the *Essais* and reducing the malpractice and injustice around him to general, descriptive formulas. Nevertheless, his irony notably concerning the *hommes de robe*, his own colleagues, is biting and reminiscent of Montaigne's.

> Elles [les lois] sont souvent faictes par des sots, plus souvent par des gens qui, en haine d'equalité, ont faute d'equité, mais toujours par des hommes, autheurs vains et irresolus. (*Essais*, III, ch. 13, p. 320)

> La plupart des législateurs ont été des hommes bornés, que le hasard a
> mis à la tête des autres, et qui n'ont presque consulté que leurs préjugés
> et leurs fantaisies. (*Lettres persanes*, p. 270)

Usbek writes that legislators are discredited amongst those who
possess any common sense ("ils sont . . . décrédités auprès des gens de bon
sens"). And Montaigne's principal complaint about *hommes de robe* is also
that their common sense had degenerated: "De vray, le plus souvent ils [les
magistrats] semblent estre ravalez, mesmes du sens commun" (I, ch. 25,
p. 148). They were a scholastic, eclectic, and petty-minded group whose
pomposity (then as today they wore long black gowns and white wigs)
deserved a good tweak. Montaigne pinches them many times over in his
Essais, but never so rudely as here:

> Qui regardera de bien près à ce genre de gens, qui s'estend bien loing, il
> trouvera, comme moy, que le plus souvent ils ne s'entendent, ny
> autruy, et qu'ils ont la souvenance assez pleine, mais le jugement
> entierement creux, sinon que leur nature d'elle mesme le leur ait
> autrement façonné; . . . (*Essais*, I, ch. 25, p. 148)

In comparison to this vigorous jab at empty-headed magistrates, the first
paragraph of Usbek's letter quoted above is not as bold and daring as it
would appear at first sight.

Perhaps Montesquieu speaks in a derogatory tone about the very
respectable *hommes de robe* not so much because of their individual flaws
but because of the inane customs and traditions of the judicial system in
which they were caught up. The fault lay perhaps less in the magistrates
than in the matter with which they had to deal. Usbek uses vague, negative
terms which connote any number of specific flaws in court procedure:

> ils [les législateurs] se sont amusés à faire des institutions puériles,
> avec lesquelles ils se sont à la vérité conformés aux petits esprits, mais
> décrédités auprès des gens de bon sens.

> Ils se sont jetés dans des détails inutiles; ils ont donné dans les cas
> particuliers, ce qui marque un génie étroit qui ne voit les choses que par
> parties et n'embrasse rien d'une vue générale. (*Lettres persanes*, p. 270)

"Institutions puériles" certainly denote the learned glosses by which magistrates made each new decision. Some judges would write entire volumes of compilations where for the decision in one case he refers to innumerable analogous examples, where obscure authorities dating from the Middle Ages or near antiquity were evoked supposedly to clarify matters. Such overly emphasized scholastic tradition served only to impede actual justice. Such pedantry proved only the decadence of the judicial process. We should not be astonished to see Rica write elsewhere of "cette armée effroyable de glossateurs, de commentateurs, de compilateurs: gens aussi faibles par le peu de justesse de leur esprit qu'ils sont forts par leur nombre prodigieux" (p. 209).[1]

Montaigne speaks out at length on this subject and with indignant eloquence. Like Usbek he emphasizes how glosses distracted one from the essential matter at hand, blowing up one subject into many tiny parts and rendering a final decision more tenuous and difficult to come upon. Moreover, he concludes that the number of authorities quoted for a given case has increased the number of judges and lawyers—further extenuating an already labyrinthine legal process (see *Essais*, III, ch. 13, p. 315).

In his vague allusion to "cas particuliers" Usbek may also have had in mind the outlandish number of laws themselves which grew out of the custom of glossing. Montaigne likewise was exasperated by this mass of data:

> Qu'ont gaigné nos legislateurs a choisir cent mille *espèces et faicts particuliers*, et y attacher cent mille loix? . . . La multiplication de nos inventions n'arrivera pas à la variation des exemples. (Ibid., p. 313)

Usbek laments the "génie étroit" of the legislators "qui ne voit les choses que par parties et n'embrasse rien d'une vue générale" (p. 270). His regret reflects Montaigne's main point for judicial reform: "Les plus desirables [lois], ce sont les plus rares, plus simples et generales."

Some of Usbek's ideas on this essential matter—that judicial commentary was petty, that it hampered basic concerns—may have been inspired by Montaigne. Both critics envisaged eliminating the scattered elements of strict court procedure in order to embrace more fundamental principles of justice. And Montaigne implied that one would have to pass over certain periphera and forget the letter of the law to keep the spirit of the law:

> . . . il est forcé de faire tort en detail qui veut faire droict en gros, et
> injustice en petites choses qui veut venir à chef de faire justice ès
> grandes; . . . (Ibid., p. 319)

Thus, the essential ideas of reform in common between our two
disillusioned magistrates are the following: that the entire legal process
should be brought down from its pretentious pedestal, simplified and
reduced to a level of common sense, eliminating the artificial barriers to
justice—the learned glosses and the petty laws which sprang out of them,
the overcomplicated style of certain legal documents.

Montaigne hints that the custom of glossing might just as well be
done away with:

> Nous doubtions sur Ulpian, redoutons encore sur Bartolus et Baldus.[2]
> Il falloit effacer la trace de cette diversité innumerable d'opinions, non
> poinct s'en parer et en entester la posterité. (Ibid., pp. 314-15)

Interpreting the glossateurs of laws did not restrict the authority of judges;
paradoxically, so many contradictory authorities allowed them to decide
arbitrarily in favor of one or the other side. Under such circumstances truth
went out the window:

> nous avons en France plus de loix que tout le reste du monde en-
> semble . . . et si, avons tant laissé à opiner et decider à nos juges, qu'il
> ne fut jamais liberté si puissante et si licentieuse. (Ibid., p. 313)

In view of these absurd conditions it is no wonder that Montesquieu described legislators as men who needed only to consult their fantasy. He may
have had Montaigne in mind while doing so.

As another reform along the same line, laws should be written in
French, not Latin. How can a people know what the laws are, if they cannot read them?—a point made by both authors in the following comparison:

> quelle chose peut estre plus estrange, que de voir un peuple obligé à
> suivre des loix qu'il *n'entendit onques*, attachés en tous ses affaires
> domestiques, mariages, donations, testamens, ventes et achapts, à des
> regles qu'il ne peut sçavoir, n'estant escrites ny publiées en sa langue,
> et desquelles par necessité il luy faille acheter l'interpretation et l'usage?
> (*Essais*, I, ch. 23, p. 123)

quelques-un (des législateurs) ont affecté de se servir d'une autre langue que la vulgaire: chose absurde pour un faiseur de lois. Comment peut-on les observer, si elles ne sont pas connues? (*Lettres persanes*, p. 270)

On the Changing of Laws

Despite Usbek and Montaigne's skepticism concerning the nature of laws, paradoxically they agree that one must abide by them. As idiotic as the judicial system is ["la forme de cette justice . . . est un vray tesmoignage de l'humaine imbecillité," wrote the essayist (III, ch. 13, p. 318)], nevertheless, citizens must obey its precepts consistently to uphold the tranquillity and order of the state. One may be skeptical in thought, but in deed conformity is the rule:

> le sage doit . . . suivre entierement les façons et formes receues. . . . Car c'est la regle des regles, et generale loy des loix, que chacun observe celles du lieu où il est. (*Essais* I, ch. 23, p. 125)

> Quelles que soient les lois, il faut toujours les suivre et regarder comme la conscience publique, à laquelle celle des particuliers doit se conformer toujours. (*Lettres persanes*, p. 271)

Whereas paragraphs 1 through 3 of Usbek's letter 129 reflected Montesquieu, the reformer and social critic, paragraphs 4 through 7 suggest his conservative side. And this part of his physiognomy is related to the Montaigne of volume I (first pub. 1580), while the criticism examined above seems to be derived largely from the later, more liberal and pessimistic Montaigne of volume III (first pub. 1588). In "De la coustume et de ne changer aisément une loy receue" (I, ch. 23) the author codifies in the title a principle one finds illustrated throughout the *Essais*: that changing laws is risky and can often prove more destructive than allowing them to remain, poor though they may be. By repeating this theme Montaigne creates a veritable piece of counter-propaganda addressed to the rebellious Protestants. Through Usbek Montesquieu espouses the same principle, expressing the danger of change in terms found in "De la vanité":

> Toutes grandes *mutations* esbranlent l'estat et le *desordonnent*.
> Qui viseroit droit à la guerison et en consulteroit avant toute œuvre se refroidiroit volontiers d'y mettre la *main*. (*Essais*, III, ch. 9, p. 192)

> Ils [les législateurs] ont souvent aboli sans nécessité celles qu'ils ont trouvées établies; c'est-à-dire qu'ils ont jeté les peuples dans les *désordres* inséparables des *changements*.
>   . . . il est quelquefois nécessaire de changer certaines lois. Mais le cas est rare, et, lorsqu'il arrive, il n'y faut toucher que d'une *main* tremblante: . . . (*Lettres persanes*, p. 271)

Montesquieu would not have had to look so far back as Montaigne to produce such a conservative, skeptical formula. As the *Lettres persanes* well illustrate, John Law had created havoc through his pernicious financial reform. For all his endeavor the ignorant Scot received no gratitude, finding safety only in exile, while society underwent a major upheaval in France. Just prior to the publication of his *Lettres* Montesquieu had observed and in fact experienced first hand the turmoil produced by bold but unwise change of the nation's laws.

Nevertheless, further textual resemblances as well as the same tenure of thought both in our letter and in "De la coustume" indicate that Montesquieu was not relying on his times alone in forming of his principles. Both writers—supple politicians, not rigid conformists—admit that occasionally circumstances arrive which demand that laws pass by the board:

> Si est-ce que *la fortune*, reservant tousjours son authorité au-dessus de nos *discours*, nous presente aucunefois la necessité si urgente, qu'il est besoing que les loix luy facent quelque place. (*Essais*, I ch. 23, p. 129)

> Il est vrai que, par une bizarrerie qui vient plutôt de *la nature* que de *l'esprit des hommes*, il est quelquefois nécessaire de changer certaines lois. (*Lettres persanes*, p. 271)

Montesquieu has virtually translated the sixteenth-century terms underlined above into contemporary French, keeping Montaigne's ideas intact. "La nature" in Montesquieu's text is synonymous with "la fortune" in Montaigne's; both imply the order of things outside of man's will and intellect. "Discours" in the above context means "raisonnement," suggesting, by association, man's power of reason. It is thus very close to Usbek's expression for our mind or intelligence—"l'esprit des hommes." Both writers believe then that chance circumstances demand change which the power of reason normally resists.

Montaigne speaks of the laws made to placate the Protestants which merely offered them an excuse for more mischief, so that in the end the compromise backfired. Usbek generalizes from this example, claiming that once a supposed change for the better became a change for the worse. Montaigne refers to this illusory improvement as a *remède* for a *mal*; Montesquieu turns this vocabulary into a paradox, saying that the "remède" turned out to be "un nouveau mal":

> On lict en nos loix mesmes, faites pour *le remede de ce premier mal*, l'aprentissage et l'excuse de toute sorte de mauvaises enterprises; et nous advient, ce que Thucidides dict des guerres civiles de son temps, qu'en faveur des vices publiques on les battisoit de mots nouveaux plus doux, pour leur excuse, abastardissant et amolissant leurs vrais titres. (*Essais*, I, ch. 23, p. 126)

> Dans la suite, elles [les lois] ont été trouvées trop dures, et, par un esprit d'équité, on a cru devoir s'en écarter; mais *ce remède était un nouveau mal.* (*Lettres persanes*, p. 271)

Note also above that while Montaigne refers to 'mots nouveaux plus doux" which succeeded only in weakening the laws' authority, Usbek in turn describes the original laws as "trop dures," a state which incited legislators to alter them. In either case, change, conceived as mitigation, worsened rather than improved the state of things.

Usbek's reasons for maintaining the existing laws are a bit cynical. He writes that the solemn and conservative aura which surrounds justice serves to convince the people that laws have some holy sanction, that they are in effect untouchable. In a more negative tone Montaigne speaks of religious laws and customs designed to hold the people in check. The two passages bear comparison:

> Puis que les hommes, par leur insuffisance, ne se peuvent assez payer d'une bonne monnoye, qu'on y employe encore la fauce. Ce moyen a esté practiqué par tous les Legislateurs, et n'est police où il n'y ait quelque meslange ou de vanité ceremonieuse, ou d'opinion mensongere,

> qui serve de bride à tenir le peuple en office. C'est pour cela que la pluspart ònt leurs origines et commencemens fabuleux et enrichis de mysteres supernaturels. (*Essais*, II, ch. 16, p. 346)

> on y doit observer tant de solennités et apporter tant de précautions que le peuple en conclut naturellement que les lois sont bien saintes, puis-qu'il faut tant de formalités pour les abroger. (*Lettres persanes*, p. 271)

The solemn pomp and circumstance are maintained primarily to impress the lower classes. On the other hand, a social philosopher and noble withdrawn from the riffraff of society needn't be dazzled by ceremony. Skeptical of law's ancient authority, Montaigne expressed his reservations openly:

> Les loix prennent leur authorité de la possession et de l'usage; il est dangereux de les ramener à leur naissance; elles grossissent et s'ennoblissent en roulant, comme nos rivieres; suyvez les contremont jusques à leur source, ce n'est qu'un petit surjon d'eau à peine reconnoissable, qui s'enorgueillit ainsi et se fortifie en vieillissant. (*Essais*, II, ch. 12, p. 292)

> Or les loix se maintiennent en credit, non par ce qu'elles sont justes, mais par ce qu'elles sont loix. C'est le fondement mystique de leur authorité; elles n'en ont poinct d'autre. (*Essais*, III, ch. 13, p. 320)

So once again we return to the essential paradoxes inherent in the first half of Usbek's letter and in the *Essais*. Although law's authority is a vain, illusory one, based on solemnity and ceremony of an almost supernatural nature, one must grant it due respect. Although educated, enlightened nobles may be skeptical of many formalities of justice, nevertheless they should obey, not change its precepts, for it is only through law's stability and permanence that the people revere them. An atmosphere of sanctity and mystery impresses the masses and encourages their respect for tradition. Montesquieu, like Montaigne, proves himself to be a very balanced social critic, a paradoxical creature whom one might dub a "liberal-conservative." Too intelligent to preach conformity without first criticizing the inadequate, overly complicated trappings of justice, he is nevertheless too wise to recommend change which might upset the delicate order of the monarchy.

A Metaphor

Whenever Montaigne speaks of law, he compares it to medicine, or rather whenever discussing the state he brings up the subject of its health—and inevitably in pessimistic terms. "Nostre police se porte mal." (III, ch. 9, p. 194) The comparison of law and medicine is an ancient one, dating back to Plutarch and Plato.[3] However, Montaigne develops the metaphor considerably in his individual, rich style:

> Elle [une civile police] dure souvent contre des *maladies* mortelles et intestines . . . (*Essais*, III, ch. 9, 194)

> Ce qui me poise, le plus, c'est qu'à compter les simptomes de nostre *mal*, j'en vois autant de naturels et de ceux que le ciel nous envoye et proprement siens, que de ceux que nostre desreiglement et l'imprudence humaine y conferent. (Ibid., p. 196)

> D'autant que la discipline ordinaire d'un Estat qui est en sa *santé* ne pourvoit pas à ces accidens extraordinaires; elle presuppose un *corps* qui se tient en ses principaux membres et office . . .[4] (*Essais*, I, ch. 23, p. 129)

Montesquieu may have been inspired by Montaigne to speak of political change as disruption in medical terms. Comparing the political reformer to a doctor, Montaigne had maintained that a surgeon's purpose should not be simply to destroy the sick flesh of a patient. Montesquieu alludes in similar fashion to a cure of financial ills undertaken by the Duke of Noailles. By cutting out the "useless flesh" he did not cure the illness. Rica develops his metaphor considerably, as Montaigne is capable of doing:

> La fin du chirurgien n'est pas de faire mourir la *mauvaise chair*; ce n'est l'acheminement de sa cure. Il regarde au delà, dy faire renaistre la naturelle et rendre la partie à son deu estre. (*Essais*, III, ch. 9, p. 192)

> La France, à la mort du feu Roi, était un corps accablé de mille maux. N . . . prit le fer à la main, retrancha les *chairs inutiles*, et appliqua quelques remèdes topiques. Mais il restait toujours un vice intérieur à guérir. Un étranger est venu, qui a entrepris cette cure. Après bien des remèdes violents, il a cru lui avoir rendu son embonpoint, et il l'a seulement rendue bouffie. (*Lettres persanes*, p. 293)

At another moment Usbek compares jurisprudence with medicine, placing both in a negative light similar to the way Montaigne does:

> Le Roy Ferdinand, envoyant des colonies aux Indes, prouveut sagement qu'on n'y menast aucuns escholiers de la jurisprudence, de crainte que les procès ne peuplassent en ce nouveau monde, comme estant science de sa nature generatrice d'altercation et division; jugeant avec Platon, que c'est mauvaise provision de pays que jurisconsultes et medecins. (*Essais*, III, ch. 13, p. 314)

> Ces lois étrangères ont introduit des formalités dont l'excès est la honte de la raison humaine. Il serait assez difficile de décider si la forme s'est rendue plus pernicieuse lorsqu'elle est entrée dans la jurisprudence, ou lorsqu'elle s'est logée dans la médecine; si elle a fait plus de ravages sous la robe d'un jurisconsulte que sous le large chapeau d'un médecin; et si, dans l'une, elle a plus ruiné de gens qu'elle n'en a tué dans l'autre.[5] (*Lettres persanes*, p. 209)

Like his famous source Montesquieu uses comparisons between law and medicine to evince his skepticism concerning their effectiveness, to emphasize the danger of any so-called cures for the body politic. Montesquieu conceives and develops the metaphor with considerable originality; Montaigne offered him only the basic theme out of which grew the two ingenious variations above. Although later Montesquieu was to take an interest in the history and positive evolution of medicine, here in a witty work of his youth he treats the subject according to familiar literary tradition. One is reminded of Molière's satire of doctors' ineptitude.

In sum, it seems clear that Montesquieu composed the first seven paragraphs of letter 129 with Montaigne in mind as his model. His rather harsh remarks at the expense of lawmakers, his general criticism of the petty, hampering formalities of justice, his rejection of Latin as the official language of law—all these complaints can be found in the *Essais*, as well as the general principle of not abolishing or changing laws. Also, like the paradoxical Montaigne, Montesquieu preaches obedience to the nation's legal code despite its flaws. Although these lucid, educated philosophers did not consider laws holy and untouchable, they knew it necessary for the people to think them so; a state's tranquillity depends upon the obedience of all its citizens. Of course, Montaigne was not the only critic of judicial abuse prior to Montesquieu, for it was a commonplace already during the sixteenth century. Rabelais, Budé, Alciat, and others had criticized glossing. The humanist reformer Cujas had also pleaded for the unifying and simplification of French law. But Montesquieu chose Montaigne as his primary source for criticism because the essayist expressed himself most forcefully and eloquently on the issue. His metaphors on law and medicine struck Montesquieu's fancy, as did certain other turns of phrase. Montaigne's skill in writing inspired Montesquieu's imitation to some extent. His style as well as his ideas impressed the youthful reformer. Montesquieu tends to generalize from Montaigne, reducing the essayist's marvelous developments to their lowest common denominator. Basic principles and formulas for reform and regulation interest Montesquieu. In letter 129 he is, above all, a theoretician for the cause of common sense. The *homme de robe*'s remark in letter 68 pertains here. Having sold his library to buy his title, the nonchalant philosopher tells Rica:

> Ce n'est pas que je les regrette: nous autres juges ne nous enflons point d'une vaine science. Qu'avons-nous à faire de tous ces volumes de lois? Presque tous les cas sont hypothétiques et sortent de la règle générale. (*Lettres persanes*, p. 148)

Such wisdom and skepticism, Montesquieu shared with Montaigne.

Laws of Honor versus Laws of Justice

In letter 90 Usbek is surprised to relate what he entitles "Conflit qui existe en France entre le point d'honneur et la loi pénale." For centuries there had been two powers of jurisdiction in France which were by their nature entirely opposed to one another. Laws of honor applied particularly to the nobles who would duel to decide their differences. However, the courts of justice, headed by the more recently ennobled *hommes de robe*, condemned this unlawful procedure and punished offenders severely. Thus, the body of the nobility was split in half—the magistrates on one side, the *noblesse d'épée* on the other. Usbek phrased the conflict between these forces in dramatic antitheses, the source of which he found in the *Essais*:

> Qu'est-il plus farouche . . . qu'il se face en une police un quatriesme
> estat . . . lequel estat, ayant la charge des loix et souveraine authorité
> des biens et des vies, face un corps à part de celuy de la noblesse; d'où il
> avienne qu'il y ayt doubles loix, celles de l'honneur, et celles de la
> justice, en plusieurs choses fort contraires, (*aussi rigoureusement
> condamnent celles-là un démenti souffert, comme celles icy un démanti
> revanché); par le devoir des armes, celuy-là soit degradé d'honneur et de
> noblesse, que souffre une injure, et, par le devoir civil, celuy qui s'en
> venge, encoure une peine capitale, (qui s'adresse aux loix pour avoir
> raison d'une offence faite à son honneur, il se deshonnore; et qui ne s'y
> adresse, il en est puny et chastié par les loix);* et, de ces deux pieces si
> diverses se raportent toutesfois à un seul chef, ceux-là ayent la paix,
> ceux-cy la guerre en charge; ceux-là ayent le gaing, ceux-cy l'honneur;
> ceux-là le sçavoir, ceux-cy la vertu; ceux-là la parole, ceux-cy l'action;
> ceux-là la justice, ceux-cy la vaillance; ceux-là la raison, ceux-cy la
> force; ceux-là la robbe longue, ceux-cy la courte en partage. (*Essais,*
> I, ch. 23, p. 124)

> Ainsi les Français sont dans un état bien violent: car *les mêmes lois de
> l'honneur obligent un honnête homme de se venger quand il a été
> offensé; mais, d'un autre côté, la justice le punit des plus cruelles
> peines lorsqu'il se venge. Si l'on suit les lois de l'honneur, on périt
> sur un échafaud; si l'on suit les lois de la justice, on est banni pour
> jamais de la société des hommes. Il n'y a donc que cette cruelle alterna-
> tive, ou de mourir, ou d'être indigne de vivre.* (*Lettres persanes,* p. 188)

Montesquieu both abridged and refined Montaigne's brilliant and lengthy
accumulation of contrasts, providing a climactic ending to Usbek's letter.[6]

Tracing a bit of French history, the Persian explains how once
("autrefois") the system of seconds brought others into the fray who should
not have been involved:

> Mais ce qu'il y avait de mal, c'est que souvent le jugement se rendait
> entre d'autres parties que celles qui y étaient intéressées.
>
>   Pour peu qu'un homme fût connu d'un autre, il fallait qu'il entrât
> dans la dispute, et qu'il payât de sa personne, comme s'il avait été lui-
> même en colère. (*Lettres persanes,* p. 188)

Is Montesquieu remembering Montaigne's criticism of the custom of
battling seconds, thirds, even fourths, or more precisely a specific instance

of such absurdity? The essayist's brother, Matecolom, while in Rome was called upon to second a gentleman he hardly knew ("*qu'il ne coqnoissoit quere*") against another whom he knew better and was closer to (see II, ch. 27, p. 417). Perhaps Montesquieu had this incident in mind when he generalized concerning the past custom of entering the fight, no matter how little acquainted one was with one's partner ("*pour peu qu'un homme fût connu d'un autre*").

Reacting to the particularly absurd situation his brother fell into, Montaigne interjects, "je voudrais qu'on me fît raison de ces loix de l'honneur qui vont si souvent choquant et troublant celles de la raison" (II, ch. 27, p. 417). Montesquieu's reflection on the subject is more ironic and caustic:

> Il se sentait toujours honoré d'un tel choix et d'une préférence si flatteuse; et tel qui n'aurait pas voulu donner quatre pistoles à un homme pour le sauver de la potence, lui et toute sa famille, ne faisait aucune difficulté d'aller risquer pour lui mille fois sa vie. (*Lettres persanes*, p. 188)

Montaigne's criticism of dueling was limited to eliminating its defects and abuse. He endeavored to convince the nobility that there was no honor in killing one's opponent, that victory need not mean murder. But not once does the essayist question the essential principle on which the "justice" of dueling stood: that the man who was stronger or more skilled was right, his weaker opponent wrong. However, the more enlightened Montesquieu cuts the ground from under this false premise with one sharp blow:

> Cette manière de décider était assez mal imaginée: car, de ce qu'un homme était plus adroit ou plus fort qu'un autre, il ne s'ensuivait pas qu'il eût de meilleures raisons. (*Lettres persanes*, p. 188)

Despite this rational objection, Montesquieu, like Montaigne, had a strong sentiment for a form of justice which signified a man's strength, skill, courage, and, above all, his class. One should remember the author's scathing remark at the expense of that man who was delighted by the edict condemning duels: "il l'observe si bien," someone whispers in Rica's ear, "qu'il y a six mois qu'il reçut cent coups de bâton pour ne le pas violer" (p. 124). Later in *Mes Pensées* Montesquieu will say almost the same thing about Voltaire subsequent to the Rohan affair (see *pensée* 1589; 931).

The theme of letter 90 revolves around a positive issue, the *point d'honneur*, which Usbek tells us is particularly pronounced "chez les gens de guerre." Montesquieu admired the military for its sturdy virtues. Moreover, it was his father's profession. A poor but clever and courageous man, Jacques de Secondat acquired a certain reputation as a soldier, whereas Jean Louis, his eldest son, found his career in the courts of justice. In recent family tradition the house of Secondat was thus split between *la robe longue* and *la robe courte*, as Montaigne calls them. Montesquieu felt a tug from both sides of the nobility and offered his son a choice of either one as a profession, saying that in the military there was more opportunity for glory, in law more chance of independence (see *pensée* 5; 69). With what patriotism Rica speaks of the *Invalides*! He would like to see the names of all those who gave their life for their country inscribed in the temples of the state as a sign of their glory and nobility. Montesquieu's admiration for military virtues and traditions was too great for him to refute categorically the custom of dueling. Like his fellow magistrate of Bordeaux, Montaigne, he stood back and criticized but did not reject the status quo. He wrote that there were three kinds of tribunals which were almost never in agreement, that of law, honor and religion (see *pensée* 51; 1905). Such had been the state of things for hundreds of years. Prior to 1721 Montesquieu was not about to ignore reality of the past and present by dreaming up some ideal system for the future.

V
THE THEME OF RETIREMENT

INVALUABLE TO THE NOBILITY'S HONOR and glory is his independence from the Court, his power to determine his own destiny without interference from the king. We shall see that this is an important theme in the *Lettres persanes*, but first one should emphasize how dominant the trait was in terms of Montesquieu's psychology and how he found a strong ally in Montaigne. These two representatives of the landed gentry naturally sought to excel according to their own industry and merit, not by means of subservience to the crown. Never were they more content than on Gascon soil where they were rulers of themselves. Montaigne pledges allegiance to his king, but always clarifies the limitations of his service, declaring strangely enough that he is the servant of the monarch only out of free choice.[1] He seeks no vain honors or wealth from the crown, for they would cost him the price of his precious liberty. It was clearly a noble's choice as to whether or not he wanted to live in "slavery."[2] His demands are modest, for essentially the essayist wishes only to live in peaceful freedom without debts and obligation to anyone:

> Les princes me donnent prou s'ils ne m'ostent rien, et me font assez de bien quand ils ne me font point de mal; c'est tout ce que j'en demande. *O combien je suis tenu à Dieu de ce qu'il luy a pleu que j'aye receu immediatement de sa grace tout ce que j'ay,* qu'il a retenu particulierement à soy toute ma debte! Combien je supplie instamment sa saincte misericorde que jamais je ne doive un essentiel grammercy à personne! Bienheureuse franchise, qui m'a conduit si loing. Qu'elle acheve! (*Essais*, III, ch. 9, pp. 203-04)

Montesquieu speaks in a similar manner and even in like terms of his own good fortune:

> Je n'ai point aimé à faire ma fortune par le moyen de la Cour; j'ai songé à la faire en faisant valoir mes terres, et à tenir ma fortune immédiatement de la main des Dieux. (*Pensée* 973; 5)

Wishing to give service and not receive it, Montesquieu's demands are likewise modest. Like the essayist he seeks no honors or recompense from the crown; to be indebted would be humiliating to a free man:

> Je ne demande à ma patrie ni pensions, ni honneurs, ni distinctions; je me trouve amplement récompensé par l'air que j'y respire. Je voudrois seulement qu'on ne l'y corrompît point. (*Pensée* 2229; 42)

(Following, Montesquieu addresses his son):

> Et notre fortune, quoique médiocre, est telle que moi, vous et les vôtres aurons toujours à aimer, à honorer, à servir notre prince, et rien à lui demander. (*Pensée* 1659; 70)

> Je disois: "Je souhaite avoir des manières simples, recevoir des services le moins que je puis, et en faire le plus qu'il m'est possible." (*Pensée* 595; 12)

Thus we see that these two *gentilhommes* were linked by a pride in their status and fought against the current of servitude in which many other nobles fell notably during the century that separated them, that period epitomized by Louis XIV, the great "centralizer" and uprooter of the nobility.

Understanding Montesquieu's insistence of freedom from the Court, it is no wonder to us that the theme of retirement—that is, living at home in the province of one's birth—acquires considerable importance in the *Lettres persanes*. The very number of times this subject reappears should make us stop and take notice. In letter 89 Usbek speaks of a French noble's prerogative to retire from the king's service, if his honor is offended:

> . . . si un sujet se trouve blessé dans son honneur par son prince, soit par quelque préférence, soit par la moindre marque de mépris, il quitte

sur-le-champ sa cour, son emploi, son service, et se retire chez lui.
(*Lettres persanes*, p. 186)

This escape hatch for the French nobility is in striking contrast to the servitude in which Persian citizens are forced to live. The Sultan can dispose of the lives of his subjects as he will. But, writes Usbek in letter 102:

> Il n'en est pas de même des grands d'Europe, à qui la disgrâce n'ôte rien que la bienveillance et la faveur. Ils se retirent de la Cour et ne songent qu'à jouir d'une vie tranquille et des avantages de leur naissance.
> (*Lettres persanes*, p. 213)

Also the *Guèbre* of *Aphéridon et Astarté* withdraws from his homeland, thereby enhancing his character which acquires the virtues of retirement— heroism and courage. The modesty and obscurity of this state seem to foster such qualities (see *Lettres persanes*, p. 138).

Most illustrative and significant, the very basis of Usbek's voyage and correspondance is his initial retirement from the corrupted and menacing Court of Persia. There is probably a great deal of fiction in the hyperbole of Usbek's confession (the number and strength of his enemies, for instance), yet one cannot overlook the autobiographical note within the basic points of this important letter (8). Barrière has already emphasized several of them.[3] He proposes that the "maison de campagne" to which Usbek retires symbolizes *La Brède*. On a broader scale one might add that Usbek's self-imposed exile and his desire to instruct himself in "les sciences de l'Occident" signifies Montesquieu's voyage into the world of knowledge and wisdom through live observation and especially through literature—in brief, his decision to write the *Lettres persanes* and the double source of his inspiration in order to do so. "Tout ceci," interjects Barrière, "fait incontestablement songer à la retraite de Montaigne, et ce sont presque les mêmes termes que l'on trouvait dans la fameuse inscription de 1570" (sic).[4] Somewhat like Montesquieu who is transformed into Usbek, Montaigne declared himself long weary of the servitude of the court and of public employment; thus, he chose to retire to the bosom of the learned virgins. (Similarly, Usbek decides not to busy himself with any worldly affairs, seeking to instruct himself in "les sciences de l'Occident.) Barrière also believed that in letter 8 Montesquieu is already contemplating his own retirement—that is, the selling of his presidential office. Such will actually take place only a few years later in 1725-26. Therefore, in letter 8 his veiled alliance with Montaigne seems even more evident; the latter was also a disillusioned and idealistic magistrate who retired to his country estate to begin composing the *Essais*.

Usbek's behavior at court prior to his withdrawal suggests Montesquieu's elevated purpose in writing his *Lettres*. Underneath the surface of the Persian court lies Versailles which our author intended to awake with the honesty of his criticism:

> j'y parlai un langage jusqu'alors inconnu [Usbek writes]; je déconcertai
> la flatterie, et j'étonnai en même temps les adorateurs et l'idole. (p. 21)

As a matter of fact, we find that in letter 88 Montesquieu, still in the guise of Usbek, attacks "les adorateurs et l'idole" of the French court, revealing the pernicious ceremony of servitude there with a dry and gripping metaphor; it suggests the barbaric ignorance of pagan times:

> La faveur est la grande divinité des Français. Le ministre est le grand-
> prêtre, qui lui offre bien des victimes. Ceux qui l'entourent ne sont
> point habillés de blanc; tantôt sacrificateurs et tantot sacrifiés, ils se
> dévouent eux-mêmes à leur idole avec tout le peuple. (p. 185)

What a mockery our daring author makes of the ancient Divine right of kings! For this is not worship, but pure idolatry.

To return to letter 8, Usbek also declares about the court:

> j'osai y être vertueux. Dès que je connus le vice, je m'en éloignai;
> mais je m'en approchai ensuite pour le démasquer. *Je portai la vérité
> jusques au pied du trône*: . . . (p. 21)

As Barrière suggests, Montesquieu may thereby be alluding to certain criticism he had made of state affairs before 1721. But one can associate Usbek's sincerity and idealism as well with the aim of our author in his *Lettres persanes*. It resembles the function of the *parlements* which Rica describes ironically:

> Ces compagnies sont toujours odieuses: elles n'approchent des rois que
> pour leur dire de tristes *vérités*, et, pendant qu'une foule de courtisans
> leur représentent sans cesse un peuple heureux sous leur gouvernement,
> elles viennent démentir la flatterie, et *apporter aux pieds du trône* les
> gémissements et les larmes dont elles sont dépositaires. (p. 295)

Like these important bodies of government of which they were members, Montaigne and Montesquieu wished to serve as intermediaries between the crown and the people and as educators of the prince, revealing courtisans for what they truly were: vile flatterers who milked kings for any and every favor. The entire letter 124 is a criticism of royal liberality. One of its paragraphs may be a commentary on a passage in the *Essais*. Speaking of the ancient king Hyero, Montaigne expresses his sympathy for the monarch's plight—being continually surrounded by an annoying court, never permitted the freedom and solitude necessary for any man's sanity and good judgment. Montaigne "pities" him and French kings like him. Usbek also "pities" kings who are enveloped by greedy courtiers. But his sympathy is evoked primarily for different reasons:

> . . . combien il sent d'incommoditez en sa royauté, pour ne pouvoir aller et voyager en liberté, estant comme prisonnier dans les limites de son païs; et qu'en toutes ses actions il se trouve *enveloppé d'une facheuse presse*. De vray, à voir les nostres tous seuls à table, *assiegez de tant de parleurs et regardans inconnuz*, j'en ay eu souvent plus de *pitié* que d'envie. (*Essais*, I, ch. 42, p. 296)

> Quand je pense à la situation des princes, toujours *entourés d'hommes avides et insatiables*, je ne puis que les *plaindre*, et je les plains davantage lorsqu'ils n'ont pas la force de résister à des demandes toujours onéreuses à ceux qui ne demandent rien. (*Lettres persanes*, p. 261)

Montesquieu's reaction to Montaigne's sympathy is ironic, if not sarcastic. He has little patience with royalty which cannot control its liberality:

> Quel peut être le motif de ces libéralités immenses que les princes versent sur leurs courtisans? Veulent-ils se les attacher? Ils leur sont déjà acquis autant qu'ils peuvent l'être; et, d'ailleurs, s'ils acquièrent quelques-uns de leurs sujets en les achetant, il faut bien, par la même raison, *qu'ils en perdent une infinité d'autres en les appauvrissant*. (Ibid.)

But we should not forget that the progressive essayist was also critical of this royal extravagance:

> . . . les gouverneurs de l'enfance des princes, qui se piquent à leur
> imprimer cette vertu de largesse, et les preschent de ne sçavoir rien
> refuser et n'estimer rien si bien employé que ce qu'ils donneront
> (instruction que j'ay veu en mon temps fort en credit), ou ils regardent
> plus à leur proufit qu'à celuy de leur maistre, ou ils entendent mal à qui
> ils parlent. Il est trop aysé d'imprimer la liberalité en celuy qui a
> dequoy y fournir autant qu'il veut, *aux despens d'autruy*. . . .
>
> *L'immoderée largesse est un moyen foible à leur acquerir bien-*
> *veuillance; car elle rebute plus de gens qu'elle n'en practique.* (*Essais*,
> III, ch. 6, pp. 130-31)

Both critics make one essential point in common: that through immoderate liberality a king alienates more subjects than he gratifies; that enriching a select few only leaves the vast majority of others impoverished. One should add that Montesquieu's tone is harsher and more caustic than Montaigne's; the latter professed to respect the tradition of *largesse*, lamenting only its abuse. More bold and daring, Montesquieu puts on no such reverent, deferential manners.

Thus when Usbek writes in letter 8: "je portai la vérité jusques au pied du trône: . . . je déconcertai la flatterie," he is speaking for one of Montesquieu's ideals in the *Lettres persanes*—a cause he shares with another eloquent and sensible reformer, Montaigne. And it is through retirement from the court and freedom from duties to the crown that both nobles best cultivate and develop their powers of criticism and impartiality. To speak of government objectively and provide some therapy for the state, Montesquieu must play the role of retirement; he must age rapidly into the character of Usbek (closer to Montaigne's age than Montesquieu's) and gain the wisdom of detachment. Retirement, like the voyage itself, is one of spirit and state of mind. Therein lies the "utilité de mes voyages" Usbek hopes to provide the monarch. Very likely Montesquieu felt a partnership with Montaigne when retreating from the court to examine both it and society at large from a fresh point of view.

VI

GENIAL SATIRE

IN HIS ANALYSIS OF MONTESQUIEU'S physiognomy Albert Sorel brought out certain traits that both nobles share, one of which is "les percées de malice et de raillerie." Like the essayist, implies Sorel, Montesquieu "se complaît aux anecdotes significatives, aux traits qui caractérisent un homme ou un pays, aux historiettes même qui ne sont que divertissantes et ne peignent que la sottise ou la bonté de l'homme de tous les temps." Sorel attributes these characteristics not only to Montesquieu's predilection for Montaigne but to their native Gascon verve, "une sorte de point d'honneur sur l'article de l'esprit."[1] One finds in the *Lettres persanes* certain moments of wit which are highly suggestive of Montaigne, passages that compare favorably to the essayist's genial satire of mankind's myopia in all its forms.

Anthropomorphism and Beauty

Rica's brief discussion of man's conception of God and beauty in letter 159 appears to be inspired by Montaigne's treatment of these dual themes in the *Apologie*. First, the well-organized Montesquieu introduces his subject with a general remark on man's subjectivity. We find its equivalent in the *Apologie*:

> L'homme ne peut estre que ce qu'il est, ny imaginer que selon sa portée. (*Essais*, II, ch. 12, p. 215)

> Les yeux humains ne peuvent apercevoir les choses que par les formes de leur cognoissance. (Ibid., p. 233)

> Il me semble, Usbek, que nous ne jugeons jamais des choses que par un
> retour secret que nous faisons sur nous-mêmes. (*Lettres persanes*,
> p. 124)

However, the more analytical Montesquieu points out how unconscious is
our subjectivity. The words "retour secret" suggest that we are unaware of
the bias of our judgment.

There follows a remark about Negroes' prejudiced idea of God and
the devil (Montesquieu's reflection on slavery and colonialization so common in his era?). This sentence bears at least some comparison with the
African ideal of beauty described in the *Essais*. Here the treatment of one
theme rubs off on another (ideal beauty turning into divinity), when Montesquieu perhaps unconsciously uses Montaigne as a springboard for his
own personal wit:

> Les Indes la *peignent* [la beauté du corps] noire et basannée, aux levres
> grosses et enflées, au nez plat et large. (*Essais*, II, ch. 12, p. 210)

> Je ne suis pas surpris que les Nègres *peignent* le diable d'une blancheur
> éblouissante et leur dieux noirs comme du charbon; . . . (*Lettres
> persanes*, p. 124)

Next Rica continues to reflect on primitive bias with a risqué observation
inspired rather clearly by Montaigne. The size, or more precisely, the
length of breasts had no limits among certain peoples, grotesque as it may
seem:

> Les Mexicanes content entre les beautez la petitesse du front . . . et ont
> en si grande recommendation la grandeur des tetins, qu'elles affectent de
> pouvoir donner la *mammelle* à leurs enfans par dessus l'espaule.
> (*Essais*, II, ch. 12, p. 170)

> Je ne suis pas surpris . . . que la Vénus de certains peuples ait des
> *mamelles* qui lui pendent jusques aux cuisses: (*Lettres persanes*,
> p. 124)

Leaving the subject of ideal Beauty, Rica returns to that of pagan anthropomorphism, summing up somewhat like Montaigne. Here the essayist is
ironic:

L'ancienneté pensa, ce croy-je, faire quelque chose pour la grandeur
divine, de l'apparier à l'homme, la vestir de ses facultez et estrener de
ses belles humeurs . . . (*Essais*, II, ch. 12, p. 215)

Je ne suis pas surpris . . . qu'enfin tous les idolâtres aient représenté
leurs dieux avec une figure humaine et leur aient fait part de toutes leurs
inclinations. (*Lettres persanes*, p. 124)

With a final sally Rica accuses man's biased viewpoint by comparing him to
triangles. One feels the same spirit and wit in Montaigne's quotation from
Xenophanes:

Pourtant disoit plaisamment Xenophanes, que si les animaux se forgent
des dieux, comme il est vraysemblable qu'ils facent, il les forgent
certainement de meme eux, et se glorifient, comme nous. (*Essais*, II,
ch. 12, p. 230)

On a dit fort bien que, si les triangles faisaient un dieu, ils lui
donneraient trois côtés. (*Lettres persanes*, p. 124)[2]

It is above all the spirit of gay satire which unites our two authors on
this ancient theme. Man receives a pinch where he deserves it, for he has
been presumptuous enough to form God in his own image. Vernière states
that the origin of Montesquieu's "attack against anthropomorphism" comes
from Spinoza (see *Lettres persanes*, p. 124, fn. 1). Not wishing to dispute
ground with this scholar, we might nevertheless say that Rica's words are
not so much of an attack against as a jovial satire of man's eternal myopia.
There is good-natured fun here. The witty Persian is far from dogmatic.
He has no ax to grind, unless it is the foolishness of man himself.

In letter 69 Usbek takes another sally at man's broad and varied
concept of ideal beauty. The choice of vocabulary, forming brief but striking antithesis is highly suggestive of Montaigne's style in another passage
devoted to the same subject:

Les Italiens la façonnent [la beauté du corps] grosse et massive, les
Espagnols vuidée et estrillée; et, entre nous, l'un la fait *blanche*, l'autre
brune; l'un molle et delicate, l'autre forte et vigoureuse; qui y demande
de la mignardise et de la *douceur*, qui y demande de la *fierté* et magesté.
(*Essais*, II, ch. 12, p. 170)

> Les poètes d'Occident disent qu'un peintre, ayant voulu faire le portrait
> de la Déesse de la Beauté, assembla les plus belles Grecques et prit de
> chacune ce qu'elle avait de plus agréable, dont il fit un tout pour
> ressembler à la plus belle de toutes les Déesses. Si un homme en avait
> conclu qu'elle était *blonde* et *brune*, qu'elle avait les yeux noirs et
> bleus, qu'elle était *douce* et *fière*, il aurait passé pour ridicule. (*Lettres
> persanes*, p. 150)

One should observe, however, that Montesquieu attributes the contradictory
facets of Beauty to one man's judgment, thus outdoing Montaigne who
conceived the opposing qualities according to the prejudices of various
peoples. The author of the *Lettres persanes* heightens the paradox.

Provinciality

Both authors are given to anecdotes which demonstrate man's
provinciality. We have seen above how mankind as a species is short-
sighted, when it comes to the conception of God. He is equally inadequate
when judging other lands from the standpoint of his own.

Letter 44 is a collection of three amusing stories designed to
illustrate prejudice and vanity. The first concerns a rather ridiculous lady
from Erivan. She is certainly reminiscent of Montaigne's *Savoyard*:

> Et disoit le Savoiart que, si ce sot de Roy de France eut sceu bien
> conduire sa fortune, il estoit homme pour devenir maistre d'hostel de
> son Duc. Son imagination ne concevoit autre plus eslevée grandeur que
> celle de son maistre. *Nous sommes insensiblement tous* en cette erreur:
> erreur de grande suite et prejudice. (*Essais*, I, ch. 26, p. 169)

> *Les hommes ressemblent tous*, plus ou moins, à cette femme de la
> province d'Erivan qui, ayant reçu quelque grâce d'un de nos monarques,
> lui souhaite mille fois, dans les bénédictions qu'elle lui donna, que le
> Ciel le fît gouverneur d'Erivan. (*Lettres persanes*, p. 90)

Our gay philosophers do not find a scapegoat in these two localities only.
Rather they find provincial vanity to be one of the most universal flaws of
mankind. "Nous sommes . . . tous en cette erreur," writes Montaigne.

"Les hommes ressemblent tous . . . à cette femme de la province d'Erivan," Montesquieu seems to answer.

One can draw the comparison out further. Usbek's King of Tartary is a blood-cousin to Montaigne's kings of Persia:

Nature nous a mis au monde libres et desliez; nous nous emprisonnons en certains destroits; comme les Roys de Perse, qui s'obligeoient de ne boire jamais autre eau que celle du fleuve de Choaspez, renonçoyent par sottise à leur droict d'usage en toutes les autres eaux, et assechoient pour leur regard tout le reste du monde. (*Essais*, III, ch. 9, p. 209)

Quand le Khan de Tartarie a dîné, un héraut crie que tous les princes de la Terre peuvent aller dîner, si bon leur semble, et ce barbare, qui ne mange que du lait, qui n'a pas de maison, qui ne vit que de brigandage, regarde tous les rois du monde comme ses esclaves et les insulte regulièrement deux fois par jour. (*Lettres persanes*, p. 91)

Thus, not only provincial characters like the lady from Erivan and the Savoyard reveal their stupidity; powerful monarchs do so as well. Persian kings believed that, simply because superstition prohibited them from drinking water other than in the Choaspez River, all the rest of the world was dried up. Similarly ignorant and foolish, the Khan of Tartary thinks that all the kings of the earth regulate their mealtimes according to his own.

The longest tale of Usbek's letter also bears comparison with Montaigne's wit:

J'ai lu, dans une relation, qu'un vaisseau français ayant relâché à la côte de Guinée, quelques hommes de l'équipage voulurent aller à terre acheter quelques moutons. On les mena au roi, qui rendait la justice à ses sujets sous un arbre. Il était sur son trône, c'est-à-dire sur un morceau de bois; aussi fier que s'il eût été sur celui du Grand Mogol; il avait trois ou quatre gardes avec des piques de bois; un parasol en forme de dais le couvrait de l'ardeur du soleil; tous ses ornements et ceux de la reine, sa femme, consistaient en leur peau noire et quelques bagues. Ce prince, plus vain encore que misérable, demanda à ces étrangers si on parlait beaucoup de lui en France. Il croyait que son nom devait être porté d'un pôle à l'autre; et, à la différence de ce conquérant de qui on a dit qu'il avait fait taire toute la Terre, il croyait, lui, qu'il devait faire parler tout l'Univers. (*Lettres persanes*, pp. 91-92)

We are reminded of Montaigne's humorous account of his village priest. Like Montesquieu, the essayist regrets that most of humanity can see no farther than the tip of its nose and measures the glory and misfortune of others only in relation to itself:

> Il se tire une merveilleuse clarté, pour le jugement humain, de la frequentation du monde. Nous sommes tous contraints et amoncellez en nous, et avons la venue racourcie à la longueur de nostre nez. . . . Quand les vignes gelent en mon village, mon prebstre en argumente l'ire de Dieu sur la race humaine, et juge que la pepie en tienne des-jà les Cannibales. (*Essais*, I, ch. 26, pp. 168-69)

Although Montesquieu did not quote Montaigne to write letter 44, like the essayist he pilfered the anecdotes from others and placed them in humorous array. The same overall flavor of style and theme in common between the two authors leads one to suspect that Montesquieu actually modelled letter 44 after Montaigne. Particularly the picturesque detail which Montesquieu himself added to the King-of-Guinea tale may have been inspired by the rich and precise style one finds in certain of Montaigne's historical anecdotes.

The theme of prejudice pervades the *Lettres persanes* as well as the *Essais*. Grinning behind their characters, both moralists mock short-sighted alarmists, those who think the world is coming to an end simply because they are not lucid and sensible enough to know that catastrophe is a relative affair. The *nouvelliste* in the letter 132 is pale and dried up with worry over the nation's wars. This absurd character has practically wasted away thinking that France will lose an entire province in a single battle, whereas an astrologist nearby predicts that a sunspot might cause the end of the world. These two fools are comparable to Montaigne's village priest described above, or to the average French citizen of his day who thought that the day of judgment had come because of the violence of France's civil wars (see I, ch. 26, p. 169).

Pierre Barrière has suggested how much of Montesquieu himself can be seen transposed into Rica and Usbek.[3] The young, provincial Baron of La Brède with his strong accent and rustic manner looked undoubledly a bit queer to Parisians and courtiers alike. Some of Rica's and Usbek's jabs at Parisians can be interpreted as Montesquieu's retorts to citizens of the nation's capital. This *Bordelais* considered them provincial. As objective, perspicacious observers of the French, Rica and Usbek follow the tradition of other foreigners visiting France in works by Marana, Bernard, and

Cotolendi. However, one might add Montaigne to this list, for his focus upon his fellow citizens, being clear and removed from prejudice, was often ironic. Montaigne is also capable of pointed thrusts at French myopia. Like his fellow *Bordelais* the essayist seems to share the viewpoint that those members of society reputed to be the most sophisticated and urbane are the least so when confronted with a character from another environment. Montaigne felt at court the way Rica, and by extension, Montesquieu did in Paris:

> [Noz jeunes courtisans] *ne tiennent qu'aux hommes de leur sorte, nous regardent comme gens de l'autre monde,* avec desdain ou pitié. Ostez leur les entretiens des mysteres de la court, ils sont hors de leur gibier, aussi neufs pour nous et malhabiles comme nous sommes à eux.[4] (*Essais*, III, ch. 9, p. 224)

> Les habitants de Paris sont d'une curiosité qui va jusqu'à l'extravagance. Lorsque j'arrivai, je fus *regardé comme si j'avais été envoyé du Ciel* . . . Je souriais quelque fois d'entendre des gens *qui n'étaient presque jamais sortis de leur chambre,* qui disaient entre eux: "Il faut avouer qu'il a l'air bien persan." (*Lettres persanes,* p. 68)

Note above that both Montaigne's courtisans and Montesquieu's Parisians are similarly ignorant and naïve, never having set foot outside their restricted environment. Both groups react to a foreigner or a man from the provinces as though he were some strange creature from another planet. One feels a provincial pact underlying the rapport between our two Gascons here. Rica becomes a universal symbol, reflecting Montaigne and all *provinciaux,* while at the same time representing Montesquieu.

Is Rica's famous, concluding *pointe* to the same letter—"comment peut-on etre persan?"—not reminiscent of Montaigne's jab at the end of "Des cannibales"? Speaking of an African monarch's privileges and superiority among his people, Montaigne interrupts: "Tout cela ne va pas trop mal: mais quoy, ils ne portent point de haut de chausses!" (I, ch. 32, p. 245).

Rica makes the acquaintance of a lady from the court who is very curious to know all about Persians but too narrow and prudish to find a harem anything but disgusting: "elle trouvait de la répugnance à voir un homme partagé entre dix ou douze femmes" (p. 296). Usbek can also be witty, given the right occasion. "Les Français," he writes, "n'imaginent pas que notre climat produise des hommes"[5] (p. 98). One calls to mind Montaigne's ironic and biting criticism of French tourists abroad who think ways of living different from their own "barbaric." "Pourquoy non barbares, puis qu'elles [les mœurs] ne sont françoises?" he asks with a grin (III, ch. 9, p. 224).

If native citizens have the least insight into the vices and virtues of their culture, then conversely foreign visitors are often embarrassingly perceptive about them. So were Marana's Turkish voyager, Cotolendi's Sicilian traveler and Dufresny's Siamese visitor among other certain or possible models of Rica and Usbek. Like these puppets our two Persians are struck, astounded even, by French customs; their shock is contagious. Seeing France through their eyes, we (or rather the French) realize suddenly our own relativity. A familiar environment becomes at once strange and mystifying. What one took for granted demands reexamination.

In Montaigne's essay, "Des cannibales," three savages make some remarkable observations about the French monarchy. They are paradoxically both naïve and perceptive; like children they speak their mind openly and frankly, surprising us with the truth of their remarks. They belong to the same family of foreign observers mentioned above, and compare favorably with Montesquieu's Persians. For instance, like Rica they felt that the French king possessed magic qualities. Little 12-year-old Charles IX is already a predecessor of the powerful Louis XIV, for his power seems illusory and unreal:

> Ils [les cannibales] dirent qu'ils trouvoient en premier lieu fort estrange que tant de grands hommes, portans barbe, forts et armez, qui estoient autour du Roy (il est vray-semblable que ils parloient des Suisses de sa garde), se soubs-missent à obeyr à un enfant, et qu'on ne choisissoit plus tost quelqu'un d'entr'eux pour commander; . . . (*Essais*, I, ch. 32, p. 244)

> D'ailleurs ce roi est un grand magicien: il exerce son empire sur l'esprit même de ses sujets; it les fait penser comme il veut. S'il n'a qu'un million d'écus dans son trésor, et qu'il en ait besoin de deux, il n'a qu'à leur persuader qu'un écu en vaut deux, et ils le croient. (*Lettres persanes*, p. 56)

Or one might compare the surprising age of the Renaissance ruler with that of Louis XIV's minister. What a topsy-turvy body politic is that of the

French! Rica writes:

> J'ai étudié son caractère, et j'y ai trouvé des contradictions qu'il m'est impossible de résoudre. Par exemple: il a un ministre qui n'a que dix-huit ans, et une maîtresse qui en a quatre-vingts; . . . (*Lettres persanes,* p. 80)

One must admit that the above comparison only goes so far. Montesquieu is to some extent a social critic (if only of a past reign) in the guise of Rica. Montaigne is merely an ironic historian as the recorder of his cannibal's observations. However, both authors use foreign visitors to point out their country's laughable relativity, and turn an ordinary custom into a most extraordinary one: in poking fun at their own monarchs, they remain detached in a light-hearted way.

Here and elsewhere, as we have seen, Montesquieu demonstrates the jovial mood of his satire. "Il ne faut pas mettre du vinaigre dans ses écrits," he states; "il faut y mettre du sel" (*pensée* 2012; 806). His definition of *raillerie* explains the mechanics of his humor to us, the Gascon verve which he shares with the gay philosopher Montaigne, not with the acidic Voltaire:

> il y a de certaines règles qu l'on peut observer dans la raillerie, qui bien loin de rendre le personnage d'un railleur odieux, peuvent le rendre très aimable. . . . On doit répandre la raillerie également sur tout le monde, pour faire sentir qu'elle n'est que l'effet de la gaieté où nous sommes, et non d'un dessein formé d'attaquer quelqu'un en particulier. . . . Enfin, il faut avoir pour but de faire rire celui qu'on raille, et non pas un tiers. (*Pensée* 1274; 623)

Montesquieu may have been inspired directly by the cannibals' second observation to speak of the great gap between the rich and the poor:

> secondement (ils ont une facon de leur langage telle, qu'ils nomment les hommes moitié les uns des autres) qu'ils avoyent aperceu qu'il y avoit parmy nous des hommes pleins et gorgez de toutes sortes de commoditez, et que leurs moitiez estoient mendians à leurs portes, decharnez de faim et de pauvreté; (*Essais*, I, ch. 32, p. 244)

Il n'en est pas de meme des pays soumis au pouvoir arbitraire: le
Prince, les courtisans et quelques particuliers possèdent toutes les rich-
esses pendant que tous les autres gémissent dans une pauvreté extrême.
(*Lettres persanes*, pp. 258-59)

It is very possible that Montesquieu modelled the above paragraph on the
cannibals' remark. The style of the two passages is similar, for the contrast
is made by a rather stark antithesis. Both writers exaggerate the miserable
condition of the poor and the privileged, overstuffed situation of the upper
classes. In reality, things were not quite so simply divided, but hyperbole
serves to speak the truth in the strongest fashion. And the very acute problem of the impoverished peasantry never ceased to concern Montesquieu.[6]
In the above letter 122 Usbek discusses in a serious tone how in the
monarchy the rich remain rich, while the poor become poorer. This more
involved context conceals the small debt that Montesquieu owes to
Montaigne for the wording of the peasants' plight.

It is clear that the ideal of our two philosophers was not to fall into
the category of the common man, not to be hoodwinked by the region or
country of their birth. Characters like the *Savoyard* and the lady from
Erivan may be amusing, but they are twice as foolish. French royalty
appears a bit ridiculous, when one examines it from an unbiased viewpoint.
The social fabric of the monarchy is by no means perfect; nor does the rest
of the "barbaric" world revolve around Paris and the court, regardless of
what their residents may think.

Montesquieu and Montaigne insist upon giving the reader's *idées
reçues* a sharp jolt, to wake him up and snap him out of mental lethargy.
The rhythm of surprises and paradoxes in the *Essais* and the *Lettres persanes* is quite similar. The comical is blended in with the serious; or even
the serious may possess a certain humor about it, just as the comical can in
reality reveal some very serious truths about mankind. *Serio ludere*. This
supple interplay of style in both works creates a great part of their charm.

VII
TWO CITIZENS OF THE WORLD

AS OPPOSED TO THE FOOLISH PITFALLS of the common man, Montaigne and Montesquieu seek to judge and inquire about the world impartially and with an eye for the common ties between all peoples. "We Frenchmen must learn to see our relative place among mankind," they seem to say.

In the first book of *Essais* Montaigne praises the universal bonds of brotherhood, using Socrates as his model. When asked what was his homeland, the Greek philosopher did not reply "Athens," but "the world." Like his illustrious predecessor, Montaigne proclaimed his universal citizenship out of understanding and affection for the human race, out of an ideal love for all nations, not from actual experience within them:

> Luy [Socrates], qui avoit son imagination plus plaine et plus estandue, embrassoit l'univers comme sa ville, jettoit ses connoissances, sa societé et ses affections à tout le genre humain, non pas comme nous qui ne regardons que sous nous. (*Essais*, I, ch. 26, pp. 168-69)

Later Montaigne remembers and answers the above passage, proving to us that he could put theory into practice. The actual experience of travel has not belied or erased his old ideal. His heart has remained open to all peoples, the national bond never assuming greater importance than the universal one:

> Non parce que Socrates l'a dict, mais parce qu'en verité c'est mon humeur, et à l'avanture non sans quelque excèz, j'estime tous les hommes mes compatriotes, et embrasse un Polonois comme un François, postposant cette lyaison nationale à l'universelle et commune. Je ne suis

> guere feru de la douceur d'un air naturel. Les cognoissances toutes
> neufves et toutes miennes me semblent bien valoir ces autres com-
> munes et fortuites cognoissances du voisinage. Les amitiez pures de
> nostre acquest emportent ordinairement celles ausquelles la communica-
> tion du climat ou du sang nous joignent. (*Essais*, III, ch. 9, p. 209)

With similar accents of warmth and love for nations other than his own,
Montesquieu indirectly proclaims his own universal citizenship in the
Lettres persanes. A Persian speaks for him the way Socrates had for
Montaigne:

> La cœur est citoyen de tous les pays. Comment une âme bien faite
> peut-elle s'empêcher de former des engagements? Je te l'avoue: je
> respecte les anciennes amitiés; mais je ne suis pas fâché d'en faire
> partout de nouvelles. (*Lettres persanes*, p. 137)

Both writers reflect that voyage allows one to form "new" acquaintances
and friendships. The "old friendships" to which Ibben alludes are those he
had made in his native land—the ones Montaigne calls "les amitiez . . .
ausquelles la communication du climat ou du sang nous joignent." Carried
away by his enthusiasm, Montaigne declares that the new friendships made
abroad surpass those of his native land, whereas the more reasonable Ibben
replies that he honors old acquaintances but is happy to acquire new friends.
"C'est mon caractère, Usbek," he writes; "partout où je trouverai des
hommes, je me choisirai des amis.[1]

Voyage

Travel is the great molder of an open and universal mind. Usbek
and Rica represent Montesquieu's dual nature (the serious and the playful)
in quest of knowledge within and without the borders of France. Their
voyage is the author's own—an imaginary one, yet no less real and
significant. In the first letter of the collection Usbek expresses the elevated
purpose of his travels: to deepen his understanding of man's complex
nature through experience in foreign lands. His words are a kind of *credo*
on which the entire work is built:

Nous sommes nés dans un royaume florissant; mais nous n'avons pas cru que ces bornes fussent celles de nos connaissances, et que la lumière orientale dût seule nous éclairer. (*Lettres persanes*, p. 12)

In "De l'institution" Montaigne preaches the value of voyaging before his actual visits to other countries of Europe. (Socrates had hardly set foot outside of Attica before declaring himself citizen of the world). He expects more of his young noble than of the average French nobility:

A cette cause [l'éducation de l'enfant] le commerce des hommes y est merveilleusement propre, et la visite des pays estrangers, non pour en rapporter seulement, à la mode de nostre noblesse Françoise, combien de pas a Santa Rotonda, ou la richesse des calessons de la Signora Livia, ou, comme d'autres, combien le visage de Neron, de quelque vieille ruyne de là, est plus long ou plus large que celuy de quelque pareille medaille, mais pour en rapporter principalement les humeurs de ces nations et leurs façons, et pour frotter et limer nostre cervelle contre celle d'autruy. (*Essais*, I, ch. 26, p. 163)

Even during his travels, taking pride in his ability to adapt to any new environment, Montaigne underrates the manners and customs of his own country in order to accept more fully those of his neighbors:

Au rebours, je peregrine très saoul de nos façons, non pour cercher des Gascons en Sicile (j'en ay assez laissé au logis); je cerche des Grecs plustost, et des Persans. (*Essais*, III, ch. 9, p. 224)

Montaigne's grasp exceeds his reach (for he did not travel to Sicily even in his longest voyage). He sees further than he traveled, not stopping at the limits of actual experience. The lands and peoples he encountered are only a sampling of those he would like to have known.

Montesquieu shares in Montaigne's humanist doctrine of looking to other lands before judging his own. Thus he developed his unbiased and critical eye so apparent in the *Lettres persanes*. Usbek and Rica serve as filters which assure their creator's objectivity and freedom from prejudice when examing French or foreign *mores*. ("Je parle des différents peuples d'Europe, comme des différents peuples de Madagascar," writes the author proudly in *Mes Pensées* [*pensée* 609; 85].) It is through a knowledge of other cultures—their customs, laws, religion, their tastes and prejudices—

that one acquires the wisdom to see one's own country as it truly is. Through ancient and modern history we can best place ourselves in perspective and calculate our relative flaws or virtues. Both Montaigne and Rhédi express how invaluable history is to appreciate man's infinite diversity. Books provided our authors the "fourth dimension" of travel beyond the limits of firsthand experience. History revealed the exciting relativity of their own nation and others:

> En cette practique des hommes, j'entends y comprendre, et principalement, ceux qui ne vivent qu'en la memoire des livres. Il [l'enfant dans "De l'institution"] practiquera, par le moyen des histoires, ces grandes ames des meilleurs siecles. (*Essais*, I, ch. 26, p. 167)

> Ce grand monde, que les uns multiplient encore comme especes soubs un genre, c'est le mirouer où il nous faut regarder pour nous connoistre de bon biais. Somme, je veux que ce soit le livre de mon escholier. Tant d'humeurs, de sectes, de jugemens, d'opinions, de loix et de coustumes nous apprennent à juger sainement des nostres, et apprennent nostre jugement à reconnoistre son imperfection et sa naturelle foiblesse: qui n'est pas un legier apprentissage. Tant de remuements d'estat et *changemens de fortune publique* nous instruisent à ne faire pas grand miracle de la nostre. (Ibid., p. 169)

> Pendant le séjour que je fais en Europe, je lis les historiens anciens et modernes: je compare tous les temps; j'ai du plaisir à les voir passer, pour ainsi dire, devant moi, et j'arrête surtout mon esprit à ces *grands changements* qui ont rendu les âges si différents des âges, et la Terre si peu semblable à elle-même.[2] (*Lettres persanes*, p. 232)

The revolution or evolution of many civilizations is the framework in which one's own history should be seen. A detached and objective point of view develops only with a knowledge of man's entire and often contradictory social nature. Both Gascons are not only citizens of the world but philosophers and moralists within it, removed from the fray like Pythagoras's spectators at the Olympic games (see *Essais*, I, ch. 26, p. 170).

Universal minds naturally possess an insatiable curiosity. Rejuvenated by the French environment, old Usbek compares himself to a child who is struck by all he sees around him. In making this comparison, could Montesquieu have been inspired by the child with whom Montaigne identifies himself in "De l'institution"? The young man in this essay should

ideally be eager to absorb the world around him and be instructed by it. He
is quite comparable to Usbek:

> Qu'on luy mette en fantasie une honeste curiosité de s'enquerir de toutes
> choses; tout ce qu'il y aura de singulier autour de luy, il le verra: un
> bastiment, une fontaine, un homme, le lieu d'une bataille ancienne, le
> passage de Caesar ou de Charlemaigne . . . Il s'enquerra des meurs, des
> moyens et des alliances de ce Prince, et de celuy-là. Ce sont choses
> très-plaisantes à apprendre et très-utiles à sçavoir. (*Essais*, I, ch. 26,
> p. 167)

> Ceux qui aiment à s'instruire ne sont jamais oisifs: quoique je ne sois
> chargé d'aucune affaire importante, je suis cependant dans une occupa-
> tion continuelle. Je passe ma vie à examiner, j'écris le soir ce que j'ai
> remarqué, ce que j'ai vu, ce que j'ai entendu dans la journée. Tout
> m'intéresse, tout m'étonne: *je suis comme un enfant, dont les organes
> encore tendres sont vivement frappés par les moindres objets.* (*Lettres
> persanes*, p. 98)

If it is the extraordinary which should excite Mme de Foix's son, then much
of the world—past and present, that in books and that in reality—*is* extraordinary. Various and sundry details of the earth's rich texture appear stim-
ulating to both Montaigne's noble boy and to Usbek because their minds are
active and alert. "Un bastiment une fontaine, un homme, le lieu d'une
bataille ancienne," etc., appear to be the precise equivalent of Usbek's
generalization, "les moindres objets." Usbek's words above recall a remark
in Montesquieu's self-portrait which would also apply to Montaigne (when
he was not afflicted by ill health): "Je m'éveille le matin avec une joie
secrète; je vois la lumière avec une espèce de ravissement. Tout le reste du
jour je suis content" (*pensée* 213; 4). In peace of mind there is sanity and
stability. It is the foundation on which to build one's intellectual faculties.

Montesquieu reveals his thirst for knowledge in universal tones
similar to Montaigne's above. There is no worthwhile subject which cannot
excite his curiosity in some way and draw him out of his provincial skin and
limiting native land:

> Je m'instruis des secrets du commerce, [writes Rhédi] des intérêts des
> princes, de la forme de leur gouvernement; je ne néglige pas même les
> superstitions européennes; je m'applique à la médecine, à la physique, à

l'astronomie; j'étudie les arts; enfin je sors des nuages qui couvraient
mes yeux dans le pays de ma naissance. (*Lettres persanes*, p. 70)

A Disagreement over the Arts

Montesquieu found a particularly invigorating intellectual atmosphere in his contact with the *Académie de Bordeaux* to which he was elected
in 1716 and of which he became director in 1718 and several times thereafter. The various fields of science Rhédi indulges in above reflect Montesquieu's activity in the Academy as well as his own private and leisurely
research in his libraries of La Brède and Paris. He may do humanistic
research into the past, studying famous philosophers and historians, or
(unlike Montaigne) scientific research for the future. Montesquieu, like
Usbek, was continually busy and thoroughly involved in the liberal arts.
He felt that they provided great hope for civilization, and in 1725 he spoke
out for them in a speech before the Academy, *Discours sur les motifs qui
doivent nous encourager aux sciences.*

However, his first interesting apology for the arts and sciences can
be found four years earlier in the *Lettres persanes*. Usbek defends them in
letter 107, answering Rhédi's previous attack. But on another level Montesquieu is defending cultural activities from the disdain of certain *gentilhommes* of his era (common prejudice still ran high against intellectuals and
scholars) and, in particular, Montaigne. Usbek refers to Rhédi's criticism
in terms quite similar to those we find in the *Essais*. Thus the dialogue and
disagreement occur not only between two Persians, but also between two
learned nobles. Montaigne claims,

> Les exemples nous apprennent, et en cette martiale police et en toutes
> ses semblables, que l'estude des sciences *amollit et effemine les
> courages*, plus qu'il ne les fermit et aguerrit. (*Essais*, I, ch. 25, p. 154)

Usbek retorts:

> Tu crois que les arts *amollisent* les peuples et, par là, sont cause de la
> chute des empires? . . . Quand on dit que les arts rendent les hommes
> *efféminés*, on ne parle pas du moins de gens qui s'y appliquent,
> puisqu'ils ne sont jamais dans l'oisivité qui, de tous les vices, est celui
> qui *amollit le plus le courage.* (*Lettres persanes*, p. 221)

To illustrate their opposing theories both philosophers use history as an example:

> Quand les Gots ravagerent la Grece, ce qui sauva toutes les librairies d'estre passées au feu, ce fut un d'entre eux qui sema cette opinion, qu'il faloit laisser ce meuble entier aux ennemis, propre à les destourner de l'exercise militaire et amuser à des occupations sedentaires et oysives. (*Essais*, I, ch. 25, p. 154)

> Tu parles de la ruine de celui [i.e., l'empire] des anciens Perses, qui fut l'effet de leur mollesse. Mais il s'en faut bien que cet exemple décide, puisque les Grecs, qui les vainquirent tant de fois et les subjuguèrent, cultivaient les arts avec infiniment plus de soin qu'eux. (*Lettres persanes*, p. 221)

Although they refer to the fall of two different empires, both writers use one country, Greece, in order to prove opposite theories. The essayist suggests that the Greeks were overrefined, degenerate, and thus vulnerable to the more powerful and bellicose nation of the Goths. With a taste for the contradictory, Montesquieu seems to reply that originally, when they overthrew the great Persian empire, the Greeks were both cultivated and powerful. Thus, through both texts the reader glimpses the beginning and ending points of the great Hellenistic empire. Montesquieu does not so much disagree with Montaigne as he does comment on him. His example merely serves to complement the essayist's. In reality, Montesquieu saw the truth in his source's original point of view that overemphasized arts and sciences could untimately weaken a nation:

> Presque toutes les nations du monde roulent dans ce cercle; d'abord elles sont barbares; elles conquièrent et elles deviennent des nations policées; cette police les agrandit et elles deviennent des nations polies. La politesse les affaiblit; elles sont conquises et redeviennent barbares. (Quoted by Vernière in *Lettres persanes*, p. 218, fn. 1)

The actual point of view of the author is as global as that of Montaigne or the two Persians. However, in the *Lettres persanes* Montesquieu skillfully employs his thought to speak against Montaigne's theory.

To conclude briefly on our two learned citizens of the world, one should say that essentially they shared the same philosophical vision, the same humanistic wisdom. Endeavoring to see man and society from the outside, they mock prejudice and parochialism in all its forms and embrace the world as a whole. Espousing travel and learning, they hope that their own example will encourage Frenchmen to live a fuller life and profit from the riches every nation has in store not only for itself but for its neighbors and visitors. Montaigne and Montesquieu seek brotherhood—and enlightened unity of mankind. Those who ignore their relative unimportance on this earth are laughed at. Those who open their minds to the riches of learning and their hearts to the people from every nation will rejuvenate themselves like Usbek who feels many years younger when transplanted onto French soil.

VIII
APPRENTICESHIP TO *HONNETETE*

Mania versus Universality

AMIDST A GROUP OF OLD *COQUETTES* Rica exclaims (after hearing their catty remarks made at each other's expense): "Ah! bon Dieu, ne sentirons-nous jamais que le ridicule des autres?" (p. 111). Rica, of course, ridicules good-naturedly every eccentricity noticeable in French society, every foible visible in mankind. The Persian, or more precisely, his creator Montesquieu is not sparing in his satire and criticism of social wits, young and old, pedantic scholars and scientists, haughty nobles and the like. In painting his tableau of French society Montesquieu would appear on first sight to exteriorize his wit, and like the "vieilles coquettes" find victims only in relation to his stable and perfect puppets of irony, Usbek and especially Rica. But such is not the case. Pierre Barrière has discovered the author's introspection and humor at his own expense notably apparent in letter 142 ("Lettre d'un savant"), in the comical scientist's letter within letter 145, and in the satirical depiction of two "impoverished" nobles (letter 132).[1] Letters 142 and 145 are essentially Montesquieu's "Du pedantisme." Constantly fearful lest his public judge him a pedant, he is eager to mitigate any such opinion, and thus mocks narrow-minded scholars and scientists. Like Montaigne who exhorts his young noble in "De l'institution" not to travel to Italy with the intention of noting the different proportions of Nero's face on a medal or a ruin (I, ch. 26, p. 163), Montesquieu satirizes the absurd occupations of his "amateur de la vénérable antiquité." The latter writes:

> Vous y remarquerez entre autres une dissertation où je fais voir que la couronne dont on se servait autrefois dans les triomphes était de chêne,

> et non pas de laurier. Vous en admirerez une autre où je prouve, par de doctes conjectures tirées des plus graves auteurs grecs, que Cambyse fut blessé à la jambe gauche, et non pas à la droite; une autre où je démontre qu'un petit front était une beauté très recherchée par les Romains. (*Lettres persanes*, p. 306)

Fact rubs closely against fiction, for the humanistic activity above is not far from the sort of research that Montesquieu performed for the Academy of Bordeaux. And when the scholar writes, "Je vous enverrai encore un volume in-quarto, en forme d'explication d'un vers du sixième livre de l'*Enéide* de Virgile," we are reminded to what length Montesquieu himself could go in an analysis of a verse or even a few words of Ovide.[2] There is a great deal of the "amateur de la vénérable antiquité" in Montesquieu.

Robert Schackleton has said that among the various portraits in the *Lettres persanes* one finds none of the *honnête homme*.[3] It is true that there is no letter bearing such a title: "Portrait de l'honnête homme." But the rather sensible and nonchalant *homme de robe* of letter 68 serves pretty well as one. (Montesquieu entitled this letter ironically "Légèreté et ignorance des magistrats.") And the noble from the court of Persia described in letter 74 is a perfect example of the virtuous, lovable French provincial *gentilhomme*. But, most important, Rica and Usbek themselves embody the various qualities of their creator's *honnêteté* and reveal them here and there as they react to and reflect upon their environment.

One of the most important traits inherent in this type of gentleman is his modesty, his natural, unpretentious air. It is the very foundation of his character. "Le vrai honnête homme," wrote La Rochefoucauld, "est celui qui ne se pique de rien." He, La Bruyère, Pascal, and even Molière, praise men of universal talents and dethrone the pedants and specialists who are overbearing or snobbish. However, the original concept of this social wisdom and grace (in French literary terms, at least) goes back to Montaigne, who examined himself and others according to the universal norm. Montesquieu's treatment of the theme reflects the essayist's because he searches in himself to ferret out any superior air or special pride that might alienate him from popular approval. When Rica meets the know-it-all *décisionnaire*, he endeavors to engage him on familiar ground, the subject of his homeland:

> Je lui parlai de la Perse [he writes]. Mais, à peine lui eus-je dit quatre mots, qu'il me donna deux démentis, fondés sur l'autorité de MM. Tavernier et Chardin. (P. 156)

Is Montesquieu not present in these words? Tavernier and Chardin are among his principal sources of authority. It is as though he were admonishing himself not to flaunt such scholars or use them pedantically.

The *honnête homme* should not be opinionated and narrowminded like the two "savants" in letter 144, one who claims that what he says is true because he said it, the other (a worse type) who refutes what others say because he hasn't said it. Rica laments their vanity and cries out in a kind of apotheosis to the *honnête homme*:

> Hommes modestes, venez que je vous embrasse: vous faites la douceur et le charme de la vie. Vous croyez que vous n'avez rien, et, moi, je vous dis que vous avez tout. Vous pensez que vous n'humiliez personne, et vous humiliez tout le monde. Et, quand je vous compare dans mon idée avec ces hommes absolus que je vois partout, je les précipite de leur tribunal, et je les mets à vos pieds. (P. 317)

The two dogmatic fools of the above letter have relatives scattered throughout the *Lettres persanes* in various portraits. A great quantity of these characters are as though all cut out of the same piece of cloth. Like the *maître à chanter* in *Le Bourgeois Gentilhomme* they cannot see farther than their specialties—neither the geometrician who measures a beautiful park and château in purely quantitative terms, nor the translator who explains idiotically, "je viens de donner Horace au public" (p. 269), nor a *nouvelliste* who can think only in terms of current events, nor an astrologist who sees the end of the world in a single sunspot, nor the poet who is ostentatiously and obnoxiously witty, nor the genealogist who enriches himself through spurious documents of nobility. All these men and others are entrenched in their tiny profession, the symbol of their class, ignorant and unwilling to communicate with their fellowman on a broad scale of moral and social values. They are the antithesis of the *honnête homme*. Either Montesquieu scorns them, or he laughs at them.

Concerning one particular specialist, Montesquieu joins Montaigne. Neither philosopher could abide the pretentions of geometry. Mathematicians were synonomous with professional vanity and uselessness. Being an abstract science, it was removed from the real world of man with which they were concerned. Of what use are theories, they ask, if they are not put into practice? Quoting an anecdote of Plutarch's, Montaigne recounts that a certain geometrician of Syracuse was once persuaded by the government to use his contemplation for the defense of his city. This he did, "desdaignant toutefois luy mesme toute cette sienne manufacture, et pensant en cela avoir corrompu la dignité de son art de laquelle ses ouvrages n'estoient que l'aprentissage et le jouet" (I, ch. 25, p. 143). We are reminded of a trait in Rica's portrait of the geometrician—his indifference to reality. "Rien pour lui n'était indifférent, pourvu qu'il fût vrai" (p. 268). When a man complains of having been ruined last winter by a flood, this oblivious scientist replies:

> "Ce que vous me dites là m'est fort agréable . . . je vois que je ne me suis pas trompé dans l'observation que j'ai faite, et qu'il est au moins tombé sur la Terre deux pouces d'eau plus que l'année passée." (P. 269)

But more than this special case we must recall Montaigne's disdain of all specialists—particularly those in the art of writing—the grammarians, logicians, rhetoricians, etc. The essayist was afraid that he and his work might be confused with such pedantic scholars. His satire of these artisans reveals a noble's prejudice against certain of the bourgeoisie who were vain about their particular craft and who, seeking money as their primary goal, could not or would not look beyond their specialty. Montaigne sought to understand the world on a broader level and communicate his universal nature to the public; he prides himself on being capable of adapting to the demands of many fields. The fulfillment of this objective is the great originality of the *Essais*, and it is a large part of the total concept of *honnêteté*:

> Les autheurs se communiquent au peuple par quelque marque particuliere et estrangere; moy, le premier, par mon estre universel, comme Michel de Montaigne, non comme grammairien, ou poëte, ou jurisconsulte. (*Essais,* III, ch. 2, p. 19)

The essayist admired certain scholars—Adrianus Turnebus and Justus Lipsius—because they were versed in subjects outside their specialty. Anyone who preferred to be known as a logician or grammarian rather than a *gentilhomme* was a ridiculous creature in the eyes of the well-rounded nobility. The virtue of possessing knowledge and personal qualities on a broad scale was no less desirable than it was rare at that time. Montaigne writes,

> Je connoy des hommes assez, qui ont diverses parties belles: qui l'esprit; qui, le cœur; qui l'adresse; qui, la conscience; qui, le langage;

qui, une science; qui, un'autre. Mais de grand homme en general, et ayant tant de belles pieces ensemble, ou une en tel degré d'excellence qu'on s'en doive estonner, ou le comparer à ceux que nous honorons du temps passé, ma fortune ne m'en a fait voir nul. (*Essais*, II, ch. 17, p. 380)

In the wake of the essayist Pascal writes:

Les gens universels ne sont appelés ni poètes, ni géomètres, etc.; mais ils sont tout cela, et juges de tous ceux-là. . . .

Il faut qu'on n'en puisse dire, ni: "Il est mathématicien," ni "prédicateur," ni "éloquent," mais "il est honnête homme." Cette qualité universelle me plaît seule.[4]

Pascal is the most obvious link between Montaigne of the sixteenth and Montesquieu of the eighteenth century; the latter is continuing a tradition which has never ceased to exist in the French literary world, once it became established.

Not only must the *honnête homme* be knowledgeable, but he must be tolerant of other's ideas and careful not to glow too brightly as an authority on any subject,

Car la precellence rare et au dessus du commun messied à un homme d'honneur en chose frivole. Ce que je dy en cet exemple se peut dire en tous autres: chasque parcelle, chasque occupation de l'homme l'accuse et le montre egalement qu'un'autre. (*Essais*, I, ch. 50, p. 336)

Un personnage sçavant n'est pas sçavant par tout; mais le suffisant est par tout suffisant, et à ignorer mesme. (*Essais*, III, ch. 2, p. 19)

A wealthy noble Montaigne meets reminds us of the two foolish scholars in letter 144—those who measure truth according to the limits of their own knowledge. This bigot begins a conversation thus: "Ce ne peut estre qu'un menteur ou ignorant qui dira autrement que, etc. . . ." Montaigne interrupts and warns us under his breath, "Suivez cette pointe philosophique, un pouignart à la main" (III, ch. 8, p. 168). He recommends a modest approach to conversation as a foil to the opinionated majority around him. "Il n'y a que les fols certains et resolus" (I, ch. 26, p. 161). His advice to the boy of "De l'institution" reflects Rica's behavior on two occasions: "Le silence et la modestie," writes the essayist, "sont qualitez tres-commodes à la conversation" (I, ch. 26, p. 165). The prudent Persian allows the *décisionnaire* to make a fool of himself. After one vain attempt to meet him on his own level Rica admits, "Mon parti fut bientôt pris: je me tus, je le laissai parler, et il décide encore" (p. 156). And hearing about the haughty Parisian noble who makes everyone feel inferior around him, Rica writes: "Si cela est, je n'ai que faire d'y aller: je la lui passe [la supériorité] tout entière et je prends condamnation" (p. 157). To fight stupidity with its own arms would be foolish indeed. Rica prefers to withdraw from the matter altogether, as though following the principle set by Montaigne for Mme de Foix's "son": "On luy apprendra de n'entrer en discours ou contestation que où il verra un champion digne de sa luite . . ." (I, ch. 26, p. 165).

What if Montesquieu were to pose as the perfect member of his class, withdrawn from the struggle for survival and looking down on those beneath him, which in his function as moralist he does to a certain extent? He would scarcely be likeable. To pose as an exemplary *honnête homme*, one is bound to be dethroned by the public. To insist upon one's modesty betrays the very virtue of modesty. Montesquieu was aware of this paradox; it is the subject of letter 50. His own ironic self-portrait is concealed beneath the sketch of the foolish noble who answers the first voice below:

> "Quoi! toujours des sots qui se peignent eux-mêmes, et qui ramènent tout à eux?—Vous avez raison, reprit brusquement notre discoureur. Il n'y a qu'à faire comme moi: je ne me loue jamais; j'ai du bien, de la naissance; je fais de la dépense; mes amis disent que j'ai quelque esprit; mais je ne parle jamais de tout cela. Si j'ai quelques bonnes qualités, celle dont je fais le plus de cas, c'est ma modestie." (*Lettres persanes,* p. 106)

Aware of the hypocrisy inherent in his own pose as *honnête homme* in his own self-portrait, Montesquieu is the object of his own satire. Such self-examination, be it sheer ritual, attests to the author's lucidity and honesty.

Be that as it may, Montesquieu does not cease to acclaim at least indirectly the value of a natural, unaffected virtue. Montaigne had done likewise, and he may have been a source for the introduction to letter 50. Rica writes:

> J'ai vu des gens chez qui la vertu était si naturelle qu'elle ne se faisait pas même sentir: ils s'attachaient à leur devoir sans s'y plier et s'y portaient comme par instinct. (P. 105)

Montaigne counsels the governor of the young noble in "De l'institution" with a similar precept:

> Il luy fera cette nouvelle leçon, que le prix et hauteur de la vraye vertu est en la facilité, utilité et plaisir de son exercice, si esloigné de difficulté, que les enfans y peuvent comme les hommes, les simples commes les subtilz. . . . Socrates, son premier mignon, quitte à escient sa force, pour glisser en la naiveté et aisance de son progrèz. (*Essais*, I, ch. 26, p. 174)

Rejecting pretentious discourse which indicates only the vanity of the speaker, Rica praises a man who is as though unaware of his merit:

> Bien loin de relever par leurs discours leurs rares qualités, il semblait qu'elles n'avaient pas percé jusques à eux. (*Lettres persanes*, p. 105)

One is reminded of Montaigne's repeated complaints about specialists in the art of language—orators, grammarians, architects, poets, and especially magistrates who tried to impress their listeners with pompous, pedantic language. Like Rica the essayist sought more down-to-earth, accessible, and sociable virtues. Like Rica he found that many nobles wanted only to show off their "exceptional qualities" by their discourse:

> la pluspart de ceux qui jugent les discours des grans debvroient dire: "je n'ay point entendu son propos, tant il estoit offusqué de gravité, de grandeur et de majesté." (*Essais*, III, ch. 8, p. 167)

Simplicity and *Grands Seigneurs Français*

Montesquieu is cautious not to force his character in the path of virtue. Behind his Persian mask, he playfully understates the role of the nobility in letter 88. His least aim is to overwhelm us with the image of his class:

> Un grand seigneur est un homme qui voit le roi, qui parle aux minis-
> tres, qui a des ancêtres, des dettes et des pensions. S'il peut, avec cela,
> cacher son oisiveté par un air empressé ou par un feint attachement pour
> les plaisirs, il croit être le plus heureux de tous les hommes. (*Lettres
> persanes,* p. 185)

We find evidence that the author is incorporated into this portrait.
As for hiding his leisure with a hurried air, we are reminded of Montesquieu's clairvoyance into his own tendency in this direction: "Je dis; 'j'ai
un nombre innombrable d'affaires que je n'ai pas' " (*pensée* 2158; 26). To
illustrate Montesquieu's own "feint attachement pour les plaisirs" we need
only quote from his self-portrait: "Lorsque je goûte un plaisir, j'en suis
affecté, et je suis toujours étonné de l'avoir recherché avec tant d'indiffé-
rence" (*pensée* 213; 4). The concluding remark—"il croit être le plus
heureux de tous les hommes"—suggests Montesquieu's healthy self-
satisfaction, one of the most prominent traits of his character. The author of
a fine essay on happiness is himself a happy man, basically free of chagrin
and immune to depression:

> Je n'ai presque jamais eu de chagrin, et encore moins d'ennui.
> Ma machine est si heureusement construite que je suis frappé par
> tous les objets assez vivement pour qu'ils puissent me donner du
> plaisir, pas assez pour me donner de la peine. (*Pensée* 213; 4)

There is a certain nonchalance inherent in our young noble author,
for in addition to a feigned attachment to pleasure, he only affects an interest
in the sciences. Usbek speaks for the casual, undogmatic Montesquieu
here: "je feignis un grand attachement pour les sciences, et, à force de le
feindre, il me vint réellement" (p. 22). A true *honnête homme* must not embrace any cause with too much ardor nor seek any goal with too much zeal.
    Simplicity also played an important role in Montesquieu's character.
In Paris he was glad to see that liberty and equality prevailed over class
prejudice:

> A Paris règnent la liberté et l'égalité. La naissance, la vertu, le mérite
> même de la guerre, quelque brillant qu'il soit, ne sauve pas un homme
> de la foule dans laquelle il est confondu. La jalousie des rangs y est
> inconnue. On dit que le premier de Paris est celui qui a les meilleurs
> chevaux à son carrosse. (*Lettres persanes,* p. 184)

Through Usbek's words above, Montesquieu could be saying that in spite of his station in life, his noble birth, he could hardly pretend to shine in the nation's capital. Thereby the author lowers his image to the level of the people. Like the average Parisian described above he does not stand out from the crowd; rather he is lost in it, happy to be so. One must not confuse Montesquieu's attitude toward Paris with another concerning the court:

> Je hais Versailles, parce que tout le monde y est petit. J'aime Paris, parce que tout le monde y est grand. (*Pensée* 998; 33)

On an equal footing with his fellow citizens Montesquieu felt dignified enough, it is clear. Maupertuis and other contemporaries expounded on Montesquieu's simplicity: "ses habits étaient fort négligés et les étoffes en étaient des plus simples; il avait deux assez mauvais chevaux de carosse . . ."[5] Jean Louis was not one to give airs in society—not even in upper-class circles. He found a flagrant display of wealth repugnant; it reminded him of American colonialists who came back to France, their pockets jingling with money. Through Usbek Montesquieu flatters himself that it was the relatively impoverished landed gentry who enjoyed the greatest credit with the king:

> Ici, il y a des gens qui sont grands par leur naissance; mais ils sont sans crédit. Les rois font comme ces ouvriers habiles qui, pour exécuter leurs ouvrages, se servent toujours des machines les plus simples. (*Lettres persanes*, p. 185)

The theme of simplicity is nowhere more important than in its relationship to Montesquieu's function as a moralist. In the first letter (number 48) where Usbek is introduced to numerous representatives of Parisian society, the observer who actually judges these outlandish types congregated in a villa near the capital is the very double of Montesquieu himself. With conscious coyness the author defines his analyst in terms which ally him with Usbek. The two figures are in reality one, and are synonomous with their creator. Usbek writes:

> Je remarquai d'abord un homme dont la simplicité me plut; je m'attachai à lui, il s'attacha à moi; de sorte que nous nous trouvions toujours l'un auprès de l'autre. (p. 99)

In this union of two unaffected, unspoiled, and almost naïve characters Montesquieu is alluding to those very same traits of his personality which, he implies, justify his role as moralist. To calculate the pretentions and idiosyncrasies of others (those inherent in the General Farmer, the gallant abbot, the poet, the old soldier, and the fortune hunter who will pass in review in this letter) one should possess the least possible pretentions and idiosyncrasies. Thus, the point of view emanates from a man whose simplicity is pleasing. It is on this basic premise that the nature of the *honnête homme* is founded.

The Double Image of Honnêteté

In letter 74 Usbek contrasts a haughty, conceited Parisian noble with the ideal specimen from the court of Persia. The oriental veil is a thin one; it serves only as a buffer to our author's vanity, for clearly Persia is a pseudonym for Gascony or Bordeaux. To illustrate the "vraie dignité des grands" Montesquieu apparently chose Montaigne as his model, although he worked the essayist's principles into his own style of thought. Both authors insist on the double image of *honnêteté* among the nobility. It can reveal itself in a manner in sympathy with the common people, or it can don the honor and pomp of its high rank. Pompous it must never be. Reacting to the snobbish Parisian grand seigneur Usbek exclaims,

> Ah! bon Dieu! dis-je en moi-même, si, lorsque j'étais à la cour de Perse, je représentais ainsi, je représentais un grand sot! Il aurait fallu, Rica, que nous eussions eu un bien mauvais naturel pour aller faire cent petites insultes à des gens qui venaient tous les jours chez nous nous témoigner leur bienveillance: ils savaient bien que nous étions au-dessus d'eux, et, s'ils l'avaient ignoré, nos bienfaits le leur auraient appris chaque jour. N'ayant rien à faire pour nous faire respecter, nous faisions tout pour nous rendre aimables: nous nous communiquions aux plus petits; au milieu des grandeurs, qui endurcissent toujours, ils nous trouvaient sensibles; ils ne voyaient que notre cœur au-dessus d'eux: nous descendions jusqu'à leurs besoins. (*Lettres persanes*, p. 158)

Montaigne also sought to be human and familiar in his dealings with the common people. To show off the prerogatives of his class before his servants would have been unthinkable:

Je louerois un' ame à divers estages, qui sçache et se tendre et se desmonter, qui soit bien par tout où sa fortune la porte, qui puisse deviser avec son voisin de son bastiment, de sa chasse et de sa querelle, entretenir avec plaisir un charpentier et un jardinier; j'envie ceux qui sçavent s'aprivoiser au moindre de leur suitte et dresser de l'entretien en leur propre train.

Et le conseil de Platon ne me plaist pas, de parler tousjours d'un langage magistral à ses serviteurs, sans jeu, sans familiarité, soit envers les masles, soit envers les femelles. Car, outre ma raison, il est inhumain et injuste de faire tant valoir cette telle quelle prerogative de la fortune; et les polices où il se souffre moins de disparité entre les valets et les maistres, me semblent les plus equitables. (*Essais*, III, ch. 3, p. 37)

When Usbek declares, "nous faisons tout pour nous rendre aimables," he may be answering Montaigne who is proud to have lived without undergoing a single lawsuit or duel, having consistently maintained good relations with his fellow citizens. Montesquieu does everything in order to be liked; Montaigne did anything not to be hated:

Mes meurs molles, ennemies de toute aigreur et aspreté, peuvent aysément m'avoir deschargé d'envies et d'inimitiez; *d'estre aimé, je ne dy, mais de n'estre point hay, jamais homme n'en donna plus d'occasion.* (Ibid., p. 36)

But there is the other side to the coin, for if a noble is familiar and relaxed with those beneath his station, he may put on a certain dignity when playing a more official role among his peers. Usbek continues, saying that to act out a part is sometimes one's duty:

Mais, lorsqu'il fallait soutenir la majesté du prince dans les cérémonies publiques; lorsqu'il fallait faire respecter la Nation aux étrangers; lorsque, enfin, dans les occasions périlleuses, il fallait animer les soldats, nous remontions cent fois plus haut que nous n'étions descendus: nous ramenions la fierté sur notre visage, et l'on trouvait quelquefois que nous représentions assez bien. (*Lettres persanes*, p. 158)

Montaigne considers the dignified mask of profession in a more skeptical light, reminding his colleagues that they should not play the magistrate at home but that at work it was a natural necessity:

> La plus part de nos vacations sont farcesques. . . . Il faut jouer deument
> nostre rolle, mais comme rolle d'un personnage emprunté. Du masque
> et de l'apparence il n'en faut pas faire une essence reelle, ny de
> l'estranger le propre. (*Essais*, III, ch. 10, pp. 252-53)

And in the same context he declares:

> Le Maire et Montaigne ont tousjours esté deux, d'une separation bien
> claire. Pour estre advocat ou financier, il n'en faut pas mesconnoistre la
> fourbe qu'il y a en telles vacations. Un honneste homme n'est pas
> comptable du vice ou sottise de son mestier, et ne doibt pourtant en
> refuser l'exercise; c'est l'usage de son pays, et il y a du proffict. (Ibid.,
> p. 253)

Montaigne's double personality is parallel to Usbek's in letter 74.
Or more precisely it is the one which Montesquieu felt best reflected his
own ideals of *honnêteté*. Montaigne had written:

> En general, elle [la grandeur] a cet evident avantage qu'elle se ravalle
> quand il luy plaist, et qu'à peu près elle a le chois de l'une et l'autre
> condition; (*Essais*, III, ch. 7, pp. 145-46)

His successor prides himself on having a similar nature, supple enough to
fit into both roles—or rather into the "role" of his professional status and
into his natural skin as a Gascon baron at ease on his lands, friendly to his
peasants. On the other hand, concerning official functions Usbek writes:
"on trouvait quelquefois que nous représentions assez bien" (p. 158). Is he
not echoing the essayist who had said: "Il faut jouer deument nostre rolle,
mais comme rolle d'un personnage emprunté" (*Essais*, III, ch. 10, pp. 252-
53). The *honnête* Baron of La Brède is a different character altogether from
the *président à mortier* who is required to appear in public ceremonies and
support the majesty of the monarchy. Like his predecessor he might have
said, "Le président et Montesquieu ont toujours été deux." Such is the
personal message of letter 74.

Both Montaigne and Montesquieu recognize that if a *gentilhomme*
should do all in order to be respected and liked by the common folk, if his
manner should be direct and down-to-earth in society at large, nevertheless
he must maintain a certain noble bearing which reflects a natural pride in his
rank and status. He must not forget that he is a representative of his class

and has the responsibility to uphold it in the eyes of others. The essayist clarifies this point in directing the young noble in "De l'institution." "La philosophie" he alludes to below is in truth synonymous with *honnêteté:*

> L'ame qui loge la philosophie doit, par sa santé, rendre sain encores le corps. Elle doit faire luire jusques au dehors son repos et son ayse; doit former à son moule le port exterieur, et l'armer par consequent d'une *gratieuse fierté*, d'un maintien actif et allegre, et d'une contenance contente et debonnaire.[6] (*Essais*, I, ch. 26, p. 173)

It is precisely this quality of bearing which the *fermier* in letter 48 lacks. Montesquieu does not conceal his class prejudice against such a *nouveau riche* and has his Persian visitor speak the truth through naive, spontaneous observation:

> Il faut bien que ce soit un homme de qualité; mais il a la physionomie si basse qu'il ne fait guère honneur aux gens de qualité; et, d'ailleurs, je ne lui trouve point d'éducation. Je suis étranger; mais il me semble qu'il y a en général une certaine politesse commune à toutes les nations; je ne lui trouve point de celle-là. Est-ce que vos gens de qualité sont plus mal élevés que les autres? (*Lettres persanes*, pp. 99-100)

Both Montaigne and Montesquieu believe in the essential dignity of their class. Any intruder was unveiled as a fake. A minimum of *politesse*, the natural polish and grace of an *honnête homme*, was a prerequisite for respect within the aristocracy. Breeding was invaluable and immediately apparent to the perceptive Montesquieu. The ruling class must emanate an air that inspires not only familiarity (for familiarity breeds contempt) but also respect.

Class awareness is one of the deepest ties between Montaigne and Montesquieu even to the point of being prejudiced. Anyone familiar with the essayist knows this leitmotiv running throughout his work—disdain for "vils artisans," pretentious merchants, and other riffraff of society. True learning was only fit for the aristocracy. True aristocracy was determined only be an old and entrenched lineage. Montesquieu did not know that his illustrious predecessor was less of an established noble than he pretended to be. And we imagine that his identity with Montaigne was as complete as it was subconscious. And yet how much sharper are Montesquieu's jabs at the *arrivistes* of his era. ("Le corps des laquais est plus respectable en

France qu'ailleurs; c'est un séminaire de grands seigneurs.") Helvétius's criticism of Montesquieu in 1747 ("Avec le genre d'esprit de Montaigne, il a conservé ses préjugés d'homme de robe et de gentilhomme") is as valid for the same man twenty years younger.

Ties with the People

A proud bearing was more common among the nobility than a modest, sociable air. It is this latter trait that pertains especially to our two nobles, for they sought to make themselves acceptable to the masses. Anecdotes on Montesquieu's informal, good-natured personality at home attest to the image of himself he wished to leave posterity. Like Montaigne he was familiar with his servants who must have found their master an affable fellow. Tradition has it that one day a peasant presented himself at the door of Montesquieu's estate at Clairac. He asked to see "le sire de Montesquieu."

> L'honnête homme ou le coquin? interrogea celui qui avait ouvert.
> —Le coquin, précisa le paysan.
> —Le coquin, c'est moi. Parle . . . répondit le sire de Montesquieu.[7]

Although René Cruchet tells us that one cannot date this dialogue to know whether it is *our* Montesquieu in question here, or another one, such a playful answer to his servant fits into the image we have of Jean-Louis. *Bonhomie* was surely a family trait. The eighteenth-century historian Garat drew up a portrait of Montesquieu that the latter would have sanctioned, even encouraged:

> Nul homme à talent ou sans talent ne fut jamais plus simple que Montesquieu dans son ton et dans ses manières: il l'était dans les salons de Paris autant que dans son domaine de La Brède, où, parmi les pelouses, les fontaines et les forêts dessinées à l'anglaise, il courait du matin au soir, un bonnet de coton sur la tête, un long échalas de vigne sur l'épaule, et où ceux qui venaient lui présenter des hommages de l'Europe lui demandaient plus d'une fois, en le tutoyant comme un serviteur, si c'était là le chateau de Montesquieu.[8]

Montaigne cultivated this modest pose as carefully as Montesquieu. In the same light one cannot help but remember the essayist's self-effacing remarks on the subject of his physical appearance. They bear a striking resemblance to the portrait of Montesquieu which Garat has left us:

> C'est un grand despit qu'on s'adresse à vous parmy vos gens, pour vous demander: "Où est monsieur?" et que vous n'ayez que le reste de la bonnetade qu'on fait à vostre barbier ou à vostre secretaire. (*Essais*, II, ch. 17, p. 359)

The essayist had described himself as below average height and suggested that he was slightly less than handsome. But we can imagine that it was his informal dress (he wore simple black and white attire, as his father had before him) and modest demeanor which made visitors mistake the noble for one of his servants. Montaigne had no need for courtly style and elegance on his own domain. In fact, the pomp and circumstance of the court annoyed him in general. At Montaigne among his friends or acquaintances, he writes, "il s'y fait trefve de ceremonie" (III, ch. 3, p. 39). He was not only amused but flattered to be confused with the common folk. We must remember that as a baby little Michel was given by his father to the care of peasants and remained among them beyond the nursing stage. Montaigne explains his father's intent in doing this and in choosing paupers as his godparents:

> de me ralier avec le peuple et cette condition d'hommes qui a besoin de nostre ayde; et estimoit que je fusse tenu de regarder plutost vers celuy qui me tend les bras que vers celuy qui me tourne le dos. (*Essais*, III, ch. 13, p. 354)

Such symbolic acts were not wasted on Montaigne, for he adds:

> Son dessein n'a pas du tout mal succedé: je m'adonne volontiers aux petits, soit pour ce qu'il y a plus de gloire, soit par naturelle compassion, qui peut infiniement en moy. (Ibid.)

Historians have noted that Montesquieu was brought into society under a similar banner. He was held over the font by a beggar of the village and during his early years was reared by peasants at La Brède. Among this family he acquired a *frère de lait* with whom he remained in touch throughout his life. More significant, like Montaigne, he cultivated an attitude of compassion and tenderness towards the poor. "Je m'adonne volontiers aux petits," says the essayist. "Nous nous communiquions aux plus petits," writes Usbek (p. 158).

An account from one of Montesquieu's contemporaries, Latapie, shows that the principle of love for the people espoused by Usbek in letter 74 was more than a mere theory in Montesquieu's life:

> Il chérit toujours ses tenanciers, et (je lui ai ouï dire quelquefois) une de ses jouissances les plus pures était de les revoir. On le devinait aisément à l'air de satisfaction qui se peignait sur son visage chaque fois qu'il revenait de Paris . . . Il n'allait jamais dans ses terres sans en visiter les habitants de toutes les classes. Il parcourait chaque jour tantôt un village, tantôt un autre, et savait le nom de tous ses paysans, auxquels il ne parlait jamais qu'en gascon. Il se plaisait à s'occuper de leurs intérêts: pour mieux les connaître il s'informait aux enfants des facultés de leurs parents. On l'a vu souvent aller vers ces derniers leur proposer les moyens de pacifier leurs querelles domestiques, pour arranger leurs affaires particulières et même pour leur porter des secours pécuniaires, sans que ces bonnes gens puissent savoir comment il avait pu être instruit de leur position.[9]

It is not suprising then that Montesquieu's heart should go out to those less fortunate than he. If they were afflicted with sorrow, his compassion was aroused that much more. Is Ibben not speaking for the author in the following words?

> j'ai eu . . . la même compassion ou plutôt la même tendresse pour les malheureux, la même estime pour ceux que la prospérité n'a point aveuglés. (*Lettres persanes*, p. 137)

Such are the fruits of a precedent for both our philosophers at the very commencement of their life. Granted, the custom of choosing impoverished godparents for sons of the nobility was a widespread one. Buffon as well had a beggar as godfather. But Montaigne and Montesquieu succeeded more noticeably in communicating to the public and to posterity the liberal ideal of their class, when dealing with those less fortunate than they. Sympathy for the afflicted and the unfortunate reflects their innate humanity and kindness:

je me compassione fort tendrement des afflictions d'autruy [writes Montaigne], et pleurerois aiséement par compaignie, si, pour occasion que ce soit, je sçavois pleurer. Il n'est rien qui tente mes larmes que les larmes . . . (*Essais*, II, ch. 11, p. 109)

Je te l'avoue, Usbek [Rica writes], je n'ai jamais vu couler les larmes de personne sans en être attendri:[10] je sens de l'humanité pour les malheureux, comme s'il n'y avait qu'eux qui fussent hommes, et les grands mêmes, pour lesquels je trouve dans mon cœur de la dureté quand ils sont élevés, je les aime sitôt qu'ils tombent. (*Lettres persanes*, p. 265)

Another episode in Montesquieu's life attests to his conscientious concern and care for the people. How ready he was to come to their aid in time of need! In the winter of 1747-48 Guyenne ran short of cereals because of the war. On December 7th when Montesquieu was at La Brède, he was told that on another area of property certain of his vassals were threatened with famine. Immediately Montesquieu traveled to this place, assembled the curés of the four nearby villages and asked that all the grain in his stores be distributed to them, seeing as they knew best the needs of their parishioners. "Il ne faut pas qu'on manque de nécessaire chez moi, quand j'y ai du superflu," he declared. Thereupon Montesquieu departed so as to escape the thanks of both curés and vassals. The sum contributed free was a large one (6,400 pounds at the time). And to top it all off, in order to guard against any future misfortune of this sort, Montesquieu had specific amounts of grain set aside for the unique purpose of charity.[11]

Both Montaigne and Montesquieu realized that they were ultimately responsible to the *peuple* and thus fashioned themselves in life and in art according to a style which could offend the fewest and attract the most. Without the vast public's good will either writer would have passed into oblivion or scorn. They were aware of this:

Nous vivons et negotions avec le peuple; si sa conversation nous importune, si nous desdaignons à nous appliquer aux ames basses et vulguaires, et les basses et vulguaires sont souvent aussi reglées que les plus desliées (est toute sapience insipide, qui ne s'accomode à l'insipience commune), il ne nous faut plus entremetre ny de nos propres affaires ny de ceux d'autruy; et les publiques et les privez se demeslent avec ces gens là. Les moins tandues et plus naturelles alleures de nostre ame sont les plus belles; les meilleures occupations, les moins efforcées. (*Essais*, III, ch. 3, p. 35)

---

il n'y a guère d'heure dans le jour où un honnête homme n'ait affaire avec le bas peuple, et, quelque grand seigneur que l'on soit on y aboutit toujours. (*Pensée* 32; 1802)

Je disois: "J'ai compris une chose dont je me doutois déjà: c'est que pour vivre bien avec tout le monde, il ne faut pas avoir de prétentions. Si vous sortez des quatre murailles de votre chambre, on vous arquebuse. Si je revenois au Monde, je ne voudrois que me chauffer l'hiver et prendre des glaces l'été." (*Pensée* 2011; 1067)

And in a slightly different context Montesquieu chastizes the aristo-cracy for forgetting its responsibilities to the common people:

Nous ne pouvons nous attacher à tous nos concitoyens. Nous en choisissons un petit nombre, auquel nous nous bornons. Nous passons une espèce de contrat pour notre utilité commune, qui n'est qu'un retranchement de celui que nous avons passé avec la société entière, et semble même, en un certain sens, lui être préjudiciable. . . . borner un homme véritablement vertueux à un certain nombre d'amis, c'est détourner son cœur de tous les autres hommes; c'est le séparer du tronc et l'attacher aux branches. (*Pensée*, 1253; 604)

Montesquieu thus shares Montaigne's democratic ideals of the nobility. He was lucid enough to know that the people deserved more attention than they received; and yet paradoxically he knew also that they could exercise great power in determining one's own reputation. In *Mes Pensées* again, he speaks of "le plus précieux de tous les biens, qui est la bienveillance du peuple." Without it, he adds, one is bound to suffer "le fléau de ridicule dont il couvre ceux qui se sont offerts à ses mépris" (*pensée* 1387; 1135).

In letter 145 Montesquieu makes a passing allusion to his success in remaining within the people's good graces. The following remark is lost in his bitterness at seeing the *Lettres persanes* censored by certain opinionated conservatives from the upper stratas of society: "Il a beau etre absous par le peuple . . ." (p. 320), cries Usbek in defense of the "homme d'esprit" who is none other than Montesquieu himself. We believe that the author took note of Montaigne's popular stance among his entourage at Montaigne and declared him his model after the fact. Following his own individual inclination, Montesquieu walks in the essayist's footsteps among the servants and peasants of La Brède. His gate should appear as relaxed and natural as Montaigne's.

In conclusion on this broad subject, it is apparent that an *honnête homme* combines qualities of an almost contradictory nature. First of all, as applied to our two provincial barons, he is of a certain rank in society; although he may understate the nobility's importance, he must nevertheless remember that he is one of its representatives. If his bearing should be unpretentious and natural among the common people, he must not be totally devoid of pride and grace when exercising his profession as magistrate or when appearing in royal functions. The nobility has a certain role to play in society. One must at times put on the mask of greatness.

At court both these provincial *gentilshommes* were obliged to transform their personalities. In their castles near Bordeaux we find them more as they were by nature—the most unaffected nobility imaginable, casually dressed and relaxed in their bearing so that one might take them for servants. As for matters of learning, in writing and particularly in conversation, to be pedantic is in the worst taste. One must make no special show of knowledge and learning. Let erudite snobs make fools of themselves, while you maintain a respectful (if ironic) silence. General approbation will be on your side, not on that of a man who is domineering and dogmatic. To take special pride in one's profession or specialty or to flaunt one's talents is sure to provoke the public's scorn. The mass's widespread range of specialties requires that you meet them on all levels of thought—not just one or two. An *honnête homme* is well rounded and universal in his knowledge so that he can communicate in a natural manner with all stations of society either in writing or in speaking. ". . . on dit bien vray," wrote Montaigne, "qu'un honneste homme, c'est un homme meslé" (III, ch. 9, p. 224). An old formula finds new expression in the *Lettres persanes*, where the author visits the widest possible scope of ranks and types, sometimes evaluating them, sometimes appraising himself and them simultaneously, for in this quest of familiarity with the world around him he does not forget that he is not only the observer but the observed. The measure of his own *honnêteté* is at stake relative to those around him. Before judging others one must first know oneself. If our gaze is by nature directed outwards, we must at least consider our own vantage point. We must realize our own relativity before discussing that of society at large.

Such, in broad terms, are the qualities at the core of both men's characters. They do not constitute merely a literary pose, but are a part of their very being. Montesquieu writes in *Mes Pensées:*

> Je me souviens que, sortant d'une pièce intitulée *Esope à la Cour*, j'en sortis si pénétré du désir d'être plus honnête homme, que je ne sache jamais avoir formé une résolution plus forte; bien différent de cet ancien qui disoit qu'il n'étoit jamais sorti des spectacles aussi vertueux qu'il y étoit entré. (*Pensée* 217; 45)

It is apparent that upon reading the *Essais*, Montesquieu was inspired by a positive example to fashion his literary personality and to know himself according to the ideals of *honnêteté* embodied in Montaigne. Usbek and Rica attest to their creator's self-portrait drawn very much along the same lines as the essayist's.

IX

THE DISPUTE OVER *DE L'ESPRIT:*
MONTESQUIEU'S SELF-PORTRAIT
IN SOCIETY

MONTESQUIEU'S SELF-DISCOVERY IS apparent on many levels in the *Lettres persanes.* The author devotes so much time to one facet of honnêteté—his role as a gallant courtier and social wit—that we must examine it separately from the previous, general discussion. Montesquieu comes especially to grips with his place in the fashionable circles that Paris opened to him. We have no better way of knowing the tenure of his life and character in the years prior to 1721 than through his work:

> C'est lui-même que Montesquieu a peint dans les *Lettres persanes* et la trame du livre est constituée par les surprises de jeune provincial faisant ses premières armes dans les salons parisiens.[1]

Robert Shackleton speaks of the baron's interest in penetrating into metropolitan society during the years 1721-28.[2] However, there is every indication that Montesquieu spent a great deal of his time socializing in Parisian salons, cafés, participating in royal functions as well as informal social outings in the years preceding 1721. Already then he shows what interest various types of Parisian social life held for him. Montesquieu was surely trying to penetrate into the proper circles. Although he had been married since 1715, he remained relatively free from the constraints of this union. In Paris he was independent, quite busy and active, it appears. The *Lettres persanes* seem to reflect Montesquieu's examination of his environment and his own relationship to it. Although obliged to follow certain social formulas, Montesquieu the author seems to mock Montesquieu the man for his somewhat embarassing situation as a wit and gallant courtier. And Montesquieu the man is ashamed that Montesquieu the author endeavors to portray himself as a witty *faiseur de livres* in the *Lettres persanes*.

Two *Beaux Esprits*

Letter 54, "Conversation de deux beaux esprits," is not so much social satire as self-appraisal. Montesquieu, who could not abide petty *beaux esprits,* creates here a sort of interior dialogue, drawing his inspiration from La Bruyère's portrait of Le Cydias. (See *Lettres persanes*, p. 114, fn. 1.) On the surface the conversation is a simple one. Two social wits decide to work together so that they will glow in the various salons of Paris. Their scheme is to calculate every *bon mot*, every *saillie*, every anecdote, every verse that they offer in society, and even the amount of approval or laughter which should follow such recitals. They support each other in the fulfillment of this task and endeavor to make their hoax appear as authentic as possible. However, the comic element is apparent, for they merely disfigure the most natural of arts—conversation. The observer of this farce is Rica who represents the alter ego of his creator, Montesquieu. While the two *beaux esprits* convey the rumblings of a social plot to impress his avid listeners, Rica is the objective author in this instance, separated from the witty Frenchmen only by a thin partition:

> J'étais ce matin dans ma chambre, qui, comme tu sais, n'est séparée des autres que par une cloison fort mince et percée en plusieurs endroits; de sorte qu'on entend tout ce qui se dit dans la chambre voisine. (*Lettres persanes*, pp. 113-14)

Clearly the two rooms symbolize two distinct levels of thought in Montesquieu's own mind, and the Persian Rica serves as a useful tool in the knowing of himself. Jean Louis's introspection begins to take concrete form when one *bel esprit* speaks of "models," suggesting the art of writing almost more than that of speaking:

> Il faudra acheter de certains livres qui sont des recueils de bons mots composés à l'usage de ceux qui n'ont point d'esprit, et qui en veulent contrefaire: tout dépend d'avoir des modèles. (p. 115)

Is this not our author's method in composing his *Lettres?* We have seen that Montaigne is one of his models, a source for certain letters. Montesquieu has a debt to La Bruyère for the form of the present letter. Elsewhere Molière, Pascal, Fénelon or others may determine the writer's style. When the same *bel esprit* adds, "Ce n'est pas assez de dire un bon mot; il faut le répandre et le semer partout," we believe the metaphysical "sowing" grains of wit symbolizes the act of writing. In hoping to publish his *Lettres persanes* the author is seeking a wider audience and smiles at his vanity in so doing.

　　　Thus, Montesquieu's gaze turns inward. He does not exclude himself from the artificial tricks required to be witty, implying that if he is the satirist of fake *beaux esprits*, then one has the right to reproach him for the same foible. In the style of his *Lettres* the author tries to reproduce a natural conversational tone—often casual and bantering. He is in conversation with the reader. And although his efforts to emulate conversation are sincere enough, Montesquieu is admitting here playfully that in reality he can hardly pretend to be a natural wit any more than the two *beaux esprits*. The confession is disguised, but no matter, an honest one.

　　　One of the two wits continues with the following remarks:

> Fais ce que je te dirai, et je te promets avant six mois une place à l'Académie. C'est pour te dire que le travail ne sera pas long: car pour lors tu pourras renoncer à ton art; tu seras homme d'esprit malgré que tu en aies. (p. 115)

We are familiar with young Montesquieu's satire of the *Académie Française*. One of his *Lettres* (number 73) pokes fun goodnaturedly at this body which put so much emphasis on the vain matters of words. But during these years when the author was composing the *Lettres persanes*, was he not a candidate or possible candidate to the Academy? He will be elected at any rate in 1727 after some delay and difficulty. The above words might point out Montesquieu's realization of his status as a candidate prior to 1721. He makes it rather clear that the artificial display of wit did not please him as a prerequisite to being accepted as a member of this august body. We feel the mild disdain of a Gascon noble for the pretentious atmosphere in the French Academy. In saying "le travail ne sera pas long," he is perhaps hoping that his own functions in society designed to have himself admitted would not continue to cost him the price of his sincerity and freedom. (Undoubtedly Montesquieu was obliged to visit members and present a certain image of himself in order to be accepted.) And the words "tu seras homme d'esprit malgré que tu en aies," suggests his hope that the pretentiousness of the Academy would not rub off on him. "Helvétius reports that Montesquieu once said that he was favorably received in French society as a man of wit, until the *Lettres persanes* showed that perhaps he was in fact such; thereafter he suffered a thousand ills."[3] Montesquieu is reflecting that he would rather be himself, relaxed, unimposing, and unaffected in society. Thus, two themes of our letter unite to reveal the author's concern over his own reputation as a *bel esprit*—one he paradoxically encouraged by being a candidate for the Academy and by writing such witty letters. In his self-portrait of *Mes Pensées* we find these doubts expressed openly and clearly:

> Je suis (je crois) presque le seul homme qui ait fait des livres, ayant sans cesse peur de la réputation de bel-esprit. Ceux qui m'ont connu savent que, dans mes conversations, je ne cherchois pas trop à le paroître, et que j'avois assez le talent de prendre la langue de ceux avec qui je vivois. (*Pensée* 213; 4)

Letter 54 is the result of Montesquieu's self-examination on the question of social wits, one that as a young man he felt to be somewhat unresolved. Only a part of himself felt truly comfortable amidst the *beaux esprits* of Parisian salons. By nature Montesquieu was a more natural conversationalist. He did not want an affected, clever style to exert an influence on his own:

> J'aime les maisons où je puis me tirer d'affaire avec mon esprit de tous les jours. (*Pensée* 1417; 25)

And we might add that although Montesquieu accumulated models of wit to form the base of his *Lettres*, he ardently hoped that they would appear neither affected nor pretentious. To realize the danger of obnoxious wit assures one best of avoiding it. However, as author of a witty work, the sole merit on which to base his literary standing and possible election to the French Academy, Montesquieu found himself in a bind. In letter 54 he seems to muse that perhaps he was moving in a direction contrary to common sense. Joining forces with the very *beaux esprits* he tended to disdain was sure to affect his own self-esteem as well as others' opinion of him.

Diseurs de Riens

We must distinguish Montesquieu from the two absurd *beaux esprits* of letter 54. He feared his presence in these characters the way Gide in *Les Faux-Monnayeurs* fears his alliance with the antagonist, Passavant. But can we separate our author from the "diseurs de riens" in letter 82? Here he is more directly involved. Rica has a few sharp words concerning these agreeable chatterboxes who are the delight of ladies. Following is his definition:

> Ce sont ceux qui savent parler sans rien dire, et qui amusent une conversation, pendant deux heures de temps, sans qu'il soit possible de les déceler, d'être leur plagiaire, ni de retenir un mot de ce qu'ils ont dit. Ces sortes de gens sont adorés des femmes; mais ils ne le sont pas tant que d'autres, qui ont reçu de la Nature l'aimable talent de sourire à propos, c'est-à-dire à chaque instant, et qui portent la grâce d'une joyeuse approbation sur tout ce qu'elles disent. (*Lettres persanes*, p. 173)

Ironically enough we find that Montesquieu was himself the most talented *diseur de riens* in the company of ladies. François Hardy in his *Mémoires de Charlemont* describes our sociable baron:

> On était étonné de ses prévenances et de ses entretiens avec les femmes. Le petit maître le plus accompli n'était pas auprès d'elles plus avenant par la gaieté de la causerie, ou plus inépuisable à trouver et à dire *les mille riens qui leur plaisent.*[4]

What sort of gallant nothings was Montesquieu capable of producing which charmed women so? We have only to search in *Mes Pensées* where the artist collects many of his *bons mots*. Does Montesquieu not pride himself on his *esprit*?

> Je disois à Mme de . . . : "Je veux avoir la meilleure part dans votre amitié: il me faut la part du lion." (*Pensée* 1155; 491)

> La pr . . . d'Au . . . me disoit de parler. Je lui répondis: "Madame, si je parlois, vous ne parleriez pas." (*Pensée* 1220; 492)

I said to a lady : "Vous n'avez aucune des qualités qui vous empechent d'être aimable; vous pouvez en avoir de celles qui vous empêchent d'être aimée." (*Pensée* 1221; 493)

I said to Mme de L . . . : "Ceux qui entendent parler de vous vous admirent; ceux qui vous voient vous aiment." (*Pensée* 1311; 496)

Mme de R . . . se plaignoit de quelques boutons. Je lui dis: "Eh! que font des boutons sur un visage qui a derrière lui une si belle âme!" (*Pensée* 1646; 497)

En envoyant l'édition de *l'Esprit* d'Ecosse à Mme Dupré de Saint-Maur, je lui disois: "Je suis bien aise que vous me lisiez dans une si belle édition: je voudrois que quelque fée me donnât un habit avec lequel je pusse vous plaire." (*Pensée* 2063; 498)

So Montesquieu was also one of those *diseurs de riens* who are adored by women, smiling at the right moment, congratulating them on all they say. Rica's jab at their cleverness among women reflects the Baron of La Brède perfectly:

Mais ils sont au comble de l'esprit lorsqu'ils savent entendre finesse à tout et trouver mille petits traits ingénieux dans les choses les plus communes. (*Lettres persanes*, p. 173)

Letter 83 should not be interpreted merely as a social satire of others. "J'avois assez le talent de prendre la langue ce ceux avec qui je vivois," he writes in *Mes Pensées* (*pensée* 213; 4). So the young Baron of La Brède was also inclined to follow in the pattern of social graces of conversation when he lived in Paris. At the end of this letter he hints that this part of his nature was not apparent on his domains in Gascony, although it developed naturally when occasion demanded it in the nation's capital:

Je te promets que ces petits talents, dont on ne fait aucun cas chez nous, servent bien ici ceux qui sont assez heureux pour les avoir, et qu'un homme de bon sens ne brille guère devant eux. (p. 173)

The expression "chez nous" above can be interpreted as meaning in Gascony. Montesquieu confesses that his character in Paris (like that of many others) displays a touch of frivolity which is in sharp contrast to common sense. It is clear that by making *himself* the butt of the satire as much as his associates, the baron had ambivalent feelings about his gallant role vis-à-vis women, although in *Mes Pensées* he comments on such polite deference in a matter-of-fact tone: "J'ai assez aimé de dire aux femmes des fadeurs et de leur rendre des services qui coûtent si peu" (*pensée* 213; 4). Letter 82 expresses a general skepticism in bright colors. Montesquieu excuses himself to a certain extent by blending his own portrait into that of others. "I am merely one of a group," he seems to say. "And the gallant clichés we dole out to women please them to such an extent that the cost in terms of sincerity is perhaps worth it, after all."

Both letters 54 and 82 together form an important aspect of our author's introspection concerning his social identity. In his twenties young Montesquieu was aware of his tendency to shine and in a sense perform in chosen society; he was aware of his ability to please his entourage, especially women; he realized he was both deliberately (and yet somehow naturally) creating a reputation for himself, one that was not to cease growing throughout his lifetime. Montesquieu's contemporaries are inexhaustible in their praise for his conversation—then and still today one of France's "fine arts." D'Argenson says:

> Il portait dans la société beaucoup de douceur, assez de gaieté, une égalité parfaite, un air de simplicité et de bonhomie qui, vu la réputation qu'il s'est déjà faite, lui forme un mérite particulier.
>
> Dans le feu des conversations, raconte Maupertuis, on trouvait toujours le même homme avec tous les tons. Il semblait encore plus merveilleux que dans ses ouvrages: simple, profond, sublime, il charmait, il instruisait, et n'offensait jamais.
>
> Quand il parlait, ajoute Garat, ce dont il n'était ni prodigue ni avare, on était toujours sûr d'être avec lui. C'était tour à tour la gaieté piquante de Rica, les vues vastes et concises d'Usbek . . .
>
> Sa conversation, d'après d'Alembert, était légère, agréable et instructive par le grand nombre d'hommes et de peuples qu'il avait connus. Elle était coupée comme son style, pleine de sel et de saillies, sans amertume et sans satire; personne ne racontait plus vivement, plus promptement, avec plus de grâce et moins d'apprêt. Il savait que la fin d'une histoire plaisante en est toujours le but; il se hâtait donc d'y arriver et produisait l'effet sans l'avoir promis.[5]

This Montesquieu so skilled in the art of "saillies" and clever in recounting an "histoire plaisante," the very joy of his listeners, is he not identical to that *bel esprit* in letter 54 who confesses:

> J'avais préparé quelques saillies pour relever mon discours; . . . J'avais un conte fort joli à faire; . . . J'ai quelques bons mots, qui, depuis quatre jours, vieillissent dans ma tête . . . Hier, j'avais espéré de briller avec trois ou quatre vieilles femmes . . . (*Lettres persanes,* p. 114)

(Especially with three or four ladies, Montesquieu, the model *diseur de riens*, was at his best. Lord Chesterfield tells that in an ordinary salon the baron did not glow as he did in chosen company where "personne n'était plus aimable, plus spirituel et plus tout à tous.")[6] Is the author not the same character as one of the *diseurs de riens* who likewise calculates his charm in advance? Rica is ironically attacking Montesquieu's own contrived wit when he designs a metaphor on the "speeches" in salons where conversation is supposed to be so natural and spontaneous:

> Il est bon de commencer de la rue à se faire écouter par le bruit de carrosse et du marteau, qui frappe rudement la porte: cet avant-propos prévient pour le reste du discours, et, quand l'exorde est beau, il rend supportables toutes les sottises qui viennent ensuite . . . (p. 173)

Here indeed is our author confessing playfully to his public. As a young man he was inclined to be even more witty and vivacious than the descriptions drawn up by his contemporaries would suggest. D'Argenson, Maupertuis, D'Alembert, and others were speaking of an older, calmer, and more mature Montesquieu than the brilliant, loquacious author of the *Lettres persanes* and frequenter of Parisian salons in the years prior to 1721. In conclusion, it must be said that Montesquieu shared in the vice or virtue of creating a conversation like a work of art. ("Les conversations sont un ouvrage que l'on construit . . ." [*pensée* 1285; 1739].) In the *Lettres persanes* the author chastizes himself for the frivolity and vanity of his task.

It is only after the publication of *L'Esprit des lois* that we possess any documentation as to Montesquieu's appearance and character. But the traits which his biographers noticed then were surely valid for the man of twenty to thirty years younger. One of his most singular characteristics was his liveliness. The Abbey de Guasco, the Italian who painted Montesquieu, maintained that he had never had to portray a man whose expression changed so much from one moment to the next. Moreover, his son and D'Alembert confirmed that there was great vivacity within Montesquieu's small, lithe frame.[7] Thus one wonders if the author of letter 82 is not describing himself along with certain others when Rica discusses the art of speaking without words—another way for a *diseur de riens* to say nothing:

> J'en connais d'autres, qui se sont bien trouvés d'introduire dans les conversations des choses inanimées et d'y faire parler leur habit brodé, leur perruque blonde, leur tabatière, leur canne et leurs gants. (p. 173)

This general, open-hearted nature of Frenchmen in general cannot be disassociated from the frank, talkative Montesquieu in particular. And when Rica describes these lively people, he is also depicting Montesquieu:

> tout parle, tout se voit, tout s'entend; le cœur se montre comme le visage; dans les mœurs, dans la vertu, dans le vice même, on aperçoit toujours quelque chose de naïf. (p. 131)

In the above two excerpts Montesquieu may very well be conscious of his own inclination to use gestures while speaking and his own tendency toward candor and enthusiasm when in the right company: "Quand je me fie à quelqu'un, je le fais sans réserve; mais je me fie à peu de personnes" (*pensée* 213; 4). At any rate, such characteristics are thoroughly meridional. Montesquieu's self-portrait seems synonymous with that of his race.

When aroused on a theme, Montesquieu could speak untiringly and continually. Lord Charlement recounts that once the baron became engaged in a warm dispute during dinner. "He gave away to the servant who stood behind him seven clean plates, supposing that he had used them all.[8] What interests us here is not Montesquieu's distraction (which is, however, remarkable), but his great energy and liveliness in talking. Thus, he may have been thinking specifically of himself when he describes certain *diseurs de riens* "qui amusent une conversation *pendant deux heures de temps*" (p. 173) and the two *beaux esprits* "en état de tenir une conversation *d'une heure*" (p. 115). As a young man Montesquieu must have had great endurance and enthusiasm. Once involved in his role as the sociable baron from Gascony, like Montaigne he was all too inclined to be a *jaseur*.

Le Visiteur

Is there not also a bit of Montesquieu in his portrait of the *visiteur* in letter 87—the poor social creature who hastens from one function to the next—funerals, baptisms, marriages, etc.—totally exhausted by his continuous activity? The rhythm of life in Paris must have tired our author also at times, for he was used to the slower, calmer pace of rural Gascony where he was born and reared. Rica contrasts the great distance the *visiteur* walked in the city compared to the smaller territory covered in the country:

> le chemin qu'il a fait sur le pavé [monte] à neuf mille six cents stades; celui qu'il a fait dans la campagne à trente-six. (*Lettres persanes,* p. 184)

Is Montesquieu implying that in spite of the vast amount of land he owned in Gascony where he loved to stroll, the distance covered there was nothing compared to his "marathons" in Paris? (The great disparity between 9,600 "stades" and 36 is remarkable.)

In both the letter on *diseurs de riens* and the present epistle the author alludes to the act of knocking on the innumerable doors of the houses he visited. Is he not musing that he and his associates were wearing themselves to a frazzle with their continual visits? "Ils fatiguent plus les portes des maisons à coups de marteau, que les vents et les tempêtes" (p. 183).

The *visiteur's* conversation is as tireless as his legs:

> Sa conversation était amusante: il avait un fonds tout fait de trois cent soixante-cinq contes; il possédait, d'ailleurs, depuis son jeune âge, cent dix-huit apophtegmes tirés des Anciens qu'il employait dans les occasions brillantes. (p. 184)

The allusion to his quoting aphorisms from the ancients reflects one of Montesquieu's distinctive personal traits, for he was very familiar with the classics—especially Latin works—and apparently liked to quote them in his letters, notebooks, and in conversation when his audience was capable of understanding. The Genevan naturalist Tremblay reports a conversation that took place between himself and Montesquieu:

> J'ai beaucoup parlé agriculture avec M. de Montesquieu. Dans une conversation que nous avions eue, il s'écria:

"O fortunatos nimium sua si bona norint Agricolas . . ."

Il ajouta ensuite: "J'ai souvent pensé à mettre ces paroles au frontispice de ma maison."9

These words date from near the end of Montesquieu's life—1752—but they probably reflect a trait of his character that existed since his early manhood. Rica writes that the old *visiteur* possessed these precooked quotations and was ready to serve them since his youth ("depuis son jeune âge"). Thus Montesquieu, in his "jeune âge" as author of the *Lettres persanes* imagines himself as the *visiteur*—dead from exhaustion at age sixty, if he were to continue his social function in Paris without interruption. Our letter is again the result of self-satire and, to a certain degree, self-criticism. "Moderation in all things," the author seems to whisper to himself.

The author's presence in the same letter may also be subconscious. It is known that Montesquieu had the reputation for being a bit miserly. His two poor carriage horses and the fact that he preferred to dine at the expense of others rather than at home helped create this public opinion. The baron was aware of it, for he went so far as to defend himself in the self-portrait of his private journal. In our letter one glimpses a trace of his economical (if not downright stingy) nature when he writes concerning *visiteurs* in general: "Le Roi ne fait point de gratification à quelqu'un de ses sujets qu'il ne leur en coûte une voiture, pour lui en aller témoigner leur joie" (pp. 183-84). We can imagine just how much "joy" the young *président* felt when royal liberality cost him the sum of two horses and a carriage! It is as though Montesquieu were required to contribute his share to the king's very likely immoderate *largesse*.10

Ironic Introspection

Like the two *beaux esprits* of letter 54 the *visiteur* prepares his conversations with a host of anecdotes and classic quotations in order to glow at the right moment. He is probably a lively talker, as Rica suggests to us with his concluding remarks: "Je me tais, Voyageur. Car comment pourrais-je achever de te dire ce *qu'il a fait et ce qu'il a vu?*" (p. 184). His character resembles that of the people in society whom Rica attacks, or at least appears to attack, in letter 50. These people also are described as

hyperactive and hypercommunicative. His rather long harangue is fraught
with meaning:

> Je vois de tous cotés des gens qui parlent sans cesse d'eux-mêmes:
> leurs conversations sont un miroir qui présente toujours leur imper-
> tinente figure. Ils vous parleront des moindres choses qui leur sont
> arrivées, et ils veulent que l'intérêt qu'ils y prennent les grossisse à vos
> yeux; *ils ont tout fait, tout vu,* tout dit, tout pensé; ils sont un modèle
> universel, un sujet de comparaison inépuisable, une source d'exemples
> qui ne tarit jamais. Oh! que la louange est fade lorsqu'elle réfléchit vers
> le lieu d'où elle part! (*Lettres persanes,* p. 106)

One can interpret Montesquieu's presence in this passage on essentially two
levels. Superficially the author is attacking the vanity of those around him
who are compulsive talkers and who are themselves the vain subject of
conversation. But in another light Montesquieu is ironically considering his
own role among others and not only as a conversationalist but as a writer.
The various dialogues created in his *Lettres persanes* are a mirror which
reflects his own clever, communicative face in the live fabric of society.
Like the social bees above he speaks through his own extensive experience.
The author is scrutinizing the creative process and concludes (with an ironic
thrust at himself) that it cannot be separated from vanity. All is vanity.
Whether we speak or write of the exterior world, it is always in terms of
ourselves that we observe it. As we have seen, in letter 54, the author
wrote of plagiarizing literary models and compiling books of borrowed wit.
Here in letter 50 one sees the paradoxical results of such procedure: in
displaying knowledge and humor, one is accountable to it as its creator. As
a conversationalist and writer, implies Montesquieu, I am also a "modèle
universel, un sujet de comparaison inépuisable, une source d'exemples qui
ne tarit pas" (p. 106). The seemingly negative remark above—"ils vous
parleront des *moindres choses* qui leur sont arrivées"—reminds us of an
almost identical observation which has long been thought to symbolize a
facet of Montesquieu's character. This is found in Ibben's letter where, as
we have seen, he compares his curiosity and sensitivity to those of a child:

> tout m'intéresse, tout m'étonne; je suis comme un enfant dont les
> organes, encore tendres, sont vivement frappés par les *moindres objets.*
> (p. 98)

All of Rica's harangue above (see p. 116) is a mock attack on *amour propre*. His subsequent pretense at modesty in the same letter is pure irony. Through him Montesquieu is caught up in the satire of the exterior world, criticizing others for the faults he feels most deeply in himself—and knowing that he does so.

In *Mes Pensées* Montesquieu clarifies what disdain he felt for social wits and what an effort he made to remain above them. He goes so far as to say,

> Il n'y a point de gens que j'aie plus méprisés que les petits beaux-esprits et les grands qui sont sans probité. (*Pensée* 213; 4)

But it seems that in the *Lettres persanes* he humorously chastizes his own tendency to be a wit despite all his formulas against it in *Mes Pensées*. We should thus not take him too seriously when he writes concerning the *Querelle des anciens et des modernes*:

> Mais ce qui me choque de ces beaux esprits, c'est qu'ils ne se rendent pas utiles à leur patrie, et qu'ils amusent leurs talents à des choses puériles. (*Lettres persanes*, p. 78)

Very likely he also enjoyed taking part in these disputes. And Usbek's remarks about the effect of coffee served in a certain Parisian café apply very likely to Montesquieu as well as to his acquaintances:

> Il y . . . a une [maison publique], où l'on apprête le café de telle manière qu'il donne de l'esprit à ceux qui en prennent: au moins, de tous ceux qui en sortent, il n'y a personne qui ne croie qu'il en a quatre fois plus que lorsqu'il y est entré. (Pp. 77-78)

The proof of Montesquieu's love of disputes is his very *Lettres* themselves. Many ideas hurtle against one another here, and the sparks of contradiction are visible everywhere.

Montesquieu's presence within the characters described above—the *diseurs de riens*, the *visiteurs*, the *beaux esprits*—is the result of a dispute within himself. In examining the outside world and the various social types within French society, he is evaluating at the same time his own nature in comparison to theirs. To a certain extent their portrait is his own. Or at least in depicting them, he reveals a point of view which is personal, subjective, even vain, in that he pretends to judge objectively a matter in which he is quite subjectively involved. Rica writes:

> On dit que l'homme est un animal sociable. Sur ce pied-là, il me paraît qu'un Français est plus homme qu'un autre; c'est l'homme par excellence, car il semble être fait uniquement pour la société.
>
> Mais j'ai remarqué parmi eux des gens qui non seulement sont sociables, mais sont eux-mêmes la Société universelle. (p. 183)

Is this not Montesquieu's function as author of the *Lettres persanes*? He multiplies his being by contact with people from all walks of life—a priest, a poet, old military heros, old coquettes, nobles, lacqueys, magistrates, pedants, scholars, kings, geometricians, *nouvellistes, journalistes,* etc. The *Lettres persanes* are a marketplace of ranks and types, all passing beneath the eye of the moralist. His experiences vis-à-vis this intense variety of characters makes him into a sort of "Société universelle" himself—at least from the reader's point of view. It is through Montesquieu that we see the world of France. He is its universal creator.

There is evidence of Montesquieu's boredom and annoyance in society during or before the composition of our work. One feels that he was tired of the general monotony of his social life. The *visiteur* speaks of his "pénibles fonctions." A character in letter 50 complains about "l'ennui répandu dans les conversations" (p. 106). And letter 90 depicts Rica's boredom in informal outings with the ladies. Women must pretend to be amused, whether they are or not. Such insincerity is a part of their character which seeks constant diversion. But Rica is more frank about his sentiments and draws the line between his nature and theirs:

> Comme l'ennui me gagnait, une femme me secoua et me dit: "Eh bien! ne sommes-nous pas de bonne humeur? —Oui, lui répondis-je en bâillant; je crois que je crèverai à force de rire". Cependant la tristesse triomphait toujours des réflexions, et, quant à moi, je me sentis conduit de bâillements en bâillements dans un sommeil léthargique, qui finit tous mes plaisirs. (p. 229)

Paradoxically, uninterrupted pursuit of pleasure is wearisome and devoid of pleasure. Montesquieu's life needed greater variety. He was saturated with social activity, both the official (see the *visiteur*) and unofficial (Rica amidst the ladies). Composing his *Lettres persanes* in solitude allowed him to escape the taxing requirements of a provincial baron endeavoring to establish himself in Paris. In fact, they may have been written in part to avoid or counterbalance the hyperactivity that his social life demanded of him. At any rate, the calm of work provided an antidote to his obligations among others, even though, in writing, he was to recreate his relationship to society. Through the freedom of contemplation Montesquieu analyzed his environment and himself simultaneously. To demonstrate any insight and wisdom, he must debate his relative vanity and that of others, the usefulness of diversions, his boredom and annoyance with some (if not most) of his entourage and their right to be bored and annoyed with him. Montesquieu's aim is to be lucid as well as all-embracing. He is no harsher on others than on himself. We must simply look beneath the surface to find his self-effacing remarks, his half ironic, half serious introspection.

In interpolating Montesquieu's self-criticism into certain letters, one finds that their tone becomes warmer. It is a cold author like La Bruyère who draws only the stupidity of others into his portraits without realizing there is a bit of his own foolishness there also. Montesquieu probably was conscious of the hypocrisy inherent in his criticism of France, for instance. Could he pretend to be free of prejudice? Hardly. And letter 44—"Supériorité que les Français de toute condition s'attribuent; vanité semblable des autres hommes"—hints at his own superiority, his own vanity. It is from a biased point of view that he attacks "l'Eglise" and "l'Epée" who were prejudiced against "la Robe." He is a partisan and defender of his own constituency in these words:

> tel, par exemple, que l'on devrait mépriser parce qu'il est un sot, ne l'est souvent que parce qu'il est homme de robe. (pp. 89-90)

Moreover, he evinces a bit of a noble's prejudice against artisans in the next paragraph:

> Il n'y a pas jusqu'aux plus vils artisans qui ne disputent sur l'excellence de l'art qu'ils ont choisi; chacun s'élève au-dessus de celui qui est d'une profession différente, à proportion de l'idée qu'il s'est faite de la supériorité de la sienne. (p. 90)

As for the lady from Erivan who can imagine no greater honor than having a French king be governor of Erivan, this provincial, short-sighted character is from the capital of Armenia. We are aware of Montesquieu's prejudice against people from the capital of France—especially women. The Parisian ladies, as we have seen, bask in their provinciality, whereas a true *provincial*, Montesquieu, pretends to be a citizen of the world! The final two characters in letter 44, who demonstrate the same *sottise* (the king of Guinea and the Khan of Tartary), are both monarchs. Now, there were no members of government whom Montesquieu wanted to render more enlightened than monarchs. A passage from *Mes Pensées* shows the amount of esteem he had for the farsightedness of kings in general:

> *Presque tous les princes traitent les affaires comme Caligula traitoit les siennes.* Lors de l'ambassade de Philon, qui fut admis à son audience, l'Empereur, passant dans une galarie avec ses jeunes fous avec lui, dit à Philon: "Est-il vrai que vous ne mangez pas de cochon?" —"Ah! Ah! Ah!" dit l'empereur en passant, et les gens de sa cour, de même. (*Pensée* 569; 1840)

In letter 44 it appears very likely that the self-conscious Montesquieu was aware that any pretense at objectivity when discussing prejudice would be vain indeed. Therefore, he ironically concealed the seeds of his own bias within the letter, as if to say to any would-be critics: "I realize that as a provincial *homme de robe* I too have a prejudiced point of view." Montesquieu refuses to be the dupe of his own philosophy and does not exclude himself from "les hommes (qui) ressemblent tous, plus ou moins, à cette femme de la province d'Erivan." If we read between the lines, the title of this letter reflects back upon the author: "Supériorité que les Français de toute condition s'attribuent; vanité semblable des autres hommes." Prejudice is a relative affair and is defined always from a biased point of view. "What moralist can pretend to be without superiority and vanity?" asks Montesquieu.

Conclusion

There is no doubt that the *Lettres persanes* are the product of self-appraisal. What work does not speak for its author's psychology in one way or another? However, Montesquieu's introspection is not only deliberate, but concealed, disguised within the Persian intermediaries who stand between himself and his public. When the author is most personal, he is at the same time most elusive. In the index of the 1758 edition of the *Lettres persanes* the name of Montesquieu appears with this gloss: "se peint dans la personne d'Usbek." Such a coy item should merely arouse our curiosity to find the author here and there throughout the work. What we have endeavored to show in regard to certain letters is that Montesquieu is blending his own self-portrait into that of his fellow countrymen and Persians alike. Man, according to psychologists, is in a constant state of tension, divided between the need to reveal and conceal himself. One senses this tension in Montesquieu. He in fact plays on his presence and absence within the oriental and occidental nature of his work. He dares the reader to find the "chaîne secrète, en quelque sorte inconnue"[11] (himself) which binds the motley bunch of letters together and makes them coherent. Montesquieu combines in himself qualities of an absolutely opposing nature—his tendency toward candor and open-heartedness (the Latin side) and a need for secrecy and dissimulation (the Persian side). In Rica's description of these contrasting traits lies miraculously the antithetical personality of our author:

> La dissimulation, cet art parmi nous si pratiqué et si nécessaire, est ici inconnue: toute parle, tout se voit, tout s'entend; le cœur se montre comme le visage; dans les mœurs, dans la vertu, dans le vice même, on aperçoit toujours quelque chose de naïf. (*Lettres persanes*, p. 131)

Like Montaigne, Montesquieu might declare, "Je suis moi-même la matière de mon livre." But his *moi* has many corners and crevices in which hide the most versatile and devious of personalities. "Vous y reconnoistrez ce mesme port, ce mesme air que vous avez veu en sa conversation" (*Essais*, II, ch. 37, p. 516). Montaigne's words could have been spoken by the author of the *Lettres persanes*. We must simply be able to hear the Gascon brogue beneath a Persian costume.

In his introduction to the *Essais*, *Au lecteur*, Montaigne declares that he has written his book with the intention of communicating his portrait only to his relatives and friends so that they might not forget him after his death. Such false modesty does not fool us, for we know that posterity was his ultimate goal. The interesting fact is that Montaigne's words apply more properly to Montesquieu than to himself. Among the readers of 1721 who other than his friends and relatives (and the very few of them) would have been able to discover the author's self-portrait in the *Lettres persanes*?

Montaigne reveals himself fully and openly; Montesquieu, only hesitantly and not without a certain embarrassment. Detachment is a safeguard against blunders. And even in drawing up a self-portrait (shortly after the publication of his *Lettres persanes*), Montesquieu presents us a curious point of view: "Une personne de ma connoissance disoit: 'je vais faire une assez sotte chose; c'est mon portrait' " (*pensée* 213; 4). The author then proceeds to describe his own character, so that "une personne de ma connoissance" could just as well be Montesquieu himself. Montaigne, on the other hand, is frank, unabashed, even lavish in depicting his personal attributes. In portraying himself Montaigne draws the features of all Frenchmen and, more broadly, all mankind. In portraying others Montesquieu draws his own features. The two writers' means are diametrically opposed, but the end result is the same. We are inseparable from our environment and define ourselves through it, and it through ourselves.

If there is one quality which both authors possess, one that is at the root of their nature, it is their profound modesty. Montesquieu learned such a virtue (if virtue can be learned) through reading Montaigne. Although we believe it was ever a trait innate to his character, the young baron was influenced by the essayist to fashion a literary style and personality without pretense and without guile. This we see demonstrated above in Montesquieu's self-effacing remarks on the subject of sciences and learning, in his definition and description of the nobility, in his reflexions on the art of conversation, in Rica's satire of *beaux esprits, diseurs de riens,* and *visiteurs.* His irony is turned inward more than outward. There is sincere humility in his refusal to take himself seriously.

> Il faut voir son vice et l'estudier pour le redire. Ceux qui le celent à autruy, le celent ordinairement à eux-mesmes. (*Essais*, III, ch. 5, p. 64)

Montaigne can also be humorously self-critical, aware that we criticize others for our own faults. His complaint about contemporary writers goes in two directions:

> il y devroit avoir quelque coerction des loix contre les escrivains ineptes et inutiles, comme il y a contre les vagabons et faineants. On banniroit des mains de nostre peuple et moy et cent autres. (*Essais*, III, ch. 9, p. 178)

And though he rebuked a certain *gentilhomme* for an absurd obsession with his bowel movements and chamber pots, the essayist realized that similarly he was a compulsive writer:

> Si ay-je veu un Gentil-homme qui ne communiquoit sa vie que par les operations de son ventre; vous voyez chez luy, en montre, un ordre de bassins de sept ou huict jours; c'estoit son estude, ses discours; tout autre propos luy puoit. Ce sont icy, un peu plus civilement, des excremens d'un vieil esprit, dur tantost, tantost lache, et tousjours indigeste. (Ibid., p. 177)

It is with the above two passages that Montaigne modestly begins the essay "De la vanité," realizing that to be self-critical is to be hypocritical, and that the only true modesty is the wisdom to know all is vanity.

Aside from a certain lucidity about the self—its relative place amidst society, its manias and shortcomings, its enthusiasm and frankness—the common ground and parallels between our two Gascons should not be overly emphasized. Montesquieu's self-portrait is unique unto himself and shines with a certain wit and irony that is not found in Montaigne. A young man more busily seeking the companionship of others in Parisian salons, he is basically different from the wise old Montaigne who seems to take society as it comes to him, rarely making the effort to find it. A more active participant, Montesquieu is the analyst of his own complex nature. Montaigne's introspection merely encouraged the young baron to examine himself. Only in the general balmy atmosphere of *honnêteté* did Montesquieu interpret his character in light of the essayist.

X

TWO *PHILOSOPHES*

IF A CERTAIN CONFORMITY IS INHERENT in the *honnête homme*, if he demonstrates the basic common sense of the average man and places himself in no ostensible way above the herd, nevertheless he is not to be held accountable for the prejudices of society. He may be a modest conformist in all outward appearances, but inside he must maintain a judgment removed from the bigotry of the common man. The *honnête homme* is not only a conformist; he is a sort of *philosophe* as well. A member of society, reflecting its multiple doctrines and specialties, he is still an individual, responsible to his own high standards of reason, open to new ideas, the advocate of common sense and humanity. In his universality he is free of bias.

One of Montesquieu's *bêtes noires* throughout his life was man's intolerance. Zealots abounded around him, and few could remain cool when the majority became overheated. In *Mes Pensées* he writes:

> Un beau temple serait celui qu'on érigeroit à l'opiniâtreté. (*Pensée* 2209; 1232)

> Les hommes sont bien extraordinaires: ils aiment mieux leurs opinions que les choses. (*Pensée* 2058; 1044)

Montaigne comes onto this subject again and again:

> Qu'on luy face entendre [à l'enfant dans "De l'institution"] que de confesser la faute qu'il descouvrira en son propre discours, encore qu'elle ne soit aperceue que par luy, c'est un effet de jugement et de sincerité, qui sont les principales parties qu'il cherche; que *l'opiniatrer et contester*

> *sont qualitez communes, plus apparentes aux plus basses ames*;
> (*Essais*, I, ch. 26, p. 166)

> L'obstination et ardeur d'opinion est la plus seure preuve de bestise.
> Est il rien certain, resolu, desdeigneux, contemplatif, grave, serieux,
> comme l'asne? (*Essais*, III, ch. 8, p. 171)

> Il n'est rien à quoi communement les hommes soient plus tendus qu'à
> donner voye à leurs opinions; (*Essais*, III, ch. 11, p. 271)

> L'affirmation et l'opiniastreté sont signes exprès de bestise. (*Essais*,
> III, ch. 13, p. 324)

The *décisionnaire*, the two *savants* of letter 144 are perfect examples of pedantic, opinionated fools. By their poor example we recognize the author's
lesson of *honnêteté*. Rank and degree of learning should not separate the
individual from the broad level of humanity. One's class and position in
society are a poor indication of one's good judgment. And very often greatness is incommensurate with talent. Both Montaigne and Rica agree on this:

> Et j'ay veu de mon temps *les plus sages testes* de ce Royaume
> *assemblées*, avec grande ceremonie et publique despence, pour des traitez
> et accords, desquels la vraye decision despendoit ce pendant en toute
> souveraineté des devis du cabinet des dames et inclination de quelque
> fammelette. (*Essais*, III, ch. 10, p. 260)

> Il semble, mon cher ***, que *les têtes* des plus grands hommes s'étré-
> cissent lorsqu'elles sont *assemblées*, et que, là où il y a *plus de sages*, il
> y ait aussi moins de sagesse. (*Lettres persanes*, p. 227)

While specific vocabulary in common between these two passages suggests
that Montesquieu may have modelled his style on Montaigne's, another
excerpt from the *Essais* provides a better overall parallel in ideas to Rica's
generalization:

> On l'advertira [le jeune homme dans "De l'institution"] estant en
> compaignie, d'avoir les yeux par tout; car je trouve que les premiers
> sieges sont communement saisis par les hommes moins capables, et
> que les grandeurs de fortune ne se trouvent guieres meslées à la
> suffisance. (*Essais*, I, ch. 26, pp. 166-67)

Skepticism is a part of their wisdom, for the truth does not depend on what others think or what tradition suggests:

> Il y a du malheur d'en estre là que la meilleure touche de la verité ce soit la multitude des croians, en une presse où les fols surpassent de tant les sages en nombre. *Quasi vero quidquam sit tam valde, quam nil sapere vulgare.*

> (Comme s'il y avait rien de si répandu que le manque de jugement. [Cicéron, *De divinatione*, II, 39])

> *Sanitatis patrocinium est, insanientium turba.*

> (Belle autorité pour la sagesse qu'une multitude de fous! [Saint Augustin, *Cité de Dieu*, VI, 10]) (*Essais*, III, ch. 11, pp. 271-72)

> La verité a ses empeschemens, incommoditez et incompatibilitez avec nous. Il nous faut souvant tromper afin que nous ne nous trompons, et siller nostre veue, estourdir notre entendement pour les dresser et amender. *Imperiti enim judicant, et qui frequenter in hoc ipsum fallendi sunt, ne errent.*

> (Ce sont des ignorants qui jugent et il faut souvent les tromper, pour les empêcher de tomber dans l'erreur. [Quintilien, *Instituion oratoire*, II, 17]) (*Essais*, III, ch. 10, p. 246)

Rica's doubts serve as a point of departure for a witty "resolution" to this problem. He solves it somewhat as Montaigne and Quintilien do above:

> Dans ce tribunal, on prend les voix à la majeure; mais on dit qu'on a reconnu, par expérience, qu'il vaudrait mieux les recueillir à la mineure. Et cela est assez naturel: car il y a très peu d'esprits justes, et tout le monde convient qu'il y en a une infinité de faux. (*Lettres persanes*, p. 183)

As we have seen above, skepticism on who are the great and what is the truth is a tool by which these philosophers remove their judgment from the *idées reçues* of their times. Theirs is a playful and amusing trick of reason (paradoxical by nature), but its intent is serious enough: to be accepted as an *honnête homme* in society, one need not share the opinions of the common man. One need only possess his virtues.

"The principal intellectual aim of Montesquieu in the *Lettres persanes* was to destroy prejudice," writes Shackleton.[1] And one must add that he attacked the bigotry of his own class as well as that of the bourgeoisie. Usbek abstracts the state of vain rivalry between various stratas of society notably at the beginning of letter 44. There the author detaches himself from conflicts of interest; he demonstrates the impartiality of his judgment, endeavoring to view his own peers with the same objectivity he does the lower classes. Donning a Persian attire, he can speak that much more freely, and at times out of sheer playfulness and daring, he seems to espouse principles that contradict his own privileged status; thus a Catholic author praises Protestantism at the expense of his own church (p. 247). (We should remember, however, that Montesquieu's wife was a Protestant.) And there are times when his detached wonder at the workings of European society coincide with Montaigne's. In *De l'amité* the essayist objects vehemently to the *droit d'aînesse,* "ce meslange de biens, ces partages, et que *la richesse de l'un soit la pauvreté de l'autre.* . ." (*Essais*, I, ch. 28, p. 200). Usbek embroiders on this injustice with the fervor of a sociologist:

> C'est un esprit de vanité qui a établi chez les Européens l'injuste droit d'aînesse, si défavorable à la propagation, en ce qu'il porte l'attention d'un père sur un seul de ses enfants et détourne ses yeux de tous les autres; . . . (*Lettres persanes*, p. 252)

Montaigne's antithetical style bears comparison to Montesquieu's.[2]

Below, it appears that Usbek needed only to give a passage of the *Essais* a slight twist in order to make a sharp, ironic thrust at celibacy:

> Choisissons la plus necessaire et plus utile de l'humaine societé, ce sera le mariage; si est-ce que le conseil des saincts trouve le contraire party plus honneste et en exclut la plus venerable vacation des hommes, comme nous assignons au haras les bestes qui sont de moindre estime. (*Essais*, III, ch. 1, p. 17)

> Je trouve que leurs docteurs se contredisent manifestement, quand ils disent que le mariage est saint, et que le célibat, qui lui est opposé, l'est encore davantage; sans compter qu'en fait de préceptes et de dogmes fondamentaux, le bien est toujours le mieux. (*Lettres persanes*, p. 246)

Although one could go so far as to call Usbek's remarks "anticlerical," more evident is the author's ironic detachment from the institution of the church. Montesquieu's objectivity is a sign of his education and learning. When Usbek observes and discusses *La Querelle des anciens et des modernes,* he writes astonished:

> je les trouvai [des beaux esprits] échauffés sur une dispute la plus mince qu'il se puisse imaginer: il s'agissait de la réputation d'un vieux poète grec . . . (p. 78)

He represents none other than his creator's own impartial judgment on this subject. Montesquieu, a great connoisseur of literature both ancient and modern, wrote in *Mes Pensées*:

> je n'ai aucune prédilection pour les ouvrages anciens ou nouveaux, et toutes les disputes à cet egard ne me prouvent autre chose, si ce n'est qu'il y a de très bons ouvrages, et parmi les anciens, et parmi les modernes. (*Pensée* 1315; 101)

Our eighteenth-century *honnête homme* says the same for the sciences:

> Je n'estime pas plus un homme qui s'est appliqué à une science, que celui qui s'est appliqué à une autre, si tous deux y ont apporté également de l'esprit et du bon sens. Toutes les sciences sont bonnes et s'aident les unes les autres. (*Pensée* 765; 678)

Like his Gascon predecessor, Montesquieu sought in life and in art to be knowledgeable on all levels, not pedantic in any, to know "un peu de chaque chose, et rien du tout, à la Françoise," as Montaigne wittily expressed it (I, ch. 26, p. 155). In the *Lettres persanes* Rica and Usbek's inquiry into all levels of experience in France represents our author's quest for universality—the touchstone of truth and appeal to a broad public. This is the work of an *honnête homme,* but his striving for impartiality and objectivity is that of a *philosophe.*

To speak free of prejudice is one of Montaigne's primary aims throughout the *Essais.* Revealing the contradictory laws of justice and honor, he stands back, as Montesquieu will do later, refusing to take sides. Amidst the religious wars around him he endeavors to remain objective (not neutral), more often praising the Huguenots than the Catholics. A moderate amid fanatics, he deplores the domineering attitude of his own class whose members were all too suggestive of the *décisionnaire* in the *Lettres persanes*:

> S'ils se rabaissent à la conference commune et qu'on leur presente autre chose qu'aprobation et reverence, ils vous assomment de l'authorité de leur experience: ils ont ouy, ils ont veu, ils ont faict; vous estes accablé d'exemples. (*Essais*, III, ch. 8, p. 162)

There are few things on which we can give a sincere judgment, he writes, because there are few in which we have not in some way a private interest. Politics offers the essayist a prime example; he mocks the equal one-sidedness of both the Scottish democrat and the monarchist:

> le populaire rend le Roy de pire condition qu'un charretier; le monarchique le loge quelque brasses au dessus de Dieu en puissance et souveraineté. (*Essais,* III, ch. 7, p. 148)

Montaigne is the observant, perceptive bystander amidst the various prejudices which separate one nationality from another. Remembering that he traveled open-mindedly throughout Europe, we are not surprised by his objective appraisal concerning blind attachment to one's customs (see *Essais*, III, ch. 13, pp. 330-31). The adaptable and tolerant essayist prefigures Montesquieu who describes his own ideals through Ibben: "En quelque pays que j'aie été, j'y ai vécu comme si j'avais dû y passer ma vie"[3] (p. 137). Had Montaigne not said before him,

> le voyager me semble un exercise profitable. . . . Nulle saison m'est ennemye . . . la mutation d'air et de climat ne me touche point; tout Ciel m'est un. (*Essais,* III, ch. 9, p. 210)

> J'ay la complexion du corps libre et le goust commun autant qu'homme du monde. La diversité des façons d'une nation à autre ne me touche que par le plaisir de la variété. Chaque usage a sa raison.[4] (Ibid., pp. 223-24)

One of Montaigne's prime characteristics is his tolerant attitude towards opinions and manners different from his own. It is on this note that he ends the first edition of the *Essais* in 1580, for his last word was addressed to the inevitable critics of his work. The author makes it difficult for them to find cause of reproach, for he does not crystallize his judgment into any fixed form. In brief, Montaigne's last words for the 1580 edition amount to an escape clause:

> je ne hay point les fantasies contraires aux miennes. Il s'en faut tant que je m'effarouche de voir de la discordance de mes jugemens à ceux d'autruy, et que je me rende incompatible à la société des hommes pour estre d'autre sens et party que le mien. (*Essais*, II, ch. 37, pp. 519-20)

In book III (pub. 1588) he takes up this theme again:

> Nulles propositions m'estonnent, nulle creance me blesse, quelque contrarieté qu'elle aye à la mienne. . . . Les contradictions donc des jugemens ne m'offencent, ny m'alterent; elles m'esveillent seulement et m'exercent. (*Essais*, III, ch. 8, p. 153)

> Quand on me contrarie, on esveille mon attention, non pas ma cholere; je m'avance vers celuy qui me contredit, qui m'instruit. (Ibid., p. 154)

> Mon imagination se contredit elle-mesme si souvent et condamne, que ce m'est tout un qu'un autre le face . . . (Ibid., p. 155)

It is ironic that Montesquieu, the adversary of prejudice in his *Lettres persanes*, should become, to a certain extent, victim of it. Letter 145 concerning "l'homme d'esprit" as opposed to "l'homme médiocre," reveals the author's bitterness over the criticism hurled against him after the initial appearance of his *Lettres*. (This letter was first included in the collection in the second edition of 1721.) As Barrière has pointed out, Montesquieu depicts himself in the "homme d'esprit."[5] For his progressive ideals he is persecuted by certain opinionated specialists. Montesquieu retorts with a few remarks on their intolerance. Montaigne had squirmed at the thought of narrow-minded, captious critics; the author of the *Lettres persanes* recoils from them, for they have already stung him:

> Il voit le jour enfin, cet ouvrage qui lui a tant coûté: il lui attire des querelles de toutes parts. Et comment les éviter? Il avait un sentiment; il l'a soutenu par ses écrits; il ne savait pas qu'un homme, à deux cents lieues de lui, avait dit tout le contraire. Voilà cependant la guerre qui se déclare.
> Encore s'il pouvait espérer d'obtenir quelque considération! Non. Il

n'est tout au plus estimé que de ceux qui se sont appliqués au meme genre de science que lui. Un philosophe a un mépris souverain pour un homme qui a la tête chargée de faits, et il est, à son tour, regardé comme un visionnaire par celui qui a une bonne mémoire. (*Lettres persanes*, pp. 320-21)

It would seem that one of the main purposes of his *Lettres* passed unnoticed: to avoid pedantic ostentation and to create a work which would have broad, unspecialized appeal, combatting prejudice, lowering learning to a level comprehensible to all citizens. Montequieu's least objective was to be doctrinaire; like Montaigne he might have said:

S'il plaist à la doctrine de se mesler à nos devis, elle n'en sera point refusée: non magistrale, imperieuse et importune comme de coustume, mais suffragante et docile elle mesme. (*Essais*, III, ch. 3, p. 40)

It is no wonder that having failed to please everybody (a difficult, if not impossible achievement), Montesquieu should strike back in terms the essayist would have understood. After all, it was Montaigne who first among French writers tried to convey through his own person the image of an undogmatic *honnête homme* to the public. Letter 145 shows that the young baron was not prepared for the criticism he received. Preaching tolerance in his *Lettres persanes*, he did not expect to be the victim of the intolerant.

We shall continue our comparison of these two *philosophes* by showing how their ideals shake man out of his unthinking acceptance of things as they are, how they are intent upon showing the relative state of civilizations—their customs, institutions, and philosophies.

A fragment intended originally for the *Lettres persanes* but ultimately discarded, bears a striking comparison with an excerpt from "Des cannibales." European cruelty can exceed a savage one, no matter what popular opinion might think, says Montaigne:

Je pense qu'il y a plus de barbarie à manger un homme vivant qu'à le manger mort, à deschirer par tourmens et par géenes un corps encore plein de sentiment, le faire rostir par le menu, le faire mordre et meurtrir aux chiens et aux pourceaux (comme nous l'avons non seulement leu, mais veu de fresche memoire, non entre des ennemis anciens, mais entre des voisins et concitoyens, et qui pis est, sous pretexte de pieté et de

religion), que de le rostir et manger après qu'il est trespassé." (*Essais,*
I, ch. 32, p. 239)

Montesquieu emphasizes an identical lesson in relativity by having a Turk
converse with a cannibal:

Fragment d'une Lettre d'Usbek à *** à ***

> Je ne sais comment il arriva qu'un *Turc* se trouva un jour avec
> *Cannibale*. Vous êtes bien cruel, lui dit le Mahométan, vous mangez
> les captifs que vous avez pris à la guerre. Que faites-vous des vôtres,
> lui répondit le Cannibale? Nous les tuons, mais quand ils sont morts
> nous ne les mangeons pas.
>   Il vaut bien la peine, pour si peu de chose de se distinguer des
> sauvages. Nous trouvons de la barbarie à des coutumes presqu'indiffé-
> rentes et nous n'en trouvons pas à violer toutes les règles de l'humanité
> et à faire taire tous les sentiments de la pitié.
>   De Paris, le 10 de la Lune de Chaban, 1715[6]

How detached our two philosophers are from petty doctrines which
divide the world into many factions, each with its own superstition! The
famous letter 46, "En quoi consiste l'essence de la Religion," where we find
various sectarians arguing among themselves, has an ancestor in the
Apologie. Although one cannot forget the importance of Marana as a
predecessor on the subject of tolerance amidst religious prejudice,[7]
Montaigne stands out as Montesquieu's companion in the art of satire.
(Marana notably lacks a sense of humor when treating this theme.) Let us
compare our two Gascon wits. Usbek writes that when a *Brachmane*
found the Persian had eaten a rabbit, he cried out:

> —Ah! vous avez commis une action abominable, et que Dieu ne vous
> pardonnera jamais, me dit-il d'une voix sévère. *Que savez-vous si
> l'âme de votre père n'était pas passée dans cette bête?"* (*Lettres
> persanes,* p. 95)

We recall, in general, Montaigne's long treatise on the soul and specifically
the argument as to where it is located in man:

> Il n'y a pas moins de dissention ny de debat à la loger. Hipocrates et
> Hierophilus la mettent au ventricule du cerveau; Democritus et
> Aristote, par tout le corps . . . Epicurus, en l'estomac . . . les stoicïens,
> autour et dedans le cœur; Erasistratus, joignant la membrane de
> l'epicrane; Empedocles, au sang; comme aussi Moyse, *qui fut la cause*
> *pourquoy il defendit de manger le sang des bestes, auquel leur ame est*
> *jointe*; . . . (*Essais*, II, ch. 12, p. 243)

The idea that a soul somehow exists and is defined in physical terms, that
such superstition can determine what is proper to eat, these notions are
absurd and comical at the same time. Our philosophers are too enlightened
to bow to such ignorance. Montesquieu's irony (a stronger one than Montaigne's) is understood without any commentary on the part of the author.
But Montaigne reveals his final judgment concerning the various schools of
antiquity. It is equivalent to Usbek's unexpressed feelings on the trivial
religious dissension in letter 46:

> Il se void infinis pareils exemples, non d'argumens faux seulement,
> mais ineptes, ne se tenans point, et accusans leurs autheurs non tant
> d'ignorance que d'imprudence, ès reproches que les philosophes se font
> les uns aux autres sur les dissentions de leurs opinions et de leurs
> sectes. Qui fagoteroit suffisammant un amas des asneries de l'humaine
> prudence, il diroit merveilles. (Ibid., p. 245)

In letter 85, "Avantages qui résultent de la multiplicité des religions
dans un Etat," Montesquieu again takes up the theme of tolerance in the
form of a one-sided debate. His arguments should be seen in the context of
the times, for we remember that not long before the publication of the
Lettres persanes Louis XIV had abolished the Edict of Nantes. Without
stating so explicitly, Montesquieu is offering every possible reason ("s'il
faut raisonner sans prévention . . . " begins Usbek) that a monarch should
grant his subjects freedom of faith. To catch his attention the author
maintains that he is speaking in the ruler's self-interest: "On a beau dire
qu'il n'est pas de l'intérêt du prince de souffrir plusieurs religions dans son
état" (p. 180).

At the end of Montaigne's essay, "De la liberté de conscience," (II,
ch. 19) the author treats the same theme, praising Julian for his wisdom.
The Roman Emperor, seeing the people of Constantinople disunited and the
Christians divided, decreed that all should worship according to their faith,

pagan and Christian alike. Strangely enough, Julian did not thereby expect to end dissension among his subjects, but by favoring their differences, to keep factions from uniting and overthrowing him:

> Ce qu'il sollicitoit avec grand soing, pour l'esperance que cette licence augmenteroit les parts et les brigues de la division, et empescheroit le peuple de se reunir et de se fortifier par consequent contre luy par leur concorde et unanime intelligence; (*Essais,* II, ch. 20, p. 393)

Usbek reasons in the same paradoxical sort of way, when he states that jealousy and rivalry among various sects will actually benefit the state:

> Ce sont des rivales [les religions] qui ne se pardonnent rien. La jalousie descend jusqu'aux particuliers: chacun se tient sur ses gardes et craint de faire des choses qui déshonoreraient son parti et l'exposeraient aux mépris et aux censures impardonnables du parti contraire. (*Lettres persanes*, pp. 179-80)

Whereas the essayist sees division as an end in itself, Montesquieu, more of a positivist, seems to go a step further, explaining that the good result of disagreement between sects is their intense rivalry in wishing to set a virtuous example. This idea may have been drawn intact from Bayle.[8] Montaigne proves himself to be a predecessor on this theme, but one must establish the basic difference of tone between letter 85 and the essay. Montaigne is a tentative liberal, balancing his argument for tolerance with another one against. (It is clear, however, the former mode of reason pleased him more.) Montesquieu, on the other hand, sounds like a passionate reformer, preaching tolerance and change in every paragraph. Although the era of France's religious wars was quite another from that of the Regency, Montesquieu's propaganda is perhaps as liberal and daring for its time as Montaigne's philosophical hint that *maybe* freedom of faith would calm the Protestants better than repression: "on diroit aussi que de lascher la bride aux pars d'entretenir leur opinion, c'est les amolir et relacher par la facilité et par l'aisance . . . " (II, ch. 19, p. 393). One was a period of religious turmoil, when much of the populace was polarized; the other a time of relative tranquillity with an atheistic (if superstitious) monarch at the healm, Phillipe d'Orléans. At any rate, one cannot overlook the fact that both Montaigne and Montesquieu speak out as exceptions to the rule. They are philosophers and independent thinkers suggesting a cure that most government officials would have found thoroughly unacceptable if not downright treasonable.

First among the *philosophes* of the eighteenth century, Montesquieu spoke out against judicial torture—the horrible *question* which was designed to force the truth out of both guilty and innocent alike. His chapters in *L'Esprit des lois* are most memorable on this subject,[9] but in the *Lettres persanes* we already find a few reflections on an analogous theme— one the author entitles "Avantages de la douceur et inconvénients de la sévérité des peines" (letter 80). Usbek speaks of the relativity involved in punishment:

> Dans les pays où les châtiments sont modérés, on les craint comme dans ceux où ils sont tyranniques et affreux.
> L'imagination se plie d'elle-même aux mœurs du pays où l'on est: huit jours de prison ou une légère amende frappent autant l'esprit d'un Européen, nourri dans un pays de douceur, que la perte d'un bras intimide un Asiatique. (*Lettres persanes*, p. 170)

The paradox is clear; cruelty and harsh sentences in no way guarantee law and order: "Compte, mon cher Rhédi (writes Usbek), que dans un état, les peines plus ou moins cruelles ne font pas que l'on obéisse plus aux lois" (p. 170).

Almost alone among thinkers of sixteenth-century France, Montaigne spoke for more clemency in judicial punishments. Somewhat like Usbek, and especially in accord with the Montesquieu of *L'Esprit des lois*, he concludes that torture, besides being cruel and inhumane, in no way achieves its supposed goal of curtailing crime: "jamais police ne se trouva reformée par là. L'ordre et le règlement des meurs depend de quelque autre moyen" (II, ch. 15, p. 330). Alluding to Seneca, the essayist states that torture or harsh sentences might even encourage disobedience:

> A ce propos se pourroit joindre l'opinion d'un ancien que les supplices aiguisent les vices plustost qu'ils ne les amortissent; qu'ils n'engen-drent point le soing de bien faire, c'est l'ouvrage de la raison et de la discipline, mais seulement un soing de n'estre surpris en faisant mal. (*Essais*, II, ch. 15, p. 330)

What is striking in the comparison of Usbek's and Montaigne's ideas is not simply their humanity and progressive social awareness but the use of a paradoxical, almost playful train of thought, surprising in its nonconformity, convincing in its logic.

The importance of moderation and reason is one of the most profound links between our two philosophers, particularly on the subject of religion. Montaigne criticized Henri III's hypocritical and outrageous acts of devotion.[10] Rica will accuse certain Spaniards of the Inquisition "qui sont si dévots qu'ils sont à peine Chrétiens" (p. 167). For Montesquieu humanity's morality lies in man. And for Montaigne, although the source of good came from God, its fruit, one of the ultimate goals of any religion, can be observed in man's attitude and behavior vis-à-vis his fellowman. Thus, though in theory our two philosphers diverge, ultimately they deem the practical results of morality and religion to be most important. Faith is the result of our acts, not simply our thoughts. How often Montaigne rises up against the barbaric acts committed in the name of Christ! Notably concerning Spanish conquests of Peru and Mexico he takes sides with the conquered, helpless Indians, lamenting the murderous cruelty of our European representatives (see III, ch. 6, pp. 137 ff). And from a moralist's point of view he considers it divine justice that the conquerors ended up by fighting each other, destroying themselves after having annihilated their Indian foe:

> *Dieu a meritoirement permis* que ces grands pillages se soient absorbez par la mer en les transportant, ou par les guerres intestines dequoy *ils se sont entremangez entre eux*, et la plus part s'enterrerent sur les lieux, sans aucun fruict de leur victoire. (*Essais*, III, ch. 6, p. 143)

Rica makes a similar observation, invoking divine will as a factor in the ironic fate of the European invaders. The idea of "consuming" or "eating one another" is found in both texts:

> Depuis la dévastation de l'Amérique, les Espagnols qui ont pris la place de ses anciens habitants n'ont pu la repeupler; au contraire, par une fatalité que je ferais mieux de nommer *une justice divine*, les destructeurs se détruisent eux-mêmes et *se consument* tous les jours. (*Lettres persanes*, p. 255)

Note above that Montesquieu prefers to bring the past tense up to the present, as if to say, "The colonialists have not changed in the past century and a half." Although our two authors probably used different sources[11] for their treatment of this period in history and although Montaigne prefers to tell the reader many of the gory details involved in this massacre (Montesquieu uses only abstractions), they are in accord on the depressing treachery and barbarism in the conquests. What decent human being can sanction genocide, after all? Both writers condemn the inhumanity of such pitiless butchery committed in the name of "civilization":

> Au rebours, nous nous sommes servis de leur ignorance et inexperience à les plier plus facilement vers la trahison, luxure, avarice et vers toute sorte d'inhumanité et de cruauté, à l'exemple et patron de nos meurs. Qui mit jamais à tel pris le service de la mercadence et de la trafique? Tant de villes rasées, tant de nations exterminées, tant de millions de peuples passez au fil de l'espée, et la plus riche et belle partie du monde bouleversée pour la negotiation des perles et du poivre! mechaniques victoires. Jamais l'ambition, jamais les inimitiez publiques ne pousserent les hommes les uns contre les autres à si horribles hostilitez et calamitez si miserables. (*Essais*, III, ch. 6, p. 140)

> Les Espagnols, désespérant de retenir les nations vaincues dans la fidélité, prirent le parti de les exterminer et d'y envoyer d'Espagne des peuples fidèles. Jamais dessein horrible ne fut plus ponctuellement exécuté. On vit un peuple aussi nombreux que tous ceux de l'Europe ensemble disparaître de la Terre à l'arrivée de ces barbares, qui semblèrent, en découvrant les Indes, n'avoir pensé qu'à découvrir aux hommes quel était la dernière période de la cruauté. (*Lettres persanes*, p. 257)

It is neither extraordinary nor surprising that two humanists should condemn the inhumanity of Spanish conquests; yet Montesquieu goes further, rejecting the entire system of colonialization. Through Usbek he builds up a large framework of examples in letter 121 all designed to show the disastrous results colonialization reaped on the mother country. For one of his allusions the author had recourse probably to the *Essais*. Both he and Montaigne speak of the Carthaginian colonialization of America which dangerously decreased the former's population:

> L'autre tesmoignage de l'antiquité, auquel on veut raporter cette descouverte, est dans Aristote,[12] au moins si ce petit livret *Des merveilles inouies* est à luy. Il raconte là que certains Carthagionois, s'estant jettez au travers de la mer Athlantique, hors le destroit de

Gibaltar, et navigué long temps, avoient descouvert en fin une grande
isle fertile, toute revestue de bois et arrousée de grandes et profondes
rivieres, fort esloignée de toutes terres fermes; et qu'eux, et autres
depuis, attirez par la bonté et fertilité du terroir, s'y en allèrent avec
leurs femmes et enfans, et commenceront à s'y habiteur. Les Seigneurs
de Carthage, voyans que leur pays se depeuploit peu à peu, firent
deffense expresse, sur peine de mort, que nul n'eut plus à aller là, et en
chasserent ces nouveaux habitans, craignants, à ce que l'on dit, que par
succession de temps ils ne vinsent à multiplier tellement qu'ils les
supplantassent eux mesmes et ruinassent leur estat. (*Essais*, I, ch. 31,
p. 233)

Les Carthaginois avaient, comme les Espagnols, découvert l'Amérique
ou, au moins, de grandes îles dans lesquelles ils faisaient un commerce
prodigieux; mais, quand ils virent le nombre de leurs habitants
diminuer, cette sage république défendit à ses sujets ce commerce et
cette navigation. (*Lettres persanes*, p. 256)

We have touched on many subjects in this chapter or many sides
to one subject—the characteristics of a *philosophe*. The term is generally
used in reference to eighteenth-century thinkers—Montesquieu, Voltaire,
Rousseau, Diderot, among the most prominent French representatives.
But, defining the term in our own way, we must add Montaigne to the same
category, remembering at the same time that he represented a different era.
The most fundamental quality inherent in this type of man is the independence of his opinions. He is not held to the clichés of fixed ideas. He is
skeptical, ironic, critical, often daring. Montesquieu is supposed to have
said admiringly of Mme du Deffand, "Voyez-la, elle ne pense pas d'après
les autres."[13] This was one of his goals in the *Lettres persanes* and
throughout his life: to remain objective and impartial amidst prejudice,
pliable and open to the ideas and customs of other lands and other thinkers.
As in the case of the essayist, Montesquieu's maturity of judgment should
have a palliative effect on society. The greatest good is the help he can give
to others, correcting religious or social abuse, taking up the cause of the
mistreated. Each philospher's individuality was not an end in itself, however playful and paradoxical some of its forms may be. Rather their
ultimate aim was to instruct us and lead us toward a fuller humanity.

XI

LETTER 66, MONTAIGNE, MODEL OF THE *LETTRES PERSANES*

Now that we have dealt comprehensively with the rapport between the *Lettres persanes* and the *Essais*, let us continue our discussion of letter 66 and specifically the paragraph concerning "pièces de gazon" (see above, pp. 10-11). There is every reason to believe that the author is playfully contradicting a passage from "Des livres," since throughout the *Lettres persanes* he compiles and comments upon not only seventeenth- and eighteenth-century predecessors but also France's most influential philosopher of the Renaissance—Montaigne. With this idea in mind, we shall proceed with our interpretation of this letter, passing on to Rica's next paragraph which is in close rapport with the preceeding one:

> Quand un homme n'a rien à dire de nouveau, que ne se taît-il? Qu'a-t-on affaire de ces doubles emplois? "Mais je veux donner un nouvel ordre. Vous êtes un habile homme: vous venez dans ma bibliothèque, et vous mettez en bas les livres qui sont en haut, et en haut ceux qui sont en bas. C'est un beau chef-d'œuvre!" (*Lettres persanes*, p. 137)

Is this not the antithesis of what Rica's just condemned? The clever man who rearranges Rica's library is close kin to the two characters the writer mocked in the preceding paragraph. The book mover is first cousin to the transplanter who sticks pieces of turf in a flower garden; and he is a twin of the printer who creates words and literature from letters of the alphabet. (Both the transplanter and the printer appear in the fourth paragraph of our letter.) His manual labor is rendered more illustrious only in that he is dealing with books instead of sod or alphabet letters. His work is a masterpiece only because he is following Rica's "nouvel ordre" instead of Montaigne's old one. Our paradoxical Persian has thus taken great pleasure in contradicting himself just as he contradicted Montaigne a moment earlier. It is as though he were responding to the essayist's likewise double standard concerning plagiarism—namely, that it can be done well or poorly, depending upon the writer's skill. Seeing this paradox suggested in the *Essais*, Rica clarifies and distills it to the point of pure contradiction.

A library in itself is no guarantee of successful writing, if one is honest and if one's public is discerning. Great sources in themselves are no key to greatness. Montaigne and Montesquieu, possessing among the finest library collections of their day, surrounded by the learning of the ages, realized that they must be discreet in borrowing. "Il ne faut que l'espitre liminaire d'un alemand pour me farcir d'allegations," writes the essayist (*Essais,* III, ch. 12, p. 303). It is no surprise that a Frenchman would attribute a dull, compiling instinct to Germans. But even an ancient Roman fell into the same ridiculous excess, as we see in an anecdote recounted by Montaigne:

> Cette facon (de répéter les autres comme un perroquet) me fait souvenir de ce riche Romain, qui avoit esté soigneux, à fort grande depence, de recouvrer des hommes suffisans en tout genre de sciences, qu'il tenoit continuellement autour de luy, affin que, quand il escherroit entre ses amis quelque occasion de parler d'une chose ou d'autre, ils supplissent sa place et fussent tous prets à luy fournir, qui d'un discours, qui d'un vers d'Homere, chacun selon son gibier; et pensoit ce sçavoir estre sien par ce qu'il estoit en la teste de ses gens; et comme font aussi ceux desquels la suffisance loge en leurs somptueuses librairies. (*Essais,* I, ch. 25, p. 146)

Montaigne was hopeful that his own ability did not depend entirely upon his sumptuous library. Montesquieu hoped the same, recoiling to think he might be the dupe of his artistic method. Rica's ironic applause when someone has rearranged his library was of sufficient warning. Montesquieu is not about to fall into the category of common scholars: "ces savants qui ont toute leur science hors de leur âme, et qui annoncent la sagesse des autres sans être sages eux-mêmes" (*pensée* 983; 1309).

To follow Rica's comical debate on compilers to its logical conclusion, we reach the final, climactic paragraph of our letter:

Je t'écris sur ce sujet, ***, parce que je suis outré d'un livre que je viens de quitter, qui est si gros qu'il semblait contenir la Science universelle; mais il m'a rompu la tête sans m'avoir rien appris. (*Lettres persanes*, p. 137)

We offer the hypothesis that his book is no other than Montaigne's *Essais*, and that Rica attacks it with the same irony with which he condemned all plagiarizers above. At La Brède Montesquieu possessed Mlle de Gournay's grand in-folio edition of 1595, 766 pages thick.[1] Being as large as the most learned and ponderous tomes in his library, it easily qualifies as that book, "si gros qu'il semblait contenir la Science universelle." Note the author's irony, when he has Rica say that the *Essais* only *seemed* to hold universal knowledge. Montesquieu knew in fact that they did.

Rica finishes his sentence with an unequaled *tour de force*, lamenting with a grin: "mais il m'a rompu la tête sans m'avoir rien appris." Turning Montaigne's words against him to the end, he is alluding to or unconsciously recalling this particular passage in "Des livres": *"Il n'est rien pourquoy je me vueille rompre la teste*, non pas pour la science, de quelque grand pris qu'elle soit" (*Essais*, II, ch. 10, p. 85). Moreover, Montaigne would not wish to rack his readers' brains (*leur rompre la tête*) any more than his own. But this Golden Rule of reading and writing ricochets off Rica and returns to strike poor Montaigne.

Nothing is more logical or perhaps more equivocal than Rica's final phase, "sans m'avoir rien appris." It can be interpreted on more than one plane. Superficially Rica is referring to the previous discussion on plagiarism and puffing out his chest pompously as he did earlier: "Quand un homme n'a rien à dire de nouveau, que ne se taît-il? What can such an eclectic writer like Montaigne teach me?" Rica cries. "I'm well enough acquainted with the classics of antiquity." Looking back, then, the term "la Science universelle" takes on this sense: it is an accumulation of the wisdom of the ages, the basis of learning out of which grew the humanist tradition of commenting upon the ancients.

Yet all in the same breath Rica is cleverly alluding to Montaigne's impartiality, his refusal to take sides, or rather his insistence on taking both sides of a given issue. This characteristic, which often renders our philosopher's "opinion" ungraspable, was well understood by another eighteenth-century connoisseur of the essayist and friend of Montesquieu's—Mme du Deffand. In a letter she writes: "il (Montaigne) n'enseigne rien parce qu'il ne décide de rien; c'est l'opposé du dogmatisme" (*Essais*, I, p. *xxv*).

Montaigne himself would be the first to admit that he can teach nothing, for he is sure of nothing. Thus, Rica might also be referring to the ubiquitous though perhaps overemphasized lesson of the *Essais—Que sais-je?* In fact, in "Des livres" we read:

> la science et la verité peuvent loger chez nous sans jugement, et le jugement y peut aussi estre sans elles; voire, la reconnoissance de l'ignorance est l'un des plus beaux et plus seurs tesmoignages de jugement que je trouve. (*Essais*, II, ch. 10, p. 85)

At this moment Montaigne's great capacity for doubting leads him to recognize only his skepticism as a safeguard against error. What can such a man teach us? From Montaigne we learn nothing certain except that our knowledge is negligible in the balance of our infinite ignorance. The words, "sans m'avoir rien appris" refer then to Montaigne's skepticism so famous in the eighteenth century and still today.

Rica's remarks, "je suis outré d'un livre que je viens de quitter," suggests that the author in fact had just referred to the *Essais*, and in particular to the passage of "Des livres" out of which he devised the paragraph on the "pièces de gazon." Rica's rebuke to compilers, which squarely contradicts Montaigne's avowed plagiarism, comes as no mere coincidence. Through his Persian veil, Montesquieu is confessing that he made and is making specific reference to the *Essais*.

As a philosopher Montaigne could doubt and overturn our fixed ideas on any conceivable subject. But on one matter he remained firm, immovable. He insisted on the status quo of religion and society's basic structure. The two were inseparable pieces. Paradoxically then, although Montaigne questioned social injustice and ineptitude, as a faithful Catholic he defended its forms against the rebellious Huguenots. Not once does he doubt the religious precepts of the church. In the *Apologie* he even poses as the champion of Christianity, and yet in no other work does the philosophical doubt display itself so fully. Montesquieu found such behavior contradictory, and, we believe, had Rica protest for him in the first paragraph of our letter, where he writes: "Celuy qui doute de tout comme philosophe n'ose rien nier comme théologien."

We note that in the letter on suicide Montesquieu would seem to reflect his disagreement with Montaigne on this matter, breaking away from the religious—civil code which punished anyone who took his own life. Here is one instance where the essayist did not dare ignore the Catholic excommunication of the dead, for he reiterated their dogma. On the other hand, Montesquieu, a purer humanist rejected it categorically, proving that he could doubt where Montaigne feared to tread. It is significant that Montesquieu should claim that Montaigne doesn't "dare" deny anything theological. One should not miss the serious note of criticism in his voice. In marked contrast to the essayist, young Montesquieu prides himself on daring to attack Catholic dogma, the pope, and narrow-minded bigots of the Church: the *directeur de conscience* (letter 48), a bishop (letter 101), an *ecclésiastique* (letter 59). Perhaps Montesquieu felt an insincere piousness in Montaigne's avowals of faith, notably the one in the *Apologie* (*Essais,* II, ch. 12, p. 275) where the essayist declares to have held firm in his personal belief in Catholicism amidst France's religious strife and turmoil. For immediately following this confession he claims that all the well-known philosophical writings of the ancients inspire him and win him over, even though they contradict one another. Moreover, Montaigne felt a particularly strong attraction to the interpretation of God removed from Catholic dogma. Here is the faith of a deist:

> De toutes les opinions humaines et anciennes touchant la religion, celle là me semble avoir eu plus de vraysemblance et plus d'excuse, qui reconnoissoit Dieu comme une puissance incomprehensible, origine et conservatrice de toutes choses, toute bonté, toute perfection, recevant et prenant en bonne part l'honneur et la reverence que les humains luy rendoient soubs quelque visage, sous quelque nom et en quelque maniere que ce fut. (*Essais*, II, ch. 12, p. 206)

How can a true Catholic express such enthusiasm for worship totally devoid of dogma, a far cry from any *religion révélée* such as Catholicism? Above, Montaigne seems to profess a sort of quietism; like Usbek he suggests that God would not recognize man, were it not for the "immensity of his knowledge" (see *Lettres persanes*, p. 172). Like the anonymous God of Athens whom St. Paul admired, Montaigne's "puissance incomprehensible" is detached from the earth and man, unknowable and unattainable. On this point Montesquieu must have felt true empathy and understanding for Montaigne; after all, his own faith was so similar.[2] Parts of the *Lettres persanes* attest to the personal nature of the author's *credo*. Following is one example:

> Mon cher Rhédi, pourquoi tant de philosophie? Dieu est si haut que
> nous n'apercevons pas même ses nuages. Nous ne le connaissons bien
> que dans ses préceptes. Il est immense, spirituel, infini. Que sa gran-
> deur nous ramène à notre faiblesse. S'humilier toujours, c'est l'adorer
> toujours. (*Lettres persanes*, p. 153)

Both philosophers chastize man for defining God as a power partial to his
own disputes and quarrels. The following parallel we draw between the
Essais and *Mes Pensées* is a further extension of Montesquieu's agreement
with Montaigne:

> les dieux n'ont agi, n'ont parlé que pour l'homme; elle [la philosophie]
> ne leur attribue autre consultation et autre vacation: les voylà contre
> nous en guerre . . . les voicy partisans de noz troubles . . . (*Essais*, II,
> ch. 12, pp. 230-31)

> L'homme forge mille plaisantes societez entre Dieu et luy. Est-il pas
> son compatriote? (Ibid., p. 232)

> nous voulons que Dieu soit un être partial, qui se déclare sans cesse
> pour une créature contre l'autre et se plaît à cette espèce de guerre.
> Nous voulons qu'il entre dans nos querelles, aussi vivement que
> nous . . . (*Pensée*, 22; 2191)

How then, asks Montesquieu, can such a free thinker like Montaigne
profess also to be a Christian? As a philosopher he implies that *religions
révélées* reflect only man's vain subjectivity—the "fausses images de nos
songes" (II, ch. 12, p. 206). How can such an undogmatic metaphysician
pretend to espouse Catholic dogma?[3] Naturally he found such behavior
contradictory and concluded that the essayist simply "dared not" go on to
criticize the Church and its principles. Montesquieu assumed that Montaigne, like himself, was at heart a philosopher, that he espoused Catholicism only to escape the censors.

Next Rica adds: "Cet homme contradictoire est toujours content de
lui, pourvu qu'on convienne des qualités." With this gently biting remark
Montesquieu insinuates that Montaigne, the least dogmatic and pedantic of
French philosophers is vain, that the most sociable and unpretentious of
noble writers is haughty. Sheer irony! Rica is merely shocking the general
notion of opinions on Montaigne held over the ages, opinions like Mme de

Sévigné's: "Ah l'aimable homme (she writes), qu'il est de bonne compagnie! C'est mon ancien ami" (*Essais*, I, p. *xxii*). Rica's jab, on the other hand, reflects again Mme du Deffand's intuition into the essayist. "il (Montaigne) est vain—eh! tous les hommes sont-ils doublement vains?" (ibid., p. *xxv*). We should understand that there is not the slightest personal vindictiveness in Rica's or Mme de Deffand's accusation. Montaigne is like any moralist whose image is polished and perfected by the good judgment he uses in distinguishing between vice and virtue. "Qualités" in Rica's text has the sense of *vertus*. In having the reader agree with his interpretation of the good and the bad, in having us concur with the consistent *bon sens*, Montaigne is patting himself on the back, implies Rica. "Tout le monde se plaint de sa mémoire" (writes La Rochefoucauld), "personne de son jugement." Even though Montaigne has complained of his faulty judgment more than once, we cannot truly take him seriously: "cet homme contradictoire est toujours content de lui." Note that Rica does not write: "Cet homme contradictoire est toujours content de lui, pourvu qu'on convienne de *ses* qualités." Montaigne never speaks of his own virtues per se, but in his function as educator, he continually implies their existence. "Voulez-vous qu'on dise du bien de vous? N'en dites pas," writes Pascal. There is the gimmick to Montaigne's clever method in winning over his readers, a method of which he himself was quite aware—particularly in "De la vanité." Montaigne was no dupe of his modesty. He knew it is always a veil of one's pride, vanity, or self-assurance. Montesquieu was, however, more aware of the paradox. Various thoughts in *Mes Pensées* illustrate his preoccupation with man's *amour propre*: "On peut cacher son orgueil; mais on ne peut cacher sa modestie" (*pensée* 1347; 1066). "Ceux qui ont peu de vanité sont plus près de l'orgueil que les autres" (*pensée* 1186; 1053). "Un fonds de modestie rapporte un très gros intérêt" (*pensée* 588; 1065). "Nous louons les gens à proportion de l'estime qu'ils ont pour nous" (*pensée* 768; 1072). Montaigne judges in favor of his readers' common sense. Taking it for granted, he causes us to admire him and ourselves simultaneously. It is a happy marriage of intellects, each one congratulating the other on his good judgment. Few readers would disagree with an excellent author's opinions. And no author can escape his role as the advocate of them. In one *pensée* of Montesquieu's lies the best clarification of Rica's idea:

> Quand on lit les livres, on trouve les hommes meilleurs qu'ils ne sont
> parce que chaque auteur, ne manquant point de vanité, cherche à faire
> croire qu'il est plus honnête homme qu'il n'est en jugeant toujours en
> faveur de la vertu. Enfin, les auteurs sont des personnages de théâtre.
> (*Pensée* 845; 1070)

However, as Rica unveils Montaigne's false modesty, so we might reveal Montesquieu's. The author becomes "des personnages de théâtre" in Rica and Usbek, the superficial, almost transparent façades between himself and his public. Montesquieu is also a moralist and, as we have seen in the chapter, "Apprenticeship to *Honnêteté*," he was aware of the hypocrisy inherent in a modest pose. This is the lesson of letter 50, the first part of which may have been inspired by Montaigne. The title, "Charme de la modestie et impertinence de la vanité," is partially ironic, for in truth the letter illustrates what one might call *l'impertinence de la modestie*. The various voices within this letter echo Montesquieu's introspection into his own *amour propre* and vanity as the advocate of a natural, unaffected—in brief—a modest virtue. The author judges himself best through the use of mirrors where the image of the self is reflected and duplicated once, twice, thrice-over by exterior figures (these, at the same time, reacting to one another). Such a method of self-examination could not be more indirect or devious. One character cries: "Quoi! toujours des sots qui se peignent eux-mêmes, et qui ramènent tout à eux?" (p. 106). And we know that in reality this is Montesquieu's voice upbraiding himself for his own self-portrait concealed in the *Lettres persanes* and precisely in this letter! In the same way, when Montesquieu writes of Montaigne in a seemingly critical tone of voice, "cet homme contradictoire est toujours content de lui, pourvu qu'on convienne des qualités," he is hinting at his own role as moralist, in this instance akin to the essayist's. Rica's judgment pronounced on Montaigne turns out to be as much a judgment upon Montesquieu.

In paragraphs four and five of our letter, as we have seen, Rica is concerned with the dangers inherent in plagiarism. He fears the futility in being a belated eighteenth-century humanist and commentator. "The choice of one's themes is a delicate matter; and how many should one take from others?" he seems to ask. Now in paragraphs two and three another debate ensues, which we quote:

> La fureur de la plupart des Français, c'est d'avoir de l'esprit, et la
> fureur de ceux qui veulent avoir de l'esprit, c'est de faire des livres.

Cependant il n'y a rien de si mal imaginé: la Nature semblait avoir sagement pourvu à ce que les sottises des hommes fussent passagères, et les livres les immortalisent. Un sot devrait être content d'avoir ennuyé tous ceux qui ont vécu avec lui: il veut encore tourmenter les races futures, il veut que sa sottise triomphe de l'oubli, dont il aurait pu jouir comme du tombeau; il veut que la postérité soit informée qu'il a vécu, et qu'elle sache à jamais qu'il a été un sot. (*Lettres persanes,* p. 136)

Thus, if paragraphs four and five dealt with subject matter, paragraphs two and three concern the spirit in which any subject should be treated. What to write and how to write it—these are the essential questions posed by Rica in the central part of his letter. Books immortalize either an author's failure or his triumph, his stupidity or his wit and cleverness. We should define the term, "de l'esprit," as Montesquieu understood it, for its sense is different from the single work, *esprit. De l'esprit* is intimately associated with dialogue and conversation, the lively chatter for which our baron was so well known himself.

L'esprit de conversation est ce qu'on appelle *de l'esprit* parmi les François. Il consiste à un dialogue ordinairement gai, dans lequel chacun, sans s'écouter beaucoup, parle et répond, et où tout se traite d'une manière coupée, prompte et vive. Le style et le ton de la conversation s'apprennent, c'est-à-dire le style de dialogue. (*Pensée* 1682; 1740)

Not only does *de l'esprit* pertain to conversation but to literature as well, when such an author as Montesquieu endeavors to express his own wit (and that of Frenchmen in general) on the printed page. The *Lettres persanes* consist of dialogue on many planes—between the authors of many letters, between characters within single letters, but, most important, between Montesquieu and his environment. The *Lettres persanes* provide a familiar, gay style of dialogue; it was a conversational approach that our author most admired and tried to recreate. Louis Vian was sensitive to its importance in regard to Montesquieu's works:

La conversation était donc une manière de travailler de Montesquieu. Rentré chez lui, il recueillait, comme l'abeille, le fruit de la journée, notant le soir les observations qu'il avait faites et celles qu'il avait entendues, les saillies de ses interlocuteurs et les siennes, ce qu'il avait dit et ce qu'il avait provoqué à dire. Je me trompe, peut-etre, mais il me semble que beaucoup de livres du dix-huitième siècle ont été causés avant d'être écrits.[4]

There is no doubt but that the two paragraphs on *de l'esprit* apply to Montesquieu, that they are a further facet of his introspection as both social wit and clever writer—twin roles, as we have seen, which gave the young *président* doubts as to his proper place in society.

Moreover, Montesquieu felt that wit (*de l'esprit*) is closely linked with satire:

Tout homme qui raille veut avoir de l'esprit. . . . Il n'y a rien de si mince que ce qui sépare un railleur de profession d'un sot ou d'un impertinent. (*Pensée* 1274; 623)

Often Montesquieu's wit reflects, even duplicates Montaigne's. They laugh similarly at provincial mankind—the French in general and especially courtiers and Parisians. They attack the pompous, empty-headed *grands* of society, and in particular their own constituency—the magistrates. They mock the serious institution of marriage and expose infidelity as a veritable French custom. They isolate the pretentious know-it-alls of society and expose the opinionated and narrow-minded to ridicule. They even satirize man for thinking he is such an important cog in the universe and for creating Gods in his own image. Our writers laugh at the inconsistency of so-called atheists and the inconstancy of French fashion. Through outside observers (Montaigne's cannibals and Montesquieu's Persians) they mock the strange status quo of French society where kings are so powerful, the aristocracy so overstuffed, and the people so poor. What institution or foible in man do they leave untouched? Finally, both men laugh at themselves in their roles as *faiseurs de livres*. ("Nous mettons en dignité nos bestises quand nous les mettons en moule," says Montaigne [III, ch. 13, p. 331].) It is this wise act which Montesquieu hopes will help save him from turning from a wit into a fool or impertinent, obnoxious *bel esprit*. And it is through his alliance with Montaigne's wit that he hopes the *sottises* immortalized in the *Lettres persanes* will not designate their author as a *sot*. Such is the meaning at the bottom of Rica's second and third paragraphs of letter 66.

Montesquieu has written a brief "Comedy of Errors" in the four central paragraphs of our letter. There we see how an author, wishing to prove he is a wit, can take one step too far and become a fool (paragraphs two and three): "quand on court après l'esprit, on attrape la sottise" (*pensée* 1358; 1177). In striving to be the intelligent compiler of a "beau chef-d'œuvre" he can turn into a simple plagiarizer (paragraphs four and five). Montesquieu has stepped out of his skin and into Rica's to pose before the author of the *Lettres persanes* a problem of balance. He is detached not only for irony but for accuracy. Like Horace he finds the safeguard against literary pitfalls in a delicate sense of equilibrium and lucidity. And one must conclude that he discovered these powers of discernment reinforced through reading Montaigne. As the essayist so often does, Montesquieu has contradicted or rather corrected himself with two antitheses, thus finding the proper means between two extremes. Here is the wisdom (*ne quid nimis*) the author has chosen to draw from Montaigne and make his own. The contradictions of the four central paragraphs are not aimed at Montaigne, but at himself, for the worthy Baron of La Brède feared being taken for a *sot* on paper, and to avoid becoming a victim, he draws up a self-prosecution.

Montaigne had done something similar in spirit in his address to Mme de Duras. He was as haunted by *sottises* as Montesquieu:

> Mon Dieu! Madame, que je haïrois une telle recommandation d'estre habile homme par escrit, et estre un homme de neant et un sot ailleurs. J'ayme mieux encore estre un sot, et icy et là, que d'avoir si mal choisi où employer ma valeur. Aussi il s'en faut tant que j'attende à me faire quelque nouvel honneur par ces sotises, que je feray beaucoup si je n'y en pers point de ce peu que j'en avois acquis. (*Essais*, II, ch. 37, pp. 517-18)

Both nobles share their class's prejudice against men of letters. As members of the aristocracy they are embarrassed for having compromised their status in writing. Montaigne goes so far as to say defensively (still addressing Mme de Duras): "j'ai mis tous mes efforts à former ma vie. Voylà mon mestier et mon ouvrage. Je suis moins faiseur de livres que de nulle autre besoigne"[5] (ibid., p. 517). And Montesquieu confesses: "J'ai la maladie de faire des livres et d'en être honteux quand je les ai faits" (*pensée* 837; 83). In the light of this confession, confirmed by certain remarks in the "Introduction" to the *Lettres persanes*, one understands why the Baron of La Brède never publicly admitted being the author of the *Lettres persanes*. Who could fear more the reputation of *bel esprit* than the writer of such impertinent letters? Montesquieu then hides behind his masks, Usbek and

Rica, and in attributing authorship to them, escapes being a *faiseur de livres*. Moreover, he dons the essayist's mantle to protect himself against a critical public and to outwit an ignorant public. Clearly it was in Montaigne's wake that Montesquieu conceived his trial of "sottises." And through his total contact with Montaigne he treats the two greatest risks of a writer dialectically. Like the various forms of government in *L'Esprit des lois* Montesquieu remains poised between order and tyranny. Surely Montaigne seemed the model of order to him. In Montaigne the author discovered a man who emerged victorious from the perils of writing, a man who retained his dignity in spite of his wit, who remained himself despite his sources, who was his own best judge and the dupe of no one. Rica's letter is dedicated to him and can be justly called Montesquieu's *Des livres*, 1721.

There remains only Rica's first sentence to analyse last. It is as much a conclusion as an introduction to this letter: "On s'attache ici beaucoup aux sciences; mais je ne sais si on est fort savant." On one level Rica is speaking of the French in general. But on the literary level "on" implies that neither Montaigne alone nor Montesquieu alone is the subject of the two phrases. Rather both are. "On" is a synonym of "nous." Yet it does not exclude other Frenchmen who write in an unaffected, pleasing manner, who are attached to all *sciences* without being pedantic in any. Rica is judging from a high point of perspective and sees Montesquieu in the same boat with Montaigne, but accompanied by other figures whom the author later mentions in *Mes Pensées*. He was to feel that Rabelais, Molière, Pascal, and Montaigne, among others, all influenced the gaiety and wit of the *Lettres persanes* (see *pensée* 1553; 886). Rica's first sentence reflects Montesquieu's awareness of his many models—especially Montaigne, but not only Montaigne. These as yet unmentioned heros are those the author has chosen to emulate, for they symbolize the best in French spirit—jovial and unaffected. "De toutes les nations connues, il n'y en a point de moins pédante qu la nôtre . . . " (*pensée* 1439; 1404). Through Rica's first words Montesquieu betrays his wish to join the lineage of great writers, *honnêtes hommes* of society and literature, the natural and unpretentious examiners of the world and man. "Ordinairement, ceux qui ont un grand esprit l'ont naïf" (*pensée* 1982; 1157). Montesquieu wished that posterity would place him in such esteem, that future generations would admire his modesty and sociability. Montaigne was his principal model, but the French spirit evident in many works of art and in the living society around them was the true model and molder of both writers. "Montaigne and I," implies Montesquieu, "by our nature are conforming to the nature of our chosen public, the *honnêtes gens* of France."

However, as he plays on the word "science" at the end of his letter, Rica also includes a double meaning in "savant" at the beginning. Scholarly and pedantic (overtones of the word) our philosophers are not. Learned and well informed they are indeed. If we take "savant" to have the latter sense, then Rica is purely ironic in inferring that neither Montaigne nor Montesquieu are *savants* ("je ne sais si on est fort savant"). With their magnificent libraries they were among the most learned men of their day. The *Essais* and the *Lettres persanes* are proof of both author's erudition. But their trick was to be learned without appearing so, to use the vast culture of the past and present at their disposal without weighing down their work in a pedantic, ostentatious manner. The same essential problem posed itself for both writers: to be a *faiseur de livres* and at the same time an *honnête homme*. The ambiguity of Rica's remark—"mais je ne sais si on est fort savant"—expresses this dilemma wittily.

On reexamining our letter as a whole, one is struck by its careful arrangement of themes and its ever increasing irony. We find it a perfectly symmetrical composition, each half containing three paragraphs. In the first half Rica discusses that anonymous "homme contradictoire" and the dangers of wit when immortalized on paper. The following section on plagiarism prepares the final paragraph concerning the *Essais*. In brief, the letter's first half deals with the man, the second with the book. Thus, in the very structure of Rica's letter one finds the balance its author is seeking through literary criticism. Yet behind such proper, academic organization Montesquieu amuses himself with outlandish irony and puns. The fun begins, of course, when Rica attacks compilers. After disagreeing with Montaigne's method of composition, in the next paragraph he proceeds to compose a "chef-d'œuvre" in the very style of the essayist. And as if this inconsistent behavior were not enough, he sums up the *Essais* with the most audacious skill in a final rally of wit (paragraph six). As biting as his irony is in the concluding paragraph, it seals the pact between our two Gascons. Montesquieu's tribute to the *Essais* is the paradoxical humor in this single sentence, a *gasconnade*, if there ever was one.[6] He must have realized that "cet homme contradictoire" would have been the first to laugh heartily at Rica's irony and contradiction. Montaigne is not the victim but the accomplice of Rica's farce. He and his work are disguised like the wily Montesquieu himself.

In 1952 Dréano suspected and in a sense searched for Montaigne's role as a predecessor of the *Lettres persanes*:

> Montesquieu trouve que sa propre manière, au moins dans son premier chef-d'œuvre, revient assez à celle de Montaigne . . . Il ne dit pas que Montaigne a été son modèle—un Montesquieu a-t-il besoin de modèle?—mais il constate que la gaieté sans plaisanterie des *Essais* renouvelée dans les *Lettres persanes* s'est trouvée au goût du XVIIIème siècle.[7]

Montesquieu provided a perfect response to Montaigne's gaiety by the gaiety of his dedicatory letter. In having Rica scathe the essayist (the way he does so many important personages and institutions) Montesquieu is in reality allowing us a glance into his workshop through windows made by Montaigne. We have removed the author's mask; we have seen through his mock insults. Beneath the irony of Rica's remarks lies Montesquieu who has chosen Montaigne as model and godfather of his *Lettre persanes*.

The title of letter 66 should not be overlooked in our study of Montaigne's presence in the *Lettres persanes*. Rica calls it "Fureur qu'ont les Français de faire des livres, trop souvent *inutiles*." Montesquieu's misgivings about his first work for popular consumption are evident. He asks himself what value there is in being a compiler and *bel esprit*, a role far removed from his status as *président à mortier* and director of the Academy of Bordeaux. Of what utility is a work designed above all to please and divert? What contribution does it make to the arts and sciences or society as a whole? A skeptic on so many other issues, Montesquieu also tends to doubt the validity of his *Lettres persanes*. Had this *bel esprit* not written, "Ce qui me choque de ces beaux esprits, c'est qu'ils ne se rendent pas *utiles* à leur patrie" (*Lettres persanes*, p. 78). Probably criticized for having undertaken this composition, in letter 66 Montesquieu playfully concedes that, indeed, his *Lettres* are not useful in the common sense of the word, not like his scientific work performed for the Academy. Yet, on the other hand, of what benefit and utility are the learned dissertations and research drawn up by the *savant* of letter 145 and the *amateur de la vénérable antiquité* of letter 142? It is with thorough irony that Montesquieu has the latter write:

> je vous donnerai par-dessus le marché quelques ouvrages de ma façon, par lesquels vous verrez que je ne suis point un membre *inutile* de la République des Lettres. (*Lettres persanes*, p. 306)

There also the author is skeptical of the validity of his own scholarly work devoted to petty points of no interest to the general public and of little value to his learned associates. Obsessed by the need to make a real contribution to society, Montesquieu mocks his own illusion that he is doing so, whether in his role as academician or witty author. "What is useful?" he seems to ask. "By scholarly, scientific standards my *Lettres persanes* are of no interest. But by universal standards, neither is my humanistic research (where I prove, for example, that Cambyses was wounded in the left foot, not the right), and neither is my scientific research (where I devote myself to examining heavenly bodies, microscopic animals, keeping close track on precise temperature changes, and the like)." In either case the lucid, self-conscious Montesquieu debates over just what is useful, and seems to conclude wisely that the question cannot be resolved by a simple answer one way or the other.

However, we should not take too seriously his reflections on the uselessness of the *Lettres persanes*. In reality, of course, Montesquieu doubts only to reassure himself of the contrary. To assume that his work contributes little is more modesty and *coquetterie* than anything else. A speech for the Academy of Bordeaux delivered in 1725, only four years after the publication of his *Lettres persanes*, points out his sincere hopes for all *belles lettres*, not excluding his own. In fact, he may have been thinking of his critics, among them Marivaux, in the following words:

> Il ne faut pas juger de l'utilité d'un ouvrage par le style que l'auteur a choisi: souvent on a dit gravement des choses puériles; souvent on a dit en badinant des vérités très sérieuses.
> Mais, indépendamment de ces considérations, les livres qui recréent l'esprit des honnêtes gens ne sont pas *inutiles*.[8]

Do we attach too much meaning to letter 66? Undoubtedly not. Montesquieu is known to have agonized over the composition of a few lines. According to Madame Necker, the author of *L'Esprit des lois* "etait quelquefois des heures sans avoir une idée qui lui plût. . . . Ainsi, lorsqu'il fit le fameux chapitre sur le despotisme, il fut trois heures avant de trouver ces deux lignes."[9] In a publication of 1834 Labat, who saw the first draft of the *Lettres persanes*, relates that Montesquieu corrected and rewrote a great deal, proof that writing was sometimes an arduous task for this classicist who sought perfection at great length. Labat writes, "Il y a des passages raturés jusqu'à quatre ou cinq fois."[10] Letter 66 must have caused Montesquieu some time and trouble. How was he to sum up his debt to Montaigne and at the same time appraise him critically? (Montesquieu was not the type to lavish his praise upon anyone without tempering it with reservations.) Reason demands moderation and a critical faculty. Montaigne's hypocrisy (as Montesquieu saw it) vis-à-vis the Church did not please our young author.

Where Montesquieu outdoes himself with obscurity and density of thought is in the first paragraph of letter 66, which could almost as well have been three paragraphs, for the meanings of the sentences are so detached from one another. There we believe the writer agonized over these three separate thoughts the way he did before composing the chapter on despotism in *L'Esprit des lois*. We must remember that one of Montesquieu's artistic principles was to skip linking ideas, a practice which can create abrupt halts and sometimes an annoying lack of transition from one idea to the next. But he maintained that the method was not without a purpose: "ce sont ces suppressions heureuses qui ont fait dire à M. Nicole que tous les bons livres étoient doubles" (*pensée* 1970; 802). The "double" nature of this letter consists in Montesquieu's own playful obscurity and the reader's task to uncover the hidden meaning behind the words, providing necessary links between sentences and paragraphs, and separating one thought from another when there would seem to be a transition but isn't one. He must solve the puzzle with little help from the author.

A letter at the heart of the creative process, one containing the most important aspects of Montesquieu's self-portrait as an author, was not simply thrown into the collection at random but was placed more or less in the middle of the work. Is it not the centerpiece of the *Lettres persanes*? The author was motivated by a double concern in choosing where to place letter 66. First of all, as he does with many other satirical or ironic letters, Montesquieu surrounds it with other epistles of an entirely different nature: number 64 and 65 dealing with troubles in Usbek's harem and number 67, the tender story of Aphéridon and Astarté. Letter 66 stands out in striking contrast, a witty, obscure work stuck in between letters of simplicity and clarity. Placed in strong relief, it illustrates one of Montesquieu's literary principles: "Il ne faut pas que, dans un ouvrage, l'ironie soit continuée; elle ne surprend plus" (*pensée* 1334; 804). Secondly, he has it immediately precede one of the three *contes*, long letters compared to the average length of conversations between our various Persians. The *contes* themselves are equally spread out in the *Lettres persanes*: the first (*Histoire des Troglo-dytes*) being letter 11; the second whose title is mentioned above, letter 67; and the third (*Histoire d'Hibrahim et d'Anaïs*), letter 141. Thus, one is at the beginning, another in the middle, and the last near the end of the *Lettres persanes*. Accentuating this rough symmetry, letter 66 accompanies the second *conte*. Montesquieu possibly chose to put the story of Aphéridon and Astarté instead of another *conte* next to his *art poétique* because of their thematic rapport. The beginning of letter 67 also reflects Montaigne very deeply, for it is there that Ibben speaks of his universal citizenshp, his love for all humanity and the retirement of a friend of his which increased the latter's heroism and virtue. As we have seen, all these themes pertain to the *Essais*. Above all, it is not surprising that a *citoyen universel* (in letter 67) should seek a *science universelle* (in letter 66). Linking these two passages on universality together, is the author giving us a slight hint with whom he shares them both?

We have spoken of one of Montesquieu's motives for rendering the sense of his dedicatory letter so obscure. Clearly he wished to play a trick on his critics and censors, camouflaging himself behind the protective words of others. However, beyond this playful discretion lies a deep facet of Montesquieu's psychology—what Barrière terms appropriately "une certaine timidité fière qui ne se livre pas."[11] As the baron was very unwilling to have his portrait done by famous painters and draftsmen of his time, he was also hesitant about doing the job himself. Montesquieu complains more than once about the timidity which plagued him throughout his life. And yet, accompanying his shyness one notices an opposing character trait—his strong pride and self-respect, even a sense of superiority. Montesquieu was too proud to reveal the key of his artistic method to the average reader. He speaks to an elite group of connoisseurs, those who not only know *about* Montaigne but who *know* Montaigne. But, on the other hand, he felt too embarrassed and unworthy to blatantly associate his name with that of the great essayist. Let us remember Montesquieu's jab at his friend Pierre Coste who felt he acquired Montaigne's glory for having reedited the *Essais*. Montesquieu writes in *Mes Pensées*:

> J'ai un honnête homme de mes amis qui a fait de belles notes sur Montaigne. Je suis sûr qu'il croit avoir fait les *Essais*. Lorsque je le loue devant lui, il prend un air modeste, et me fait une petite révérence, et rougit un peu. (*Pensée* 1441; 946)

Coste deserved the fun poked at him, to be sure. But we can hear jealousy in Montesquieu's laughter. He who loved and read Montaigne till the end of his life did not have the publicity and congratulations his friend enjoyed for simply having added a few notes to the *Essais*. Montesquieu was too humble to claim Montaigne openly as his model, but he was too proud to let us follow him into the secret chamber of his creative method.

Montesquieu's last remarks in "Quelques réflexions sur les *Lettres persanes* " provide a conclusion on his secret partnership with Montaigne. Speaking primarily to his critics, he writes with characteristic duplicity:

> Certainement la nature et le dessein des *Lettres persanes* sont si à découvert qu'elles ne tromperont jamais que ceux qui voudront se tromper eux-mêmes. (*Lettres persanes*, p. 5)

On a superficial level the author is scolding his public for misreading his work, for seeing in it dangerous ideas and doctrines which he had no intention of advocating. (Displaying is not synonymous with selling.) In brief, Montesquieu upbraids his censors for ferreting out hidden heresy and treason in the *Lettres persanes*, when it was neither implied nor intended. But on another level, the author is ironic in misleading us to think that the nature and purpose of his *Lettres persanes* are thoroughly obvious. Who among his contemporaries could know that the letters consisted of a compilation and commentary modelled on the *Essais*? Who could know that, in painting certain traits of his Persians and fellow Frenchmen, he was sketching his own portrait as well? Who could realize that the most detached writer who refused to claim his authorship of his work, a man seemingly far removed from his Persian characters, was ever present as the *chaîne secrète* which bound the philosohpy, theater, and *contes* of his work together? Who would think that the most impersonal method of composition— compiling and glossing—would at the same time reveal the most personal of self-revelations and discoveries? Montesquieu smiles at these paradoxes hidden in the fabric of his work and declares that only those who *want* to be ignorant will not grasp the "obvious" nature and design of the *Lettres persanes*. Pure irony—as clear as the quiet sarcasm in another remark drawn from these "Réflexions": "on n'a pas certainement voulu frapper [le genre humain] par l'endroit le plus tendre" (p. 5). An expert satirist and mocker of mankind must have laughed inside to say this. And in deceiving us, he was simply waiting till the day when we would laugh with him.

CONCLUSION

To JUDGE BY MONTESQUIEU'S own interpretation of his alliance with Montaigne, the essayist exercised a liberating influence on the *Lettres persanes*. This we can judge by the two basic themes of letter 66. The author is free to compile and comment upon not only Montaigne and the ancients but on any number of writers before and after the *Essais*. Montesquieu remains attached to his model more in terms of *forme* than *fonds*. His belief that philosophical literature should include all subjects and all styles (see *Pensée* 1261; 612) is demonstrated in the *Lettres persanes*. Montesquieu may imitate the satirical method of Pascal, the logic of Descartes, the smooth storytelling charm of Fénelon, or the playful contradictions of Montaigne and Rabelais. Similarly Montaigne maintained that he imitated the styles of his sources—Salluste and Caesar, Seneca and Plutarch (see *Essais*, II, ch. 17, p. 356). Yet despite their similar doctrines, it is obvious that Montesquieu outdoes any predecessor; he creates veritable *pastiches* of other writer's styles. On the question of wit or satire (*de l'esprit*) Montesquieu may also base his remarks on those of other moralists, historians playwrights, etc., but this procedure does not prohibit him from developing an old theme or from inventing a new one. That the *Lettres persanes* have survived as a work of art for over two centuries is proof of the author's ingenuity and originality, the validity of his taste and judgment. The basic paradox of letter 66 which speaks for the entire work is that a commentator and compiler can have so much new to say. By nature he is not bound to be a mere eclectic. "Tout est dit, et l'on vient trop tard depuis plus de sept mille ans qu'il y a des hommes, et qui pensent," writes La Bruyère. A lucid connoisseur, Montesquieu would have recognized the truth in this observation (itself, appropriately enough, an aphorism drawn from *Ecclesiastes*). Like Montaigne, Montesquieu felt humble in the presence of so much wisdom which preceded him over the ages. What new could he hope to create? Yet, were he criticized for being a plagiarist, Montesquieu might reply with the words of Pascal:

> Qu'on ne dise pas que je n'ai rien dit de nouveau. . . . Quand on joue à la paume, c'est une même balle dont joue l'un et l'autre, mais l'un la place mieux.[1]

One realizes what immense irony is contained in Rica's final *pointe* to letter 66, where he claims that the *Essais* "taught" him nothing. On the contrary, one might say they taught him everything—more than any other single source of inspiration. They probably influenced the author to paint his own portrait in the *Lettres persanes*, a few years before he did so again, openly and frankly in *Mes Pensées*. They also encouraged him to embrace the widest possible range of topics and to display a *science universelle* in the most natural, unaffected manner. As Vernière has suggested (*Lettres persanes*, p. 183; fn. 1), the library Rica visits is a résumé of the riches in Montesquieu's own collection at La Brède. This "bibliothèque publique" as the Persian refers to it, is in reality a *bibliothèque privée*. The vague, general term merely encourages us to uncover its precise, personal nature. There Montesquieu passes in review the great variety of his readings and sources, commenting on them wittingly in the style of Pascal's *Provinciales*. We find the author's subjective taste expressed here—his love for history and theater, his distaste for poetry and novels. And again we see demonstrated his universal curiosity and playful skepticism.

Not only does Montesquieu rival Montaigne with the depth and vastness of his learning; he displays it in a rhythm similar to that in the *Essais*. Unlike La Bruyère who creates large chapters all devoted to one theme so that there is a certain monotony in the accumulation of maxims, Montaigne and Montesquieu pass from one subject to another, never allowing the reader time to become bored. It is true that Montaigne does this with greater freedom, disgressing many times in the majority of his essays. Nevertheless, one might interpret each letter in the *Lettres persanes* as a new digression. The variety and contrasts created within an essay like "De la vanité" compare favorably to the treatment of several themes throughout a number of letters. Both writers were aware of the need to vary their tone and subject matter so as to hold the reader's interest. The basic structure of the *Lettres persanes* is not so different from that of the *Essais*. They constitute Montesquieu's *jardin à l'anglaise* of literature, with contrived freedom and disorder, a dense and rich collection of thoughts organized mainly according to the esthetic principle of contrast.

Our thesis may prove nothing but the similar universal appeal and humane attitudes shared by two philosophers—each exceptional for its day. Various chapters touch on such a variety of topics that there is often very little relationship between them. What do Montaigne and Montesquieu not discuss and examine? The *Lettres persanes* reflect not only the gaiety and satire of the *Essais* but also more serious thoughts on man's morality, his abortive grasp at happiness and certainty on this spinning planet, the deception of his senses, the inconsistency of his morality, the contradiction, inadequacy, or cruelty of his law, the foolheartedness of his rulers, his provincialism and pride, or his goodness and generosity. We have compared most every aspect in the study of man and society which links our two moralists. With bold foresight they attack innumerable questions raised by ancient and contemporary philosphy. Speaking of the *Lettres persanes*, someone had written, "The introduction of relativism into French thought is the most complete achievement of the work."[2] But Montesquieu did not introduce relativism into French thought! If anyone did, it was Montaigne. And it is often from Montaigne as a base that Montesquieu debates many points: our ideas and theories are relative to the body's constitution; judgment depends on our senses; the object of love is relative to our health or whim; gods are created according to our needs; laws depend on the relative capability—or rather stupidity—of legislators.

Readers have spoken of the elegant skepticism in the *Lettres persanes*. One must recognize that it finds its roots in the *Essais*, for Montaigne was the first great European philosopher capable of using his doubt to awaken us. Montesquieu also questions many established customs and institutions, concluding, like the essayist, that the majority is not always right, that marriage does not necessarily bring about love and fidelity, that the world does not revolve around courts and capitals, that learning is not synonymous with wisdom, nor laws with justice, nor royal liberality with generosity, nor capability with nobility.

Both writers share a great freedom of judgment which often coincides. Montaigne's word applies equally well to Montesquieu:

> [je] suis tant jalous de la liberté de mon jugement que mal-ayséement la puis-je quitter pour passion que ce soit. (*Essais*, II, ch. 17, p. 380)

Montesquieu's judgment must be enslaved to no one, not even to Montaigne. The *Lettre persanes* are the testimony of the author's conversation with his model—their agreements and disagreements. In answer to the essayist Montesquieu says that he does not pity kings because they are surrounded by flatterers, but because they don't have the will to resist their flatterers; that instability of faith applies not only to pagans but to Christians as well; that infidelity is even more rife and accepted in the regency than it was during the Renaissance; that the Christian-civil code punishing suicide victims is cruel and useless and that much of the church (its superstitions and ignorance) deserves criticism; that cultivating the arts does not weaken a nation or render it effeminate; that the custom of dueling in no way guarantees justice. In conversing with Montaigne, Montesquieu contradicts him on occasion. But both writers contradict themselves as well. Their thought is a continual dialectic. In disputing with Montaigne, Montesquieu becomes his strongest ally; after all, the essayist had said:

> Quand on me contrarie, on esveille mon attention, non pas ma colère, je m'avance vers celuy qui me contredit, qui m'instruit. (*Essais*, III, ch. 8, p. 154)

In a sense it is as though Montesquieu were "instructing" Montaigne or bringing the essayist up to date on certain matters, showing him how the times had changed.

Dialectical thought cannot be diasassociated from a dialectical style. By this we mean both writer's tendency to create a particular type of *saillie*, short phrases in the form of antithesis, sometimes witty, sometimes not. Montesquieu found a model for this stylistic device in authors other than the essayist, notably in Corneille whom he greatly admired. But when Montaigne broached a subject which interested Montesquieu in this concise, clear-cut way, then the latter lifted the idea, style and all, and dropped it into his own work. Thus, we find their reflections on dueling quite similar as well as those on divorce, ideal beauty, the groveling poor, and the over-stuffed rich. In the double image of *honnêteté* style imitates idea to an extent; language structures thought. Both men oscillated between the image of grandeur and averageness—one reserved for their upper-class peers, the other for their peasants and servants.

The name of Montaigne, an alternate spelling of Montagne, is in close rapport with the etymology of "Montesquieu." If the latter means a "wild or barren mountain,"[3] then the former suggests a less abrupt, wooded rise. To us the names seem symbolic of our writer's differing styles, for Montesquieu's is more dry and clipped. There is less shade on his land, but greater brightness and clarity. And although sharp antitheses are found in Montaigne's domain, in general rich images are more abundant and sentence structure sometimes so diffuse that we lose sight of the idea, it is so drowned in rhetoric.

We have shown where the two men contrast or disagree, but it must be said that there is infinitely more on which they agree. Their tolerant, flexible attitudes are an integral part of their humanity. No cause, however highly motivated, is more important than the good of man. Morality's ultimate base is in man and for man. With sympathy and love they go out to the less fortunate, the afflicted. Far from speaking solely in the interest of their class, Montaigne and Montesquieu espouse causes which aim at the common welfare of the state. Their greatest goal was perhaps to acquire the love and respect of all their fellow citizens. To do so they needed only to be *honnêtes hommes*, without undue pride, even without undue virtue. Modesty is the best method to acquire others' respect. Knowing oneself and one's relative place in society, we are best assured of our self-esteem. The *Lettres persanes* are the fruit of probing in two contrary directions, both inward and outward, for the author could not truly know the world without knowing himself; nor could he know himself without knowing the world. Montaigne offered him the example after which he might accomplish both. Retired at La Brède, surrounded by the sciences of the universe, Montesquieu began his quest to discover himself and his environment, emulating his relative[4] Montaigne who had done the same a century and a half earlier. As we know that Cicero was the model of his *Traitée des devoirs*, Plutarch the model of his *Vies parallèles*, and Corneille the model of his dialogue *Sylla et Eucrate*, it comes as no great surprise that Montaigne should be the model of this humanist's *Lettres persanes*.

Notes

Introduction

[1]Charles Augustin Sainte-Beuve, *Les Grands Ecrivains français: études des lundis et des portraits,* ed. Maurice Allem, 2 vols. (Paris: Garnier Frères, n. d.), vol. II, p. 31.

[2]Albert Sorel, *Montesquieu* (Paris: Hachette et Cie, 1887), p. 11.

[3]Sorel, pp. 11-12.

[4]Sorel, p. 12.

[5]Sainte-Beuve, p. 58.

[6]Jean Eugène Bimbenet, "Montaigne-Montesquieu," Société d'agriculture, sciences, belles-lettres et arts d'Orléans, Séries 2, v. 24 v. 54 of collection, Rapport sur le mémoire qui précède, by L. Guerrier in séance of Dec. 15, 1882, p. 60.

[7]Fortunat J. Strowski, *Montaigne* (Paris: F. Alcan, 1900), p. 310.

[8]Pierre Barrière, *Un Grand Provincial: Charles-Louis de Secondat, baron de La Brède et de Montesquieu* (Bordeaux: Delmas, 1946), p. 123.

[9]See also Robert Shackleton, *Montesquieu, A Critical Biography* (London: Oxford University Press, 1961), p. 349.

[10]Barrière, p. 9.

[11]Barrière, pp. 81-82.

[12]Barrière, p. 156.

[13]Barrière, p. 154.

[14]Barrière, p. 137.

[15]Barrière, p. 75.

[16]Barrière, p. 224.

[17]Barrière, p. 71.

[18]Pierre Barrière, "Les Eléments personnels et les éléments bordelais dans les *Lettres persanes,*" *Revue d'Histoire littéraire,* 1951, p. 36.

[19]Barrière, *Un Grand Provincial,* p. 192.

[20]See Montesquieu, *Œuvres Complètes,* ed. André Masson, 3 vols. (Paris: Nagel, 1950), vol. II, *pensée* 2154. In all future references to *Mes Pensées* we shall refer first to the number of the *pensée* in the Masson edition followed by the number in Roger Caillois's edition of Montesquieu's *Œuvres Complètes* (n. p: Gallimard, 1949). Thus, this reference is: *Pensée* 2154; 1939.

[21]*Lettres persanes,* ed. Paul Vernière (Paris: Editions Garnier, 1975), p. 226.

[22]Ed. Elie Carcassonne (Paris: F. Roches, 1929).

[23]Ed. Antoine Adam (Geneva: Editions Droz, 1954).

[24]ed. Paul Vernière (Paris: Editions Garnier, 1975).

[25]See *Lettres persanes*: p. 52, fn. 2; p. 63, fn. 1; p. 74, fn. 2; p. 75, fn. 3; p. 79, fn. 3; p. 113, fn. 1; pp. 165-66, fn. 2 & 3; p. 172, fn. 2; p. 190, fn. 4; p. 200, fn. 2.

[26]Shackleton, p. 39.

[27]Montaigne, *Essais*, ed. Maurice Rat, 3 vols. (Paris: Garnier Frères, n. d.), vol. II, ch. 10, p. 84.

[28]See the following images of planting, transplanting, and *pièces* in the *Essais*: (a) pertaining to the structure of writing:

> . . . les escrivains indiscrets de nostre siecle, qui . . . vont semant des lieux entiers des anciens autheurs pour se faire honneur, font le contraire. (I, ch. 26, p. 156)

> . . . je vins à rencontrer une piece haute, riche et eslevée jusques aux nues (i.e., un passage plagié). (Ibid.)

> . . . sous les inventions anciennes rappiecées par cy par là . . . (I, ch. 26, p. 157)

> Que sont-cy icy aussi, à la verite, que crotesques et corps monstrueux, rappiecez de divers membres, sans certaine figure, n'ayants ordre, suite ny proportion que fortuite? (I, ch. 28, p. 198)

> Si suis trompé . . . si nul escrivain l'a semée [la matière] ny guere plus materielle ny au moins plus drue en son papier. (I, ch. 40, p. 282)

> Semant icy un mot, icy un autre, eschantillons despris de leur piece, escartéz, sans dessein et sans promesse . . . (I, ch. 50, p. 335)

> . . . les formes de parler, comme les herbes, s'amendent et fortifient en les transplantant. (III, ch. 5, p. 97)

> comme quelqu'un pourroit dire de moy que j'ay seulement faict icy un amas de fleurs estrangeres, n'y ayant fourny du mien que le filet à les lier. (III, ch. 12, p. 302)

> Ce fagotage de tant de diverses pieces (les *Essais*) . . . (II, ch. 37, p. 486)

. . . tels ravaudeurs, gens que je ne feuillette guiere . . .

. . . empilé par son industrie ce fagot de provisions incogneues . . .

Ces pastissages de lieux communs, dequoy tant de gents mesnagent leur estude . . . (III, ch. 12, p. 303)

(b) pertaining to man:
L'homme, en tout et par tout, n'est que rapiessement et bigarrure. (III, ch. 21, p. 395)

. . . toute cette nostre contexture est bastie de pieces foibles et defaillantes. (I, ch. 53, p. 214)

. . . nous sommes bastis de deux pieces principales essentielles . . . [le corps et l'âme] (II, ch. 12, p. 214)

(c) pertaining to the social structure:
Platon dict que . . . quand il ordonne son philosophe chef d'une police, il n'entend pas le dire d'une police corrompue comme celle d'Athenes, et encore bien moins comme la nostre, envers lesquelles la sagesse mesme perdroit son Latin. Comme une herbe transplantée en solage fort divers à la condition, se conforme bien plustost à iceluy qu'elle ne le reforme à soy. (I, ch. 23, p. 124)

. . . une police, c'est comme un bastiment de diverses pieces jointes ensemble, d'une telle liaison, qu'il est impossible d'en esbranler une que tout le corps ne s'en sente. (I, ch. 23, p. 125)

[29]Barrière, *Un Grand Provincial*, p. 120.

[30]Montesquieu, *Lettres persanes*, ed. Paul Vernière (Paris: Editions Garnier, 1975), p. 4.

Chapter I

[1]Inspired by Epictetus, Montaigne touched an analogous subject in the essay, "Que le goust des biens et des maux dépend en bonne partie de l'opinion que nous en avons" (*Essais*, I, ch. 14).

[2]See allusions in the *Essais* to "Nostre miserable condition humaine" (I, ch. 14, p. 47), "l'humaine condition" in the sense of man's mortality (I, ch. 20, p. 93), and "la nihilité de l'humaine condition" (II, ch. 6, p. 53).

[3]Blaise Pascal, *Pensées,* ed. Ch.-M. des Granges (Paris: Garnier Frères, 1961), pp. 109-10.

[4]Pascal, p. 119.

[5]In his edition of the *Lettres persanes,* Vernière has discussed the importance of Spinoza in regard to the second half of letter 76. (See footnote 1, p. 161.) Yet it seems that our author's inspiration was divided, for Montaigne and Stoic philosophers probably influenced the first part.

[6]On the Bordeaux copy and thus in all modern editions of the *Essais* we find the last words to read, ". . . nous sommes punis *et en cetui-cy* et en l'autre monde." But Mlle de Gournay in her 1595 edition either censored or omitted the words "et en cetui-cy et." Thus Montesquieu, who had access only to this edition (see below, ch. X, fn. 1), read the text as we have reproduced it.

Chapter II

[1]Montesquieu would have been familiar with the text through the *Saint-Evremoniana* published in 1700. See *Lettres persanes,* p. *vii.*

[2]"Vous venez de perdre votre mari; vous ne m'aimerez plus," writes Montesquieu in a letter to an anonymous mistress (*Pensée* 1040: 508).

[3]Barrière, "Eléments personnels," pp. 26-27.

[4]In certain love letters from which Montesquieu drew excerpts for *Mes Pensées* we find him reiterating in a more personal vein the schism between love and marriage:

Que la haine que vous avez pour le mariage est juste! La raison vous a fait sentir ce que l'expérience seule peut faire connoître aux autres.

Lorsque, par des noeuds solennels,
Deux fidèles amants, que même ardeur anime,
Vont s'unir l'un à l'autre, aux yeux des Immortels,
    L'Amour est toujours la victime
    Qu'on immole sur les autels.

Vous voyez, Mademoiselle, qu'il ne faut point confondre les chaînes de l'Hymen avec celles de l'Amour; il ne faut point se marier; mais il faut aimer, et tout le monde doit être là-dessus de même religion. (*Pensée,* 1047; 511)

[5]Montaigne ultimately disagreed with his source here also, and on the Bordeaux copy he eliminated the word "cens." Five hundred years of fidelity was thus quickly reduced to five.

[6]In *L'Esprit des lois* Montesquieu reiterated his reaction, but this time in response to Roman historians:

Denys d'Halicarnasse, Valère-Maxime et Aulu-Gelle rapportent un fait qui ne me paroît pas vraisemblable. Ils disent que quoiqu'on eût à Rome la faculté de répudier sa femme, on eut tant de respect pour les auspices, que personne, pendant cinq cent vingt ans, n'usa de ce droit jusqu'à Carvilius Ruga, qui répudia la sienne pour cause de stérilité. (*L'Esprit des lois,* livre 16, ch. 16)

[7]Montaigne's source is Plutarch, *Vie de Lycurque,* XI. See *Essais,* II, ch. 15, p. 326, fn. 715.

[8]The worst curse a wise old Troglodyte can cast upon a sinful member of the tribe is to deprive him of posterity: "puisse-t-il mourir le dernier de sa famille!" (*Lettres persanes,* p. 35).

Chapter III

[1]Pascal, p. 151.

[2]Not every trait of the Catholic rebel's wit is related to the *Essais.* The allusion to the influence of "esprits animaux" upon his beliefs brings to mind Descartes's *Traité des passions de l'âme* (although in *Gargantua* Rabelais refers to his hero's prodigious "esprits animaux"). If we searched further back, we would surely find this obscure motivating force in antiquity.

Chapter IV

[1]Montesquieu states his case plainly in *Mes Pensées.*

Il faut beaucoup moins de peine à un juge pour décider la question en elle-même, qu'à débrouiller toutes les autorités qu'on lui cite. . . . Les citations des avocats troublent l'esprit de décision, au lieu de l'aider. (*Pensée* 1316; 830)

[2]Famous justices of the past, authorities still quoted during Montaigne's time supposedly to determine or support court decisions.

[3]See *Essais,* III, ch. 13, p. 314, footnote 578 and III, ch. 13, p. 319, fn 592.

[4]See also *Essais,* II, ch. 37, pp. 510-11 for an anecdote on the pernicious effects of law and medicine on society.

[5]In a more serious frame of mind did Montesquieu disagree with Montaigne, King Ferdinand, and Plato, when he took down the following notes?

On a cru remarquer que, dans un certain pays, les maladies sont venues avec les médecins. Ce sont plutôt les médecins qui sont venus avec les maladies. (*Pensée* 1389; 724)

[6]Bimbenet also compared these two passages (see "Montaigne-Montesquieu,"

Séance du 5 mai, 1882, p. 40), but he did not analyze them stylistically or even place one passage next to another.

Chapter V

[1]"J'en sers plus gayment mon prince par ce que c'est par libre eslection de mon jugement et de ma raison, sans obligation particulier, et que je n'y suis pas rejecté ny contrainct pour estre irrecevable à tout autre party et mal voulu" (*Essais*, III, ch. 9, p. 227).

[2]"La subjection essentielle et effectuelle ne regarde d'entre nous que ceux qui s'y convient et qui ayment à s'honnorer et enrichir par tel service" (*Essais*, I, ch. 42, p. 297).

[3]See Barrière, "Eléments personnels," pp. 21-22.

[4]"Barrière, "Eléments personnels," p. 22.

Chapter VI

[1]Sorel, p. 12.

[2]The theme of geometric prejudice for comical effect reminds us also of this passage in the *Apologie*:

Tout ainsi que la preferance en beauté, que Platon attribue à la figure spherique, les Epicuriens la donnent à la pyramidale plus tost ou carrée, et ne epuvent avaller un dieu en forme de boule. (*Essais,* II, ch. 12, p. 170)

[3]See Barrière, "Eléments personnels," pp. 17ff.

[4]Montesquieu identified strongly with Montaigne on this subject. We quote from his unfinished essay, *Sur le bonheur*:

Retranchons donc du nombre des malheureux tous les gens qui ne sont pas de la Cour, quoiqu'un courtisan les regarde comme les plus infortunés de l'Espèce humaine.* Retranchons-en tous ceux qui habitent les provinces quoique ceux qui vivent dans la Capitale les regardent comme des êtres qui végètent. (*Pensée* 30; 549)

*On dit que tout le monde se croit malheureux. Il me semble, au contraire, que tout le monde se croit heureux. Le courtisan croit qu'il n'y a que lui qui vive. (Montesquieu's footnote)

[5]Same irony in *Mes Pensées*.

. . . la plupart des gens ne connoissent que leur siècle: un Européen est choqué des mœurs simples des temps héroïques, comme un Asiatique est choqué des mœurs des Européens. (*Pensée* 1607; 589)

[6]See *Pensée* 2134; 47. See also 1996; 661 and 1687; 1846.

Chapter VII

[1]We find further traces of Montesquieu's universal citizenship in *Mes Pensées*:
Quand j'ai voyagé dans les pays étrangers, je m'y suis attaché comme
au mien propre: j'ai pris part à leur fortune, et j'aurois souhaité qu'ils
fussent dans un état florissant. (*Pensée*, 213; 4)

Si je savois une chose utile à ma nation qui fut ruineuse à une autre, je
ne la proposerois pas à mon prince, parce que je suis homme avant
d'être François, (ou bien) parce que je suis nécessairement homme, et
que je ne suis François que par hasard. (*Pensée*, 213; 4)

Si je savois quelque chose qui me fût utile, et qui fût préjudiciable à ma
famille, je la rejetterois de mon esprit. Si je savois quelque chose utile
à ma famille et qui ne le fût pas à ma patrie, je chercherois à l'oublier.
Si je savois quelque chose utile à ma patrie, et qui fût préjudiciable à
l'Europe, ou bien qui fût utile à l'Europe et préjudiciable au Genre
humain, je la regarderois comme un crime. (*Pensée*, 741: 11)

[2]A passage in *Mes Pensées* provides a good parallel to Montaigne's understanding of his own nation's relativity amidst others:

Il faut se corriger premièrement des vices de son pays et ne pas
ressembler à ce Thrace d'Ovide: *Flagrat vitio gentisque suoque.* Sans
cela, on se montre dans l'espèce commune de ses compatriotes; par
conséquent, dans l'espèce commune des hommes. (*Pensée* 1020; 1725)

Chapter VIII

[1]Barrière, "Eléments personnels," pp. 30, 33, 35-36.
[2]See *Pensée* 1680; 878.
[3]Shackleton, p. 35.
[4]*Mes Pensées*, p. 81.
[5]Barrière, *Un Grand Provincial*, p. 53.
[6]Montesquieu treats this theme in his own way (a bit more rigidly) in his
unfinished treatise, *Des devoirs*, inspired by Cicero. And he shows us that a proud
demeanor need not be a vain and haughty one:

On aime une *noble fierté* qui vient de cette satisfaction intérieure que
laisse la vertu: elle sied aux Grands; elle orne les dignités. Une grande
âme ne sauroit s'empêcher de se montrer tout entière: elle sent la
dignité de son être. (*Pensée* 1256; 607)

[7]René Cruchet, *France et Louisiane, Médecine et Littérature, Montaigne et*

Montesquieu at Home, Romance Language Series, No. 2 (University, La.: Louisiana State University Press, 1939), p. 277.

[8]Quoted by Barrière in *Un Grand Provincial*, p. 54.

[9]Louis Vian, *Histoire de Montesquieu* (Paris: Didier, 1878), p. 142.

[10]One finds almost the very same words in Montesquieu's self-portrait: "Je n'ai jamais vu couler de larmes sans en être attendri" (*Pensée* 213; 4).

[11]Vian, pp. 169-70.

Chapter IX

[1]Montesquieu, *Œuvres complètes*, ed. André Masson, vol. II, p. xxv.

[2]Shackleton, pp. 46-47.

[3]Quoted by Shackleton in *Montesquieu*, p. 85.

[4]Barrière in *Un Grand Provincial*, pp. 141-42.

[5]Vian, pp. 219-20.

[6]Vian, p. 217.

[7]See Shackleton, p. 380.

[8]Shackleton, p. 381.

[9]Quoted by Barrière in *Un Grand Provincial*, p. 138.

[10]Other passages in the *Lettres persanes* hint at the author's economical train of mind. Take, for instance, a visitor's situation in the shops of Paris. We are reminded of Montesquieu's remark in *Mes Pensées*,

> Ce qui fait que j'aime à être à La Brède, c'est qu'à la Brède il me semble que mon argent est sous mes pieds. A Paris, il me semble que je l'ai sur mes épaules. A Paris, je dis: "Il ne faut dépenser que cela." A ma campagne, je dis: "Il faut que je dépense tout cela" (*Pensée* 2169; 34).

Here are Rica's words on the same theme:

> Toutes les boutiques sont tendues de fils invisibles où se vont prendre tous les acheteurs. L'on en sort pourtant quelquefois à bon marché: une jeune marchande cajole un homme une heure entière pour lui faire acheter un paquet de curedents.
>
> Il n'y a personne qui ne sorte de cette ville plus précautionné qu'il n'y est entré; à force de faire part de son bien aux autres, on apprend à le conserver; seul avantage des étrangers dans cette ville enchanteresse. (p. 123)

Also, speaking of the French fetish of fashion, Montesquieu reveals his concern over its cost in Rica's passing remark, "Mais, surtout, on ne saurait croire combien il en coûte à un mari pour mettre sa femme à la mode" (p. 205).

[11]One might thus interpret Montesquieu's well-known expression which appears in "Quelques réflexions sur les *Lettres persanes*" (*Lettres persanes*, p. 4).

Chapter X

[1]Shackleton, p. 41.

[2]Bimbenet caught this parallel. See "Montaigne-Montesquieu," Séance du 31 mars, p. 332.

[3]Later in *Mes Pensées* Montequieu declared that this principle expressed in the *Lettres persanes* before his actual travels was also valid after them: "Quand j'ai voyagé dans les pays étrangers, je m'y suis attaché comme au mien propre" (quoted by Vernière in the *Lettres persanes*, p. 137, fn. 1).

[4]Compare to Montesquieu's adaptability in Italy: "Lorsque j'étois à Florence, et que je voyois les manières simples de ce pays; un sénateur, le jour, avec son chapeau de paille; le soir, avec sa petite lanterne: j'étois enchanté, je faisois comme eux . . . (*Pensée* 997, 52).

[5]Barrière, "Eléments personnels," p. 34.

[6]Elizabeth Carayol, "Des lettres persanes oubliées," *Revue d'Histoire littéraire* (janvier-mars 1965), p. 23.

[7]Shackleton, p. 32.

[8]See *Lettres persanes*, p. 180, fn. 1.

[9]Book VI, ch. 9 ff.

[10]"J'ay veu tel grand blesser la reputation de sa religion pour se montrer religieux outre tout exemple des hommes de sa sorte" (*Essais*, I, ch. 30, 225).

[11]Montesquieu's sources were probably either Barthelemy de la Casas's *Brevissima Relacion de la Destruccion de las Indias*, published in 1552 (see *Pensée* 207; 1573) or Antoine de Solis's *Histoire de la Conquête du Mexique* published in Madrid, 1684 (see *Pensée* 796; 104). He may also have read the Abbot Jean-Baptiste Morvan de Bellegarde's *Histoire d'Espagne* published in 1726 (see *Pensée* 898; 1576). Montaigne's source was Gomara's *Histoire generale des Indes* and *Histoire de Cortez*, the latter an Italian translation published in Venice, 1576 (see *Essais*, III, ch. 6, p. 138).

[12]Montaigne knew Aristotle's text through the *Timée* of Benzoni (see *Essais*, I, ch. 31, p. 233, fn. 580).

[13]Vian, p. 197.

Chapter XI

[1]Louis Desgraves, *Catalogue de la Bibliothèque de Montesquieu* (Geneva: Droz, 1954), p. 264. Mr. Desgraves gives us the following entry (number 1506): "Montaigne (Michel de) *Essais*. Paris (A. L'Angelier), 1595. In-fol., 1 vol." For a description of the Angelier edition see *Essais*, ed. Maurice Rat, vol. I, pp. *xxxviii-xxxix*. Barrière claims that Montesquieu possessed a famous copy of the *Essais* annotated by Montaigne. (See *Un Grand Provincial*, p. 198.) We find no documentary evidence to verify this assertion.

[2]See Bimbenet, Séance du 5 mai, 1882, pp. 20 ff. "Montaigne and Montesquieu, les plus illustres déistes."

[3]These same questions puzzled Fortunat Strowski, who questioned the sincerity of Montaigne's faith. See *Montaigne, sa vie publique et privée* (Paris: Editions de la Nouvelle Revue Critique, 1938).

[4]Vian, p. 221.

[5]Barrière intuitively felt Montaigne's presence in letter 66, for he quoted him in pointing out Montesquieu's intentions: "Sa coquetterie de grand seigneur qui ne veut pas être pris pour un faiseur de livres s'exprime dans la lettre 66" ("Eléments personnels," p. 29)

[6]"La Gasconnade est un jeu d'esprit, un trait d'imagination, une manière fanfaronne, brillante et ingénieuse de dire les choses." (Vian, p. 322).

[7]Maturin Dréano, *La Renommée de Montaigne en France au XVIIIe siècle 1677-1802,* (Angers: Editions de l'Ouest, 1952), p. 281.

[8]*Œuvres complètes*, ed. André Masson, vol. III, p. 227.

[9]Vian, p. 227.

[10]Vian, p. 54.

[11]Pierre Barrière, *Un Grand Provincial*, p. 45.

Conclusion

[1]Pascal, p. 79.

[2]Shackleton, p. 45.

[3]Shackleton, p. 1.

[4]"Le grand-père et la grand-mère de Montesquieu sont tous les deux et l'un autant que l'autre, en rapport assez étroit avec la famille de Montaigne." Jacques de Feytaud, "Entre Montaigne et Montesquieu," *Bulletin de la Société des Amis de Montaigne*, no. 16 (1960), p. 61.

Bibliography

MONTAIGNE

I. Editions of Montaigne's works:

Montaigne, Michel Eyquem de. *Essais.* ed. Mlle de Gournay. Paris: chez Michel Sonnius, 1595.

——. *Essais.* 3 vols. Paris: Imprimerie nationale, 1906-31 (Reproduction typographique de l'exemplaire annoté par l'auteur et conservé à la bibliothèque de Bordeaux).

——. *Essais.* ed. R. Strowski, F. Gebelin, P. Villey. 5 vols. Bordeaux: Imprimerie nouvelle F. Pech and Cie, 1906-33.

——. *Essais.* ed. Pierre Villey. 3 vols. Paris: F. Alcan, 1922-23.

——. *Essais.* ed. Maurice Rat. 3 vols. Paris: Garnier Frères, n. d.

——. *Essais.* ed. Pierre Villey. (réédités par V. L. Saulnier), Paris: Presses universitaires de France, 1965.

——. *Essais.* ed. A. Micha. 3 vols. Paris: Garnier-Flammarion, 1969.

——. *Essais.* ed. Maurice Rat. 2 vols. Paris: Garnier Frères, 1967.

——. *Essais.* ed Pierre Michel. Paris: Gallimard, 1973.

——. *Œuvres complètes.* ed. Albert Thibaudet & Maurice Rat. Paris: Gallimard, 1962.

——. *Œuvres complètes.* Préface d'André Maurois. Paris: Editions du Seuil, 1967.

II. Biography and Criticism of Montaigne:

Barrière, Pierre. *Montaigne, gentilhomme français.* 2nd edition. Bordeaux: Delmas, 1949.

Bonnefon, Paul. *Montaigne, l'homme et l'œuvre.* Paris: J. Rouam and Cie, 1893.

Brunschvicg, Léon. *Descartes et Pascal, lecteurs de Montaigne.* New York: Brentano's, 1944.

Defaux, Gérard. "Un cannibale en haut de chausses. Montaigne et la logique de l'identité." *Modern Language Notes,* SCVII (1982), pp. 919-57.

Dréano, Maturin. *La Religion de Montaigne*. Paris: Nizet, 1969.

———. *La Renommée de Montaigne en France au XVIIIe siècle, 1677-1802*. Angers: Editions de l'Ouest, 1952.

Faguet, Emile, "Montaigne," *Seizième Siècle: études littéraires*. Paris: Société française d'imprimerie et de librairie, 1902, pp. 365-421.

Feytaud, Jacques de. "Entre Montaigne et Montesquieu," *Bulletin de la Société des Amis de Montaigne*, no. 16 (1960), pp. 59-61.

Frame, Donald M. *Montaigne's Discovery of Man*. New York: Columbia University Press, 1955.

Friedrich, Hugo. *Montaigne*. trans. Robert Rovini. Paris: Gallimard, 1968.

Gide, André. *Essai sur Montaigne*. Paris: J. Schriffrin, 1929.

Gray, Floyd. *La Balance de Montaigne*. Paris: Nizet, 1982.

———. *Le Style de Montaigne*. Paris: Nizet, 1958.

Heck, Francis S. "Montaigne's conservatism and liberalism. A paradox?" *Romanic Review*, XVI (1975), pp. 165-71.

Janssen, Herman Josef Joannes. *Montaigne fidéiste*. Nijmegen: N. V. Dekker and Van de Vegt, n. p., 1930.

Jeanson, Francis. *Montaigne par lui-même*. Paris: Editions du Seuil, 1957.

Keller, Abraham C. "Montaigne and Women. A Position Paper." *Papers on French 17th Century Literature*, VIII, 14, 1 (1981), pp. 69-82.

La Charité, Raymond C. *The Concept of Judgment in Montaigne*. The Hague: Martinus Nijhoff, 1968.

Lanson, Gustave. *Les Essais de Montaigne: étude et analyse*. Paris: Mellottée, n. d.

Mayer, C. A. "Stoïcisme et purification du concept chez Montaigne." *Studi Francesi*, XXIV (1980), pp. 487-93.

Michel, Pierre. "Note de lecture. Montaigne et Montesquieu devant Rome, 'métropole' éternelle et universelle." *Bulletin de la Société des Amis de Montaigne*, V, 21 (janvier-mars, 1977), pp. 45-48.

Moussat, Emile. "De Montaigne à Montesquieu." (prés. par Pierre Michel) *Bulletin de la Société des Amis de Montaigne*, V, 12 (1974, Suppl.), pp. 2-4.

Norton, Grace. *The Spirit of Montaigne; Some Thoughts and Expressions Similar to Those in His Essays*. Boston: Houghton, Mifflin, 1908.

———. *Studies in Montaigne*. New York: The MacMillan Company, 1904.

Plattard, Jean. *Montaigne et son temps*. Paris: Boivin and Cie, 1933.

Pons, Roger, "Etude sur la pensée religieuse de Montaigne. L'Apologie de Raymond Sebond." *L'Information littéraire, XXX* (1978), pp. 151-62.

Sainte-Beuve, Charles Augustin. "Montaigne," *Les Grands Ecrivains français, XVIe Siècle: Les Prosateurs*. ed. Maurice Allem. Vol. 3 (Paris, Garnier Frères), 1926, pp. 162-252.

Schonberger, Vincent L. "La conception de l' 'Honneste' homme chez Montaigne." *Revue de L'Université d'Ottawa*, XLV (1975), pp. 491-507.

Starobinski, Jean. *Montaigne en mouvement.* Paris: Gallimard, 1983.

Strowski, Fortunat J. *Montaigne.* Paris: F. Alcan, 1900.

————. *Montaigne; sa vie publique et privée.* Paris, Editions de la Nouvelle Revue Critique, 1938.

Thibaudet, Albert. *Montaigne.* ed. Floyd Gray. Paris: Gallimard, 1963.

Tournon, André. *Montaigne, la glose et l'essai.* Lyon: Presses universitaires de Lyon, 1983.

Villey, Pierre. *Les Essais de Michel de Montaigne.* Paris: Société française d'éditions littéraires et techniques, E. Malfère, 1932.

————. *Montaigne devant la postérité.* Paris: Boivin et Cie, 1935.

————. *Les Sources et l'évolution des essais de Montaigne.* Paris: Hachette 1908.

Weber, Henri. "*L'Apologie de Raymond Sebond* et la religion de Montaigne." *Réforme, Humanisme, Renaissance,* IV, 8 (décembre 1978), pp. 12-22.

MONTESQUIEU

I. Editions of Montesquieu's works:

Montesquieu, Charles-Louis de Secondat, baron de La Brède et de. *Lettres persanes.* ed. Pierre Marteau, 2 vols. Cologne: Imprimeur-libraire, près le Collège des Jésuites, 1754.

————. *Lettres persanes.* ed. Henri Barckhausen. Paris: Hachette et Cie, 1913.

————. *Lettres persanes.* ed. Elie Carcassonne. 2 vols. Paris: F. Roches, 1929.

————. *Lettres persanes.* ed. Antoine Adam. Geneva: Droz, 1954.

————. *Lettres persanes.* ed. Paul Vernière. Paris: Classiques Garnier, 1960.

————. *Lettres persanes.* ed. Jean Starobinski. Paris: Gallimard, 1973.

————. *Lettres persanes.* ed. Paul Vernière. Paris: Classiques Garnier, 1975.

————. *Lettres persanes.* ed. Réal Ouellet et Hélène Vachon. Paris: Hachette, 1976.

————. *Persian Letters.* trans. Mr. Ozell. 2 vols. London: printed for J. Tonson, and sold by Thomas Combes and James Lacey, 1722.

————. *Œuvres complètes.* ed. Roger Caillois. 2 vols. n. p.: Gallimard, 1949-51.

————. *Œuvres complètes.* ed. André Masson. 3 vols. Paris: Nagel, 1950-55.

II. Biography and Criticism of Montesquieu:

Balde, Jean. "Montesquieu, Châtelain de La Brède." *Correspondant,* Aug. 25, 1930, vol. 320, n. s. 284, pp. 481-501.

Barrière, Pierre. "Les Eléments personnels et les éléments bordelais dans les *Lettres persanes.*" *Revue d'Histoire Littéraire,* 1951, pp. 17-36.

————. *Un Grand Provincial: Charles-Louis de Secondat, baron de La Brède et de Montesquieu*. Bordeaux, Delmas, 1946.

Bimbenet, Jean Eugène. "Montaigne—Montesquieu." *Société d'agriculture, sciences, belles-lettres et arts d'Orléans*. Mémoires, séance of March 31, 1882, series 2, vol. 23 (vol. 54 of collection) pp. 313-55; rapport sur le mémoire qui précède, by L. Guerrier in séance of June 2, 1882, pp. 356-60. Second part: séance of May 5, 1882, series 2, vol. 24 (vol. 54 of collection) pp. 15-59; rapport sur le mémoire qui précède, by L. Guerrier in séance of Dec. 15, 1882, pp. 60-64.

Bouvier-Aja, Maurice. "Les Paradoxes du baron de Montesquieu." *Europe* 574 (fevrier 1977), pp. 6-17.

Carayol, Elizabeth. "Des lettres persanes oubliées." *Revue d'Histoire littéraire*, LXI (janvier-mars 1965), pp. 15-26.

Carr, J. L. "The Secret Chain of the *Lettres persanes*." *Transactions*, vol. I, 1967, pp. 333-44.

Cruchet, René. *France et Louisiane, Médecine et Littérature, Montaigne et Montesquieu at Home*. Romance Language Series, No. 2. University . La.: Louisiana State University Press, 1939.

Dalat, Jean. "Montesquieu magistrat. L'homme en lutte avec ses contradictions." (L'Académie Montesquieu - Archives Montesquieu No. 4), *Archives des lettres modernes*, no. 139, octobre 1971.

Dargan, Edwin P. *The Aesthetic Doctrine of Montesquieu: Its Application in His Writings*. Baltimore: J. H. Furst, 1907.

Dedieu, Joseph. *Les Grands Philosophes: Montesquieu*. Paris: F. Alcan, 1913.

Desgraves, Louis. *Catalogue de la Bibliothèque de Montesquieu*. Geneva: Droz, 1954.

Faguet, Emile. "Montesquieu." *Dix-huitième Siècle; études littéraires*. Paris: Boivin, n. d., pp. 137-92.

Frautshci, R. L. "The Would-be Invisible Chain in the *Lettres persanes*." *French Review* April 1967, pp. 604-12.

Gearhart, Suzanne. "The Place and Sense of the 'Outsider.' Structuralism and the *Lettres persanes*." *Modern Language Notes*, XCII (1977), pp. 724-48.

Hamilton, James F. "Reason and Sentiment in Montesquieu's Understanding of Suicide." *American Society Legion of Honor Magazine*, vol. 47 (1976), pp. 101-14.

McLelland, Jane Kyle Brumage. *The Web and the River: a Study of Montesquieu's Use of Metaphor*. Dissertation, Stanford University, 1976. *Dissertation Abstracts International*, vol XXXVI, no. 12, June, 8097-A.

Montesquieu, Baron Philippe de. "Montesquieu, gentilhomme provincial." *Revue de l'Académie du Centre*, 1973, pp. 13-38.

Novak, Otakar. "Un Montesquieuiste traducteur de Montaigne (Anton Vantuch). *Sbornik Praci filozofické Fakulty Brenske Univerzity*. D. 25-26 (1978-79), pp. 136-41.

Quoniam, Théodore. "L'humanisme de Montesquieu." *Echo judiciaries girondins*, 6 août, 2-3; 9 août, 1; 13 août, 2-3 (1973).

Raymond, Agnes G. "Encore quelques réflexions sur la 'chaîne secrète' des *Lettres persanes.*" *Studies on Voltaire and the Eighteenth Century*, vol. 89 (1972), pp. 1337-47.

Raymond, M. "L'Humanisme de Montesquieu." *Les Grands Ecrivains français, études des lundis et des portraits.* Ed. Maurice Allem. Vol. 11 (*Philosophes et savants*, I), p. 29-70.

Rosso, Corrado. "Montesquieu et l'humanisme latin." *Cahiers de l'Association Internationale des Etudes Françaises*, vol. 35, 1983, pp. 235-50.

———. "Montesquieu présent: Etudes et travaux depuis 1960." *Dix-huitième Siècle*, no. 8. pp. 373-404.

Sainte-Beuve, Charles Augustin, "Montesquieu." *Les Grands Ecrivains français: études des lundis et des portraits.* Ed. Maurice Allem. Vol. II. Paris: Garnier Frères, (*Philosophes et savants*, I), pp. 29-70.

Shackleton, Robert. *Montesquieu, A Critical Biography.* London: Oxford University Press, 1961.

Sorel, Albert. *Montesquieu.* Paris: Hachette et Cie, 1887.

Starobinski, Jean. "Les *Lettres persanes*: apparence et essence." *Néohelicon*, 1974, no 1-2, pp. 83-112.

———. *Montesquieu par lui-même.* Paris: Editions du Seuil, 1953.

Valéry, Paul. "Préface aux *Lettres persanes.*" *Variété II.* Paris, 1930, pp. 53-73.

Vantuch, Anton, "Les Eléments personnels dans les *Lettres Persanes.*" *Annales de la Faculté des Lettres et Sciences humaines de Nice.* 2ème trimestre, 1969, pp. 127-42.

Vian, Louis. *Histoire de Montesquieu.* Paris: Didier and Cie, 1878.

Young, David Bruce. *Montesquieu's Standards and His Relativism in the "Lettres Persanes": their Origins, Significance and Development.* Dissertation, Columbia University, 1971. *Dissertation Abstracts International*, vol. XXXII, no. 6, December, 3236-A.